# Public-Private Partnerships in Health Care in India

Public-private partnerships are increasingly advocated to alleviate deficiencies in the public health system as well as to reduce economic stress on those who seek services from an expensive, burgeoning and unregulated private health sector. Focusing on India, this book examines how the private sector in developing countries is tapped to deliver health care services to poor and underserved sections of society through collaborative arrangements with the government. Having emerged as a key reform initiative, aspects of public-private partnership are examined such as the genesis of private sector partnerships, the ways in which the private sector is encouraged to deliver public health services, and the models and formats that make such partnerships possible.

Based on in-depth case studies from different states of India and drawing on experiences in other countries, the authors analyse challenges, opportunities and benefits of implementing public-private partnerships and explore whether partnership with the private sector can be designed to deliver health care services to the poor as well as the consequences for beneficiaries.

This book will be of interest to scholars of public policy and development administration, health policy and development economics as well as South Asian Studies.

**A. Venkat Raman** is Reader in Human Resource Management and Health Services Management at the University of Delhi, India.

**James Warner Björkman** is Professor of Public Policy and Administration at the Institute of Social Studies, The Hague, the Netherlands, and Professor of Public Administration and Development at Rijksuniversiteit Leiden, the Netherlands.

# Routledge studies in development economics

# Public-Private Partnerships in Health Care in India

Lessons for developing countries

**A. Venkat Raman and
James Warner Björkman**

Routledge
Taylor & Francis Group

LONDON AND NEW YORK

First published 2009
by Routledge
2 Park Square, Milton Park, Abingdon, Oxon OX14 4RN

Simultaneously published in the USA and Canada
by Routledge
270 Madison Ave, New York, NY 10016

*Routledge is an imprint of the Taylor & Francis Group, an informa business*

Typeset in Times by Wearset Ltd, Boldon, Tyne and Wear
Printed and bound in Great Britain by TJI Digital, Padstow, Cornwall

*British Library Cataloguing in Publication Data*
A catalogue record for this book is available from the British Library

*Library of Congress Cataloging in Publication Data*
A catalog record for this book has been requested

ISBN10: 0-415-46728-4 (hbk)
ISBN10: 0-203-88655-0 (ebk)

ISBN13: 978-0-415-46728-5 (hbk)
ISBN13: 978-0-203-88655-7 (ebk)

# Contents

# Illustrations

## Figures

## Tables

# Acknowledgments

We are grateful to the Indian Council for Social Science Research (ICSSR) and the Netherlands Organisation for Scientific Research (NWO) for funding the research on which this book is based. We also thank the Indo-Dutch Program for Alternatives in Development (IDPAD) and its Coordinators – Dr. Sanchita Dutta in New Delhi and Dr. Marc Verhagen and Dr. Cora Govers in The Hague – who administered the grant 5.3.96 during 2003–2007 and facilitated our endeavors.

Our team of researchers – Dr. S. Kaushik, Mr. Sigamani, Ms. Shashi Rani – merit special mention for their skills and enthusiasm, and likewise the versatile skills of Mr. Jitender Panwar.

During our fieldwork legions of government officials, health staff, private sector managers and other stakeholders shared information about the practice of public-private partnership throughout India. Without compromising confidentiality, we record our gratitude for their support and cooperation – and, of course, reserve responsibility for ourselves about how we interpreted their contributions.

We received encouragement from colleagues in India at Delhi University's Faculty of Management Studies and in the Netherlands at the Institute of Social Studies who are too numerous to mention all by name. However, we express a special word of thanks to Dr. Sanjeev Singh at the Institute of Informatics and Communication for providing technological support during our entire project.

And, of course, Arpitha and Prabha share the distinction of having had to put up with both authors for a very long time!

A. Venkat Raman
New Delhi
James Warner Björkman
The Hague

# Abbreviations

| | |
|---|---|
| AB | Aktiebolag (Sweden) |
| ADBI | Asian Development Bank Institute |
| AIDS | Acquired Immuno-Deficiency Syndrome |
| AIMS | All-India Movement for Seva |
| AMI | American Medical International |
| ANC | Ante-Natal Clinic |
| ANM | Auxiliary Nurse Midwife |
| APL | Above Poverty Line |
| APOLO | NGO network (Ecuador) |
| APUSH | Andra Pradesh Urban Slum Healthcare |
| ARS | Arogya Raksha Scheme |
| ASK | Arpana Swasthya Kendra |
| BEMFAM | Sociedade Civil Bem-Estar Familiar no Brasil |
| BIMARU | Bihar, Madhya Pradesh, Rajasthan, Uttar Pradesh |
| BISR | Birla Institute of Scientific Research |
| BOO | Build, Own, Operate |
| BOT | Build, Operate, Transfer |
| BPL | Below Poverty Line |
| BROT | Build, Rehabilitate, Operate, Transfer |
| CBHI | Central Bureau of Health Intelligence |
| CBO | Community-Based Organization |
| CCO | Cancer Care Ontario |
| CCSS | Costa Rican Social Security Institute |
| CD4 | Cluster of Differentiation antigen 4 |
| CFW | Child and Family Welfare |
| CHC | Community Health Center |
| CHE | Crown Health Enterprise |
| CII | Confederation of Indian Industries |
| CLAS | Local Health Administration Committee (Peru) |
| CME | Continuing Medical Education |
| COOPESALUD | Cooperativas de Salúd |
| CROS | Canadian Radiation Oncology Services |
| CT | Computerized Tomography |

| | |
|---|---|
| DALY | Disability Adjusted Life Year |
| DANIDA | Danish International Development Agency |
| DFID | Department for International Development |
| DHFW | Department of Health and Family Welfare |
| DOTS | Directly Observed Treatment, Short-course |
| ECG | Electro-Cardio-Gram |
| ECP | Emergency Contraception Pill |
| ENT | Ear, Nose, Throat |
| FHF | Family Health Fund |
| FMC | Frontier Medical College |
| FOGSI | Federation of Obstetric and Gynecological Societies of India |
| FONASA | Fondo Naciónal de Salúd (Chile) |
| FOY | Friend of Youth |
| FPIA | Family Planning International Assistance |
| FUSAL | Fundación Salvadoreña Para la Salúd y el Desarrollo Humano |
| GF/GFATM | Global Fund to Fight AIDS, Tuberculosis and Malaria |
| GOI | Government of India |
| GP | General Practitioner |
| GTZ | Gesellschaft für Technische Zusammenarbeit |
| HFA | Health Funding Authority |
| HIV | Human Immunodeficiency Virus |
| HHS | Hospital and Health Services |
| HMO | Health Maintenance Organization |
| HRD | Human Resource Development |
| HRM | Human Resource Management |
| HSD | Health Sector Development |
| HSR | Health Sector Reform |
| ICT | Information Communication Technology |
| IIED | International Institute for Environment and Development |
| IMA | Indian Medical Association |
| IMF | International Monetary Fund |
| INSALUD | Network of NGOs (Dominican Republic) |
| IPA | Independent Practitioner Association |
| IPFA | International Project Finance Association |
| IPP-VIII | India Population Project, 8th phase |
| ISRO | Indian Space Research Organization |
| IT | Information Technology |
| JP | Jaya Prakash Narayan |
| KIITH | Karnataka Integrated Telemedicine and Tele-Health |
| KMET | Kisumu Medical and Educational Trust |
| KMF | Karnataka Milk Federation |
| LLFS | Life Line Fluid Store |
| MARCH | Management and Resources for Community Health (Haiti) |
| MCD | Municipal Corporation of Delhi |

| | |
|---|---|
| MOH | Ministry of Health |
| MOU | Memorandum of Understanding |
| MRI | Magnetic Resonance Imaging |
| MTP | Medical Termination of Pregnancy |
| NCD | Non-Communicable Disease |
| NFP | Not-for-Profit |
| NGO | Non-Governmental Organization |
| NH | Narayana Hrudayalaya |
| NHS | National Health Service |
| NL | the Netherlands |
| NMCH | National Commission on Macroeconomics in Health |
| NRHM | National Rural Health Mission |
| OAE | Own-Account Enterprise |
| OECD | Organization for Economic Cooperation and Development |
| OPEC | Organization of Petroleum Exporting Countries |
| ORT | Oral Rehydration Therapy |
| PCG | Primary Care Group |
| PFI | Private Finance Initiative |
| PHC | Primary Health Center |
| PHR | Partnership for Health Reform |
| PIC | Public Interest Company |
| PPM | Public-Private Mix |
| PPP | Public-Private Partnership |
| PROCOSI | NGO network (Bolivia) |
| PROFAMILIA | Asociación Dominicana Pro-Bienestar de la Familia |
| PROSALUD | Network of NGOs (Bolivia) |
| PSI | Population Services International |
| RCH | Reproductive and Child Health |
| RH | Reproductive Health |
| RHA | Regional Health Authority |
| RKS | Rogi Kalyan Samiti (Patient Welfare Society) |
| RNTCP | Revised National Tuberculosis Control Program |
| SAIDS | Social Action for Integrated Development Services |
| SHEF | Sustainable Healthcare Enterprise Foundation |
| SHIS | Southern Health Improvement Samity |
| SMS | Sawai Man Singh |
| STI | Sexually Transmitted Infection |
| TA/DA | Travel Allowance/Daily Allowance |
| TB | Tuberculosis |
| TBA | Traditional Birth Attendant |
| TPA | Third Party Administrator |
| TOP reseau | Franchise for Reproductive Health Care (Madagascar) |
| UK | United Kingdom |
| UMHRC | Uttaranchal Mobile Hospital and Research Center |
| UNAIDS | Joint United Nations Program on HIV/AIDS |

| | |
|---|---|
| UNDP | United Nations Development Program |
| UNFPA | United Nations Fund for Population Activities |
| UNICEF | United Nations Children's Fund |
| USAID | United States Agency for International Development |
| US | United States of America |
| VCTC | Voluntary Counseling and Testing Center |
| WHO | World Health Organization |
| YWCA | Young Women's Christian Association |

# 1 Concepts, theories and models

Public-private partnerships are increasingly popular in the field of development cooperation and sustainable development. Although not an altogether new phenomenon, the popularity of public-private partnerships in policy circles has grown steadily since the late 1980s to a point where their promotion seems to have become a dominant 'development narrative' (Entwistle and Martin 2005; Linder 1999; Roe 1991). Partnerships are promoted as the most logical solution to a variety of service delivery and development problems, and are often presented as 'technical', politically neutral solutions – a theme that parallels the Progressive Movement in the United States of America during the early twentieth century (Ferguson 1990).

Public-private partnerships reappeared after conservative governments in Europe and the US – notably the Thatcher regime and the Reagan Administration – introduced extensive privatization of government institutions. Partnerships were considered to be a 'softer' version of the same development strategy that would have less dramatic social consequences and therefore would be more palatable to the general public. In Britain the 'New' Labour Party stressed partnerships as a way to expand services without borrowing funds or raising taxes, a view welcomed by both civil society organizations and the corporate sector. Despite the debate over whether civil society is a counterweight to the market (Escobar 1995; Levine 2002), the promotion of partnerships is grounded on an acceptance of a neo-liberal growth strategy to economic development.

In the literature on public-private partnerships, two streams are notable. The first stream concerns prescriptive literature, often written with a public administration or management perspective that focuses on characteristics of partnerships and provides recommendations of how to establish them. This literature rarely addresses the ideological underpinnings of the approach nor does it question the concept itself with its inherent power relations. Much of this literature suggests that the public sector can learn from the private sector in terms of efficiency, results-orientation and flexibility (Batley 2004; Brunsson and Sahlin-Andersson 2000). The other stream concerns more critical studies, often empirically based, that document the behavior and frequent failure of many partnerships. These studies are more likely to address the ideological background of public-private initiatives and to criticize the – often implicit – assumption that all partners within partnerships are equal. Nevertheless, in-depth case studies of how power relations are shaped by and affect partnerships remain relatively rare (Laurie 2005; Mosse 2004).

Public-private partnerships have many precedents. Historical examples include the role of the church in social security and the mercantilist era of infra-structural development. The concept seems to be remarkably attractive because both governments and non-governmental organizations seize upon the idea. Part of the attraction stems from the general acceptance of economic development as the premise for development, and the widespread belief that markets are the most efficient tool to foster such growth. Private sector companies are regarded as efficient, proactive and flexible; they quickly adapt to changing situations in the market and, being results-oriented, they are held accountable. The private sector is thus seen to be more efficient in developing markets and in delivering services. But, little information exists on the costs and benefits of partnerships or how they contribute to poverty alleviation. There is lack of transparency about the distribution of results.

It is difficult to find recent literature that argues why public services should remain under the sole production of the government. Shleifer (1998) argues that the crucial issue concerns incentives to innovate and to reduce costs. Neo-classical economic theory holds that the efficiency of a sector is a function of incentive and market structures rather than ownership. As long as an enterprise operates in a competitive market without barrier to entry or exit, it doesn't matter whether an enterprise is owned privately or by the state. The owner yields autonomy to the management, instructs it to follow the signals of the market and, based on performance, rewards or sanctions the management (Nellis 1994).

States can own enterprises by ensuring that the above conditions hold. In principle, it does not matter whether a service is provided by the state or con-tracted out. A contract with the private sector, or regulation of it, should be able to enforce specific services. There are, however, two problems with state enter-prises. First, the above-mentioned conditions are often not met; second, when they are met, they are not sustained over the long term. At almost any time, politicians can impose social and commercial objectives on the state enterprise, which lead to the inefficient use of resources (Boycko *et al.* 1996).

Based on empirical evidence, private enterprises often outperform public enter-prises. The World Bank found that rates of return on equity invested in public industrial enterprises are about one-third of those in a country's industrial private sector (Nellis 1994). In this sense one can argue that ownership matters. Given the absence of explicit objectives focusing on efficiency and given organizational cul-tures and control systems to support these objectives, state enterprises are often less efficient than private enterprises (Wortzel and Wortzel 1989).

Despite the arguments in favor of shifting ownership away from the state, or suggesting that ownership doesn't matter, there are political reasons such as electoral strategies for retaining a service within state ownership. State owner-ship can be, for instance, a good way to buy votes by not privatizing the enter-prise and therefore keeping workers employed (Zahariadis 1999).

During the 1990s public-private partnerships (PPPs) emerged as a key tool of public policy across the world. PPPs refer to any form of agreement between public and private parties and can be defined as 'the combination of a public need with private capability and resources to create a market opportunity through which the public need is met and profit is made' (Heilman and Johnston 1992: 197).

Public-private partnerships present an alternative solution to full privatization. The concept comprises different types of contracts with the private sector, ranging from short-term contracts, involving only a part of the service provided (contracting out, operations, maintenance) to longer-term contacts that apply to an entire service (leasing, concession) (Edwards and Shaoul 2003). The partnerships can be with small-scale independent providers, non-governmental organizations or the private for-profit sector.

Private organizations and public sectors can realize mutual advantages from partnerships. The main rewards from partnering with the private sector for the public sector are improvements of program performance, cost-effectiveness, better service provisions and appropriate allocation of risk and responsibilities (Pongsiri 2002). On the other hand, the private sector strives to make a reasonable profit, obtain better investment potential, and have opportunities to expand its business interests (Scharle 2002). The involvement of the private sector in providing a service yields incentives that reduce costs (and prices, if competition exists), improve quality and stimulate innovation while reducing potential market failures that can occur under full privatization (Chong *et al.* 2006).

The total social benefit of public-private partnerships is affected by the degree to which risk is allocated among stakeholders so risk should be considered in the design of policies for a sector. Different types of partnerships correspond to different distributions of risks; therefore, an initial policy pertains to the choice of the type of public-private partnership. If the distribution of risks is not considered during political decisions about partnerships, it is possible that both the probability and the consequences of risks are aggravated (Luís-Manso 2005).

As a policy intervention public-private partnerships are increasingly adopted for critical urban infrastructure services where loss of control and outright privatization are considered unacceptable (Edwards and Shaoul 2003). They are perceived to remedy a persistent lack of dynamism in public service delivery. Regarding health care services, the role of partnerships lies in considering them as both economic and public goods that require a balance between social and economic considerations as well as returns generated to private shareholders.

For involving the private sector in delivering health care, a wide range of approaches exist. Some options keep the operations and ownership in public hands but involve the private sector in the construction and design of the infrastructure. Other possibilities are involving private actors in the management, operation and/or financing of assets. Hence, they involve different levels of public and private sector responsibilities for service delivery. In all these options, public authority remains responsible for overseeing the activity and for ultimately ensuring that public needs are met. For setting and enforcing performance standards, the government retains the final responsibility. A strong regulatory role is required to ensure that the interests of the consumers and the performance standards are protected. The key issue for partnerships is an adequate allocation of regulatory and managerial functions between private and public sectors in order to guarantee the resolution of conflicts between investment needs and consumer protection both in the short and long term (Luís-Manso 2005).

## Partnership with the private sector

Reaching out to the private sector and fostering a collaborative relationship for providing services to the local community has been at the center of macro-economic policies of governments across the world (Mitchell-Weaver and Manning 1992). Partnership with the private sector has emerged as a policy option with the realization that, given respective strengths and weaknesses, neither the public sector nor private sector alone is in the best interest of the health system. Involvement of the private sector is, in part, linked to wider belief that public sector bureaucracies are inefficient and unresponsive while market mechanisms promote efficiency and ensure cost effective, good quality and responsive services (WHO 2001). According to Bloom *et al.* (2000), these beliefs are predicated on the following reasons.

- Government has failed to deliver quality health care. Poor control of government spending contributes to inefficiency. Government systems are accountable only indirectly at election time rather than being responsive to customer satisfaction. They suffer from low-levels of innovation, and supervisory systems are weak (Mitchell 1986).
- Despite the notion that government is best placed to provide health services for all, in many countries government-operated health programs fail to reach significant segments of the population. Factors causing this deficiency include inadequate training and deployment of medical personnel, insufficient supply of drugs, lack of equipment and supplies, poor systems for monitoring public health practitioners, and inability to hold staff accountable for their actions, indiscipline and absenteeism.
- Due to increasing resource constraints, many governments have been forced to reduce health spending. It is unlikely that public funds alone will, in the foreseeable future, be adequate to pay for essential health care needs.
- The private sector has a large proportion of doctors, health facilities and financial capabilities. However, the private sector is poorly placed to prevent and control infectious diseases or to provide services to the poor as well as those living in remote areas.
- Governments fail to regulate the private sector. While most governments have legislation and regulations, they are not enforced. Often regulations

and laws are outdated or information necessary for enforcement is lacking. Corruption, too, is often a problem. Lack of knowledge by government officials is an especially pressing issue.

According to Agha *et al.* (2003), regulations regarding the operation of private health providers have not kept pace with the expansion of the private sector. This has caused opportunistic behavior by private providers, leading to variations in the price and quality of services (see also Hongoro and Kumaranayake 2000). Providing incentives could change these practices and improve the quality of care (Agha *et al.*1997; Foreit 1998).

The debate about public-private partnership emerged for several reasons (ADBI 2000). Apart from mounting evidence that health care in many countries is dominated by the private sector, even for the poor and the rural population, there are concerns about efficiency and the quality of care in the public health system. There is also realization that public and private sectors in health can potentially gain from one another. Apart from resource gains, there is a possibility to transfer technology, knowledge, skills and even the prestige associated with partnerships. Another critical reason for seeking public-private partnership is the rapid escalation of health care costs. Health care costs are likely to continue to rise and pose the greatest risk to the poor. It would be prudent for governments to manage resources and contain costs by improving efficiency.

Another perspective on partnership between the public and private sectors in health care assumes that the public sector must re-orient its role. Traditionally governments have both financed and delivered public services to all, whereas private spending has been on the delivery of individual services. While the private sector has rapidly increased its role in both financing and providing services, governments face challenges on both fronts due to resource constraints. There is an emerging trend in which governments are re-examining their roles in financing and delivering services. The critical distinction is between the *financing* and the *provision* of services. Mitchell (2000) generates four models to distinguish these functions in health services.

1 The conventional model is *public financing and public delivery*.
2 The second model is *private funding and private delivery* of services, in which public health services are rarely delivered. Private insurance, ambulances and specialty hospitals are examples of this model.
3 A third model is *private financing and public delivery*. Recent initiatives by global NGOs to implement disease control programs, reproductive health or other public health services are included in this category. Another form of private financing and public provision is the user-fee, when users pay out-of-pocket for public services.
4 The fourth model is *public funding and private delivery*. Argued to be the most effective model, it is believed that quality and efficiency will be better than through direct provision by government.

Two types of this fourth model are contracting and insurance programs, with contracting the most common form. Different options of contracting are possible too: pay for salary and drugs; pay per case as a reimbursement; or prepaid grant. In addition to contracting out the direct provision of service, other options include community-based health insurance programs; use of vouchers (wherein a specified amount per case, for a given period of time, for a given type of services is rendered); funding for supplies under priority programs (e.g. disease control programs in which private providers are supplied with drugs and supplies for their participation); and funding the private sector to set up private clinics in areas where no health services are available.

Combinations of financing and providing health services are provided in Table 1.1. Interaction between the public and private sectors lies on a continuum from no relationship at all to a very close interaction and synergistic relationship. The range of relationships includes (Ahmed 2000):

- Parallel activities: public and private activities are carried out without any contact with each other or acknowledgment of the existence of the other.
- Competitive activities: the activities in the public and the private sector are carried out with similar objectives, targeting common clientele and competing with each other, which may cause either wasteful duplication of activities or enlargement of choices for the beneficiaries.
- Complementary activities: activities or services from the public and the private sectors complement each other in terms of the nature and content of services or geographical and population coverage, either accidentally or by design.
- Contractual services: the government contracts the private sector to provide specified services for agreed fees, with the contractor being accountable to government authority.
- Cooperation and collaboration: collaborative relationships include elements based on shared objectives, strategies and outcomes.

*Table 1.1* Public-private financing and provision of health services

| Financing | Provision | |
|---|---|---|
| | *Public sector* | *Private sector* |
| Public | • Public health facilities<br>• Medical colleges/universities<br>• Public hospitals<br>• Health insurance | • Contracts<br>• Vouchers<br>• Community-based health insurance |
| Private | • User fees (partly)<br>• Autonomous hospitals<br>• Private health insurance<br>• Private medical colleges | • Fee for medical service<br>• Pharmacies |

Source: Bloom *et al.* 2000.

## Motives for partnership

Collaboration between the public sector and the private sector depends on many factors. One of the most critical factors is the motivation of the respective stakeholders. Generally the motive of the government is to provide health services to all at minimum cost (and free at the point of use) as well as to provide equity of access for all services. Commercial enterprises, on the other hand, seek to maximize profits rather than promote equity or access. Community-based and non-profit organizations have special concerns about reaching poor and disadvantaged parts of society that are often not reached by government.

In a review of health sector reform initiatives in Peru, Guatemala, Costa Rica, Colombia and the Dominican Republic, Abramson (1999) identified reasons why the public sector contracts with NGOs to deliver primary health services. Reasons include:

- extending coverage in the scope of services as well as geographic area for underserved populations;
- increasing the availability of medicine and medical supplies;
- improving the quality of care; and
- improving efficiency, cost-control and optimal use of resources.

NGOs were also interested in contracts to increase their financial resources while simultaneously focusing on their social mission.

While the health system as a whole has common objectives of equity, efficiency, quality and accessibility, the definition and meaning of these objectives are interpreted differently by public and private providers. According to Bloom *et al.* (2000), the notion of quality is perceived and interpreted differently in the public and the private sector. Since public and private sectors have different work cultures, the notion of efficiency would depend on availability of resources and on the quantum of services to be offered. Income inequality among patients who seek health services tends to determine the interpretation of equity in access to the health services in the private sector. In terms of financing health care, political compulsions make the public sector commit for the long term while the private sector operates on short-term profit motives.

Opinion is divided about the motives of the private sector. Opinions range from deep distrust to strong support for close cooperation. One extreme view about the for-profit sector is that private providers are only motivated by money. Private providers are unlikely to perform for the public good or contribute to the public health goals of the state (Roemer 1984). Bennett *et al.* (1994) suggest five problems that are associated with private for-profit provision of health services:

- The objectives of the private for-profit sector are geared towards maximizing profit, often by illegitimate means; profits can be increased by over-charging, over-prescribing, mystifying quality care as technology-centric, overuse of diagnostics, cutting costs by lowering quality of care, ignoring safe practices and other unethical activities.

- The for-profit private sector ignores services relevant for public health concerns such as health education, prevention and disease notification.
- Private practitioners are unlikely to be interested in integrating their information systems with that of the public sector health system.
- Due to pay differentials, the private for-profit health sector is responsible for the 'brain drain' from the public sector that causes shortages and gaps in service delivery.
- The private for-profit sector in developing countries is often unregulated and lacks control over the quality of services, due to lack of peer review or lack of an accreditation system.

Rosenthal (2000) also cites five major concerns about relying on the private health sector to meet national health goals and objectives.

- Private provision of health services is driven by consumer *willingness to pay*; allocating resources on the basis of demand may not lead to allocative efficiency (e.g., expenditure on and consumption of ineffective medications).
- Private provision is driven by *ability to pay*; therefore inequalities in health service delivery may be exacerbated as poor areas and marginalized populations remain underserved while wealthy areas gain from expanding levels of service.
- Health care suppliers may create *excessive demand* for their services (client/agent problem).
- Consumers often are *unable to judge* the quality of services rendered, so they may receive lower quality service than that for which they pay.
- *Demand* for scarce human and physical resources by the private health sector may result in understaffing and other resource scarcities in the public sector.

However, the role of the private sector is neither easy to define nor easy to neglect. Its strength is its innovativeness, efficiency and learning from competition (Bloom *et al.* 2000). But there is an important distinction between profit and non-profit organizations in the private sector. Non-profit organizations have been particularly adept at providing services at the grassroots level. Their size and flexibility allow them to achieve notable successes where governments have failed. One area in which the private for-profit sector works well is providing quality care at minimal cost. Standards of management are generally higher in the private for-profit sector where staff are better paid and more motivated. The private sector can play an important role in transferring management skills and best practices to the public sector. The private sector is also well suited for research and development and for identifying newer techniques of treatment.

Despite these differences, the public and private sectors regularly interact with one another. While the government needs the private sector's support in order to bring in more resources, expand coverage and provide diversity of services, the private sector has an incentive to approach government to influence its policies in terms of tax exemptions, accreditation and fee setting (Wang 2000). Political motivation for public-private partnerships comes from an expectation that the relative advantages of partnership-based service delivery are visible in the short run whereas their costs and problems are reflected only in the long run. Given the short-term electoral politics and the glamour of media publicity, politicians choose strategies that have short-term impacts (Keramidas and Bout-Colonna 2007).

Profitability is critical for the private sector to be attracted to a partnership (Hammami *et al.* 2006). As the commercial risk of such projects is quite high, demand for services, size of the market and level of income (or purchasing power) are important influences on private sector participation in partnerships. Risks are higher in areas where private sector providers are few, potential demand is unknown, tariffs for public services are subsidized and collection from users is poor. Partnership arrangements are by definition contractual arrangements. As such, their sustainability depends critically on the regulatory environment that in turn is shaped by the quality of institutions. Weak institutions create uncertainties about the quality of regulations and therefore increase risk. Strong institutions and effective rule of law are thus important for securing partnerships. Past experience in running partnership projects is a critical predictor of successful future arrangements. Hence, a government's reputation for having honored past public-private partnerships is important for attracting future partnerships.

When public and private partners become ready for partnerships, they seek to optimize their respective costs (Rangan *et al.* 2006). While the private partners try to economize on resource costs, the public organizations tend to economize on governance costs. Cost of resources depends on the scale or volume, experience and industry-specific expertise of the private partner. Governance costs, on the other hand, depend on sector specificity (more specialized would mean higher cost), uncertainty of volume (high uncertainty would mean high costs), and the likely future behavior of the partner. Decisions about whether to partner or not depend on relational factors:

1. when the public actor resource costs are higher than those for private actors, and when public benefits do not much exceed private actor benefits, then private actors will be willing to undertake partnerships;
2. when the public benefits significantly exceed private benefits, and when resource costs are not relatively higher, then public actors will themselves undertake activities; and
3. when public benefits significantly exceed private actor benefits but public actor resource costs are far higher than the private actor costs, then public actors would be more than willing to collaborate with the private actors.

However, government as a viable partner may be undermined by three critical factors: a political agenda about allocation of resources; absence of adequate human, financial and institutional capability; and lack of credibility due to unsatisfactory history of achievements, relationships and behavior. Under these situations multilateral organizations can be optimally involved in the partnership dynamics. In partnerships, multilateral organizations act as a catalyst, coordinator, administrator and moral watchdog.

## Public-private partnership: conceptual framework

Perspectives on what constitutes a public-private partnership vary. Often authors use the terms 'contracting' and 'public-private partnership' almost interchangeably (Hodge and Greve 2007). Disagreement is more apparent over whether a partnership is a tool of governance or a 'language game' (Teisman and Klijn 2002). Linder (1999) considers partnership as a language game with 'multiple grammars' designed to 'cloud' other purposes such as privatization and to encourage private providers to supply public services at the expense of public organizations themselves. The label may also be due to trends within the public sector to use new buzzwords, to advance the same policy under different but catchy names or a deliberate ploy to change the discourse in pursuit of policy votes.

### *Defining the public and private sector*

The terms 'public' and 'private' can be confusing because there are several ways to define them. The 'public sector' is relatively easier to define. It includes organizations and institutions that are financed by state revenue and that function through government budgets. They include ministries and departments under national and provincial governments, district administration, municipal authorities, local government bodies, para-statal corporate entities, autonomous or semi-autonomous bodies or corporations, civic agencies, law and order agencies, cooperative societies under state control, state universities and research organizations.

The term 'private sector' is less easy to characterize. Private sector is defined as all organizations and individuals working outside the direct control of the state; these include both for-profit companies and individuals and not-for-profit private organizations (Bennett 1991). Broadly the private sector includes all non-state actors, some explicitly seeking profits and others operating on a non-profit basis. The former are conventionally called 'private business' or 'private enterprise'; the latter are non-governmental organizations (NGOs) that include voluntary associations and charitable trusts. For-profit providers may include individual medical practitioners, diagnostic centers, ambulance providers, blood banks, commercial contractors, institutional agencies such as polyclinics, nursing homes and hospitals of various capacities that provide different levels of services. They may be run under trust ownership or corporate ownership. They may be located in urban or rural areas. The private sector may also include community-service extensions of industrial establishments, cooperative soci-

eties, community-based organizations, religious and philanthropic trusts, professional associations, trade unions, research and development establishments, self-
help groups, citizen forums, clubs, associations, and other types of non-state
organizations.

Non-profit non-governmental organizations vary in size, sophistication and
expertise. There are international NGOs, national NGOs and community-based
NGOs. Not-for-profit (NFP) NGOs account for a tiny proportion of health care
provision. In most Indian states, the share of the NFP sector is less than 1
percent. NFP services are clustered in charitable clinics or hospitals. Nursing
homes, which characterize the for-profit sector, are almost entirely absent in the
non-profit sector. Some NFP facilities are established on a financially sustainable basis and are funded through user-charges; however, most require the
support of philanthropic donations. NFPs often provide good quality care, need
little regulation or oversight from government, are able to attract dedicated
workers at lower than market rates and cater to the needs of the poor and those
otherwise excluded from mainstream health care. Moreover, budget permitting,
they are willing to take on health care challenges that the for-profit sector is not
willing or unable to undertake such as running tuberculosis clinics, voluntary
counseling and testing centers (VCTC) for HIV/AIDS, adopting Primary Health
Centers, and other community based health schemes.

Given these characteristics, governments have found it easy to create partnerships with the NFP sector to support or deliver state and central government programs (World Bank 2004). However, as most NGOs are not large enough or do
not have the capacity to sustain themselves for long periods without external
funding, their interventions are often at the mercy of donors who lose interest or
commitment. While in the short term they usefully complement the role of the
government in delivering services to the community through project-based
health schemes, in the long term these arrangements may not be sustainable and
their scaling up is doubtful. Given their non-profit motives and grassroots-level
presence, however, NGOs can play oversight roles in a system that involves
more for-profit private sector delivery. The NFP sector is also largely self-regu-
lating and offers high quality services at low cost to its users.

The formal for-profit sector encompasses the most diverse group of practitioners and facilities. At the top end are hospitals that provide quality care at
international standards. Since such facilities focus almost entirely on tertiary
care, however, they are too expensive to be relevant to the health care needs of
the poor. Small private clinics and nursing homes are within the reach of some
poor households but even their moderate costs can be economically arduous.
Much of the private for-profit sector is heavily underutilized with low occupancy rates in all but the most successful hospitals. Since the private for-profit
sector accounts for the largest proportion of services and resources in the health
sector, any strategy to improve public health should take them into account
(World Bank 2004).

The private for-profit sector is largely in secondary and tertiary care and in
the production of medical and pharmaceutical technology; not-for-profit NGOs

*Table 1.2* Advantages and liabilities of private sector subgroups

| Sub-sector | Advantages | Liabilities |
|---|---|---|
| Informal | • Accessible<br>• Client-oriented<br>• Low cost | • Poor quality care<br>• Difficult to mainstream<br>• Poorly educated |
| NGO | • High quality<br>• Target the poor<br>• Low cost<br>• Involve the community | • Small coverage<br>• Lack of resources<br>• Cannot be scaled-up<br>• Ad hoc interventions |
| For-profit | • High quality (in selected areas)<br>• Huge outreach/coverage<br>• Innovative | • Ad hoc interventions<br>• High cost<br>• Variable quality<br>• Clustered in cities |

derive sustenance from local communities and from their ability to introduce both innovation and flexibility at the grassroots level. The World Bank (2004) argued that each subgroup of the private sector is motivated by different objectives and behaves in a unique way. Each subgroup has its own advantages and liabilities, as Table 1.2 illustrates.

### Defining public-private partnership

Although widely used, partnership is a difficult concept to define. Poorly defined in the literature, it means many things to many people. Some definitions in the literature are so vague and general that they cover practically any type of interaction between public and private actors. Yet as a general term, partnership is often used to describe a range of inter-organizational relationships and collaborations. While there is no universally accepted definition, there is a convergence about what constitutes a partnership, as the following examples indicate:

- 'a means to bring together a set of actors for the common goal of improving the health of a population based on the mutually agreed roles and principles' (WHO 1999).
- 'collaborative activities among interested groups, based on mutual recognition of respective strengths and weaknesses, working towards common agreed objectives developed through effective and timely communication' (Paoletto 2000).
- 'a working relationship that is characterized by a shared sense of purpose, mutual respect and the willingness to negotiate' (Lister 2000).
- 'any form of joint effort or undertaking of public and private players for achieving common objectives. Sometimes sharing common objectives may not be a core condition since partners may have different views and objectives' (Wang 2000).
- 'partnerships are a useful way of engaging a wide range of stakeholders and

non-government organizations in achieving the complex set of development objectives in health' (ADBI 2001).

- 'cooperation of some sort of durability between public and private actors in which they jointly develop products and services and share risks, costs and resources that are connected with these products' (Van Ham and Koppenjan 2001).
- 'a dynamic relationship among diverse actors, based on mutually agreed objectives, pursued through a shared understanding of the most rational division of labor based on the comparative advantage of each partner' (Brinkerhoff 2002).
- 'refers to a variety of co-operative arrangements between the government and private sector. It is a method of involving the private sector in delivering public goods or services and/or securing the use of assets necessary to deliver public services. Partnership also provides a vehicle for coordinating with non-governmental actor to undertake integrated, comprehensive efforts to meet community needs. The structure of the partnership varies to take advantage of the expertise of each partner, so that resources, risks and rewards can be allocated in a way that best meets clearly defined public needs' (Axelsson *et al.* 2003).
- 'a collaborative venture between two or more organizations that pool resources in pursuit of common objectives' (Gill 2003).
- 'true partnership requires shared objectives, shared risks, shared investments, and shared rewards' (Annigeri *et al.* 2004).
- 'a partnership means that both parties have agreed to work together in implementing a program, and that each party has a clear role and say in how that implementation happens' (Blagescu and Young 2005).
- 'at the heart of the concept of partnership [is that] partners operate in the conviction that their partnership is an expression of something shared that creates extra potential and added value' (Hodgkin 2005).
- 'a form of agreement [that] entails reciprocal obligations and mutual accountability, voluntary or contractual relationships, the sharing of investment and reputational risks, and joint responsibility for design and execution' (World Economic Forum 2005).

Partnership is therefore a collaborative effort and reciprocal relationship between two parties with clear terms and conditions, well-defined partnership structures, and specified performance indicators for delivering a set of health services within a stipulated period of time. They achieve mutually understood and agreed objectives by following certain mechanisms.

Three themes emerge among these definitions. First, there is a sense of *relative equality* among the individuals and organizations involved. Second, there is *mutual commitment* to agreed objectives that provides direction for members of the partnership. And third, there is *mutual benefit* for the principal stakeholders involved in the partnership. Partnerships differ markedly from those relationships based on markets and on hierarchies (Moore 1992). Market-based relationships involve exchange when buying and selling goods and services; bureaucratic relationships involve hierarchy based on authority. Partnership is distinct from these classic forms because it involves collaboration and coordination among organizations based on trust. Without trust, there is little to distinguish a partnership from a contractual relationship or from an authority-based relationship.

When partnerships occur along the lines of a principal–agent relationship, the principal holds the authority and the agent simply receives support. A common case has been the domination of donors over recipients in bilateral aid and the demands of the former for accountability by the latter (Ashman 2001). 'In recent years, however, there has been a shift towards a more collaborative, mutually beneficial type of partnership. In this new partnership model, both parties join their resources to achieve common benefits' (Blagescu and Young 2005).

Ahmed (2000) argued that the fundamental principles of partnerships are 'non-rivalry' and 'non-exclusion' of public goods; he identified the following criteria for judging the effectiveness of any partnership:

- Universality (i.e. access for all who are eligible to a type of service);
- Equity (i.e. ensuring acceptable quality of service for all, sharing of costs equitably if imposed, and special attention to disadvantaged groups);
- Efficiency (i.e. management of an activity to achieve maximum results and benefits by expending least resources);
- Accountability (i.e. holding the providers of services answerable to the beneficiaries and other stakeholders regarding both process and outcome of a program). Transparency, participatory planning and decision-making, and evaluation are necessary conditions for accountability.

In the context of describing the benefits of partnerships in international drugs, pharmaceutical products and development, Widdus (2001: 718) observed:

> Partnership between public/governmental entities, private/commercial entities, and civil society has a contribution to make in improving the health of the poor by combining the different skills and resources of various organizations in innovative ways. Public agencies clearly benefit from working in collaboration with the private sector in areas where the public sector lacks expertise and experience. Partnerships appear to be most justified where:
>
> - Traditional ways of working independently have a limited impact on a problem.
> - The specific desired goals could be agreed by potential collaborations.
> - There is relevant complementary expertise in both sectors
> - The long term interests of each sector are fulfilled, and
> - The contribution of expertise and resources are reasonably balanced.

Public private partnerships should generally be viewed as social experiments that are attempts to learn how to tackle intractable health problems in better ways. There is no formula for constructing them and it is unlikely that a universally applicable one will be found. Public private partnership can be helpful but they are not a panacea. Action is needed to overcome weak delivery systems.

The Government of India's conceptual note (2005) on public-private partnership presupposes that partnership initiatives are aimed at the problem of poor health services delivery at two levels:

1   improved delivery mechanisms; and
2   increased mobilization of resources for health care from different sources.

The benefits of PPP are argued to be:

- Better quality of services can be achieved by setting up standard guidelines for the partners. A basic minimum level of quality health services would be maintained. Competing private health care providers would try to improve the quality as well to retain or to increase their clientele.
- Competition between the partnership facilities and other health care providers would not only provide greater choice of services to the poor but also make the private sector accessible to the poor through reduction in prices.
- By standardizing the services throughout the initiative, cost reduction can be achieved through economies of scale.
- Existing capacity of public health facilities can be improved without substantial investment in infrastructure. The resources saved can be utilized for other aspects of health care delivery.
- Synergy between public and private systems would reduce duplication of effort and wastage of funds.
- Opportunities to adopt best practices from organizational and management systems.
- Opportunities to target services to the poor and to reach inaccessible places through private initiatives
- Opportunities to work with the private sector for self-regulation and accountability.
- Flexibility in tailoring services according to community needs in order to address differences in health care needs.
- Partnerships create more channels of resource mobilization.

Many advantages of public-private partnerships arise from the relative strengths of each sector. The public sector works on a large scale and therefore can utilize economies of scale. A great deal of technical and professional expertise exists in the public system, which is considered to be more equitable than the market. Advantages of the private sector are its presence at all levels of society. Private organizations operate under robust business models, possess management and technical skills to attract and retain clients (patients), operate under intense pressures to deploy and manage resources at optimal level, thus attaining a high degree of efficiency. They are sufficiently flexible to act independently at short notice.

In summary, the key criterion in a partnership is collaboration among multiple organizations in which risks and benefits are shared in pursuit of shared goals. As Wildridge *et al.* (2004) observe, 'Most definitions of partnership include terminology such as common aim, vision, goals, mission or interest; joint rights, resources and responsibilities; autonomous and independent; equality and trust'. While contemporary rhetoric about partnerships is often symbolic and used to camouflage asymmetrical relationships, the core elements of a viable partnership are beneficence (joint gains), autonomy (of each partner), joint-ness (shared decision-making and accountability) and equity (fair returns in proportion to investment and effort).

## Key attributes of public-private partnership

All partnerships have four overlapping phases (Venkat Raman and Björkman 2006). During the *preparation phase*, abstract ideas are turned into projects. Given the goals to be achieved, the project initiator identifies possible partners and explores how risks may be shared. A critical issue is the extent to which the government is prepared to reduce its control over operational stages of the project. Public-private partnerships require governments to define the level of project control while private sector agencies need to be convinced that governments – both central and local – will stick to what is agreed.

It is also necessary for local consumers and other stakeholders to buy into the concept, including their willingness to pay. Public-private partnerships are not free. In the end, either the government or the user must pay. 'PPPs do not affect public responsibility. Government stays responsible. Under public responsibility, firms are invited to provide services either to the government or directly to the public' (UK/NL 2003). This preparation phase usually ends with a Memorandum of Understanding (MOU) by the parties.

The *negotiation phase* involves planning the project, during which all parties provide inputs to clarify the original goal and to formulate a plan for action. Feasibility studies are undertaken to analyze financial viability, socio-economic contexts, risk assessment and potential distribution of revenues. The primary interest of for-profit private actors is the return on investment because, as compensation for undertaking risks, the private sector expects a certain amount of revenue. The more varied interests of non-profit players include achieving goals of social welfare, building capacity through linkages, accessing a combined pool of resources and enhancing legitimacy. This critical phase identifies and addresses key factors for the proposed project, including a sound balance among project finances, risk-taking and additional cost-recovery. The end of the negotiation phase is usually marked by a formal agreement signed by the relevant parties and sometimes by a contract.[1]

In the *implementation phase*, the public and private partners execute the project according to their agreements. They 'get something done'. If critical elements are unavailable or if they turn out differently than expected, the negotiation phase resumes by revising the original plans. When all arrangements are operating relatively smoothly, the project enters its *operational phase* in which the expected benefits are reaped.

The single label of partnership does not do justice to the variety that exists in practice. Some authors address the problem of varied interpretations by developing distinct categories to describe differences in partnerships or presenting partnerships as a continuum based on key characteristics found in a partnership. Lewis (1998), for example, distinguishes two forms of partnership – a partnership is *active* if it involves negotiations and adaptations in the light of practice, or *passive* if it is used only to gain access to external resources by accepting externally-imposed rules. Pallavi (2005) suggests a classification that spans six different types of claims associated with public-private partnerships.

1   Often used to describe an ideal form of partnership, *collaboration* involves shared decision-making power over planning and implementation of programs. It is based on mutual respect, acceptance of autonomy, independence and pluralism of private opinions and positions (Tandon 1991). Used interchangeably with the term partnership, collaboration is more a value-based claim than an actual form of practice.

2   *Cooperation* between partners is another type of claim used interchangeably with partnership. As partners, private organizations and governments cooperate to pursue similar goals through similar strategies, thus working towards a convergence akin to collaboration. Coston's (1998) model of eight forms of NGO/government relations suggests that cooperation is a less ambitious form of collaboration that does not require an equal sharing of power. The power is assumed and not derived from expertise or contributions in a non-hierarchical set-up (Robison *et al.* 2000).

3   Based on comparative advantage, private organizations and governments work together in a *complementary* relationship to pursue similar goals but recognizing different abilities (Najam 2000). Complementarity generates synergy, whether planned or unexpected.

4   *Consultation* involves constructive dialogues between NGOs and the government in the area of program design. It need not always lead to direct financing of a private organization by the government (Newman 2000).

5   *Contracts* exist when government provides private organizations with a well-defined package of services to be implemented under conditions largely established by the government. Government may provide funds and training to encourage non-governmental organizations to operate in priority areas. Contractual relations carry risks for the autonomy of an organization and are often contrasted with partnerships.

6   *Coordination* involves hierarchy that is constructed voluntarily where one actor is given the task of leading (Robison *et al.* 2000). In practice, formal

or informal units of NGOs may be set up in relevant government departments in order to enable the government to plan its programs in full knowledge of activities by the others.

The six-fold classification identifies the different types of claims made by governments and by the private sector within the broad area of partnership. The first three claims – collaboration, cooperation and complementary relations – are sought by the private sector; the last three claims – contracts, consultation and coordination – are desired by governments. In practice, these claims are not mutually exclusive and may coexist within a single partnership between a private agency and the government.

According to Bazzoli *et al.* (1997: 535), partnerships are more useful when the net benefits of partnership exceed those of independent activity, and when the joint efforts of organizations to produce a service are more efficient or effective than independent action by individual organizations. Public-private partnership has four principal goals:

- A focus on the health status of the communities, not just patients who receive care or enrollees of a health plan.
- A seamless continuum of care with mechanisms that facilitate service delivery at the right time in the most appropriate setting based on patient need.
- Management within fixed resources as achieved through capitated payments or global budgets based on the costs of efficient care delivery.
- Community accountability.

Wang (2000) notes that formation of partnerships does not mean that the philosophies of partners must change. Rather, what partnerships hope to achieve matters most. Partnerships are not ends in themselves. The use of partnerships relies on judgments about with whom to form partnerships and how best to combine respective strengths. The value of partnerships goes beyond market efficiency and community participation.

The 'Field Guide to Environmental Partnerships' (cited in Paoletto 2000) makes the following observations on partnerships:

- Partnerships are formed among organizations but succeed because of individuals.
- A successful partnership usually has a strong leader who champions the partnership projects and goals with vision, energy and enthusiasm.
- Partnerships involve people directly affected by a partnership, usually those most willing and able to work for it.
- Shared agendas, joint decision-making and mutual benefit constitute a partnership; money facilitates the projects.
- Visible senior-level support lets a partnership operate easily within an organization; it displays the organization's commitment to other partners as well as to the general public.

- Organizations should be willing to consider new ideas and share responsibility.
- A partnership is an opportunity for organizations to work together beyond day-to-day business-as-usual activities.
- Most partnerships are proactive and involve action beyond what is required by regulation or policy.

In many countries, 'partners' in partnership have moved away from the for-profit sector to the non-profit sector. Legal and political obstacles in some countries have made any partnership with the commercial sector unacceptable. There is a fear that any partnership with the private sector is an indirect attempt at privatizing the public sector health system. As a result, the public sector has had to find creative ways to partner with NGOs, such as contracting via projects. Such fears about the private sector emerge from the perceived social image of private sector as being 'exploitative' and having 'ulterior motives'.

Ambegaokar and Lush (2004) suggest that private individuals pioneered partnerships with the public sector. Historically, due to lack of interest or even opposition by the government on issues related to women's sexual health, these pioneers initiated services related to sex education and contraceptives among women. Although begun as social movements, these initiatives eventually became independent not-for-profit businesses (domestic NGOs) and developed close links with government. Managerial independence from government while yet working to fulfill public health goals is precisely the type of management structure that some health sector reforms advocate as the ideal form of public-private partnership. Reasons for the success of NGOs are said to be that:

1   their mission was more important than the available government grant;
2   they ventured into an arena where government was yet to venture;
3   they were autonomous with strong managerial systems.

Experience in social marketing of contraceptives around the world is a pioneering example of private sector approaches in the delivery of public health services.

While there are several advantages of engaging non-profit private sector, in the Indian context partnering NGOs in the provision of public health services has been constrained by many factors. According to Mukhopadhyay (2000), the importance of NGOs in health sector was envisioned by the Government of India through successive plan periods since the mid-1960s. But since health is constitutionally a state (provincial) responsibility, this concern of the central government is often not shared by all state governments. Consequently, there has been an uneven partnership between government and NGOs, depending on the political composition of respective state governments. The NGOs are expected to implement what the government has already planned. The NGOs feel that there is a mismatch between the government health priorities compared to needs at the grassroots. Even if a partnership exists, it is complicated by the unequal nature of relationships as well as the red-tape involved in getting programs sanctioned by government and money released.

In the context of widespread involvement of NGOs with the government in providing family welfare and reproductive health services, Ahmed (2000) asks whether NGOs are true partners of the government in sharing and working together, in setting objectives and priorities, in developing strategies, in implementing programs, and in assessing results. Or are NGOs merely contractors bidding for government contracts like any commercial service providers to fulfill the contract for an agreed fee? In India concerns have been raised about the dubious nature of some NGOs, which are often established by political personalities to garner funds from the state.

There are several reasons why governments choose to contract with NGOs. They can provide services to underserved sections of the population, improve accessibility, improve the quality of care, control health care costs for the beneficiaries as well as the health system, improve the utilization level of public health institutions and reduce the overall cost escalation in health care. Collaborating with NGOs and the private for-profit sector allows the government to circumvent problems with traditional public service arrangements such as inflexible human resource management or non-amenability to performance-based incentives. It is also possible that the government would face less political resistance if it were to seek partnership with the non-profit NGO sector rather than the for-profit sector. It is also possible to hypothesize that bureaucracy is more than willing to partner with the for-profit sector for administrative efficiency whereas popular political sentiments may prevent overt collaboration with private for-profit partners.

NGOs tend to enter into partnership with the public sector for three reasons: to fulfill a social mission, to sustain themselves financially and to gain recognition from the government (Abramson 1999). Whether the private partner is a for-profit or not-for-profit organization, governance of the public sector is a key factor in partnership building. Ahmed (2000) delineates the issues pertaining to governance:

- degree of centralization or decentralization;
- presence or absence of legal and institutional framework;
- public accountability and transparency; and
- organizational (bureaucratic) culture and attitudes that encourage or discourage partnership.

## Public-private partnership: types and models

Public-private partnerships come in different forms and structures. The continuum ranges from ownership changeover to simple outsourcing for a fee. According to Moser (2000), the classic partnership types and other innovative types include:

- *Contracting in*: a public health service or institution is given autonomy and responsibility for achieving certain service targets, often through global budgeting.
- *Contracting out*: a private enterprise is contracted to provide part or all of a service (for example, contracting a firm to provide laboratory, laundry or catering services) or leasing a public institution to the private sector with service delivery targets. In some countries, the delivery of services to certain populations may be contracted to NGOs.
- *Selling or leasing public institutions or space*: hospitals, clinics or land is leased or sold to the private sector. Often these deals include obligations to provide levels of coverage for the poor and other social benefits from the lessors or buyers.
- *Private sector governance*: by appointment to Boards of Directors or other oversight structures, community leaders or private persons are included in the governance of semi-autonomous institutions.
- *Sharing technology and specialist resources:*
  - Physicians admit private patients in public facilities while private physicians provide a limited range of specialist services on a salary basis or for a fee in public institutions.
  - Based on contracting out, fee-for-service or barter, the private sector utilizes technological resources in the public sector (MRI, CT scan, laboratories) and vice versa.
  - Patient referrals from the public to the private system for specialist services or vice versa rather than physicians or institutions developing competing services.
  - Bulk purchasing of pharmaceuticals and supplies jointly by the public and private sectors in order to reap discounts due to economies of scale and stronger purchasing clout.

Aljunid (1995) suggests that the interaction between the public and private sectors occurs on four dimensions: regulation, human resources, patient referrals and disease notification. It is argued that the unregulated behavior of the private sector is a major cause of inequities in the health sector. Roemer and Roemer (1982) suggest that evidence from around the world indicates that self-regulation within the private sector is not effective in protecting the interests of the patients and that a free market in health care, without regulation, leads to monopoly or oligopoly which, in turn, would be deleterious to consumers. They propose that government is responsible for such regulation.

Other analysts argue that excessive government regulation leads to greater administrative costs, higher probability of unnecessary interventions and unjustified deployment of complex technologies (Belmartino 1994). By working with the private sector, the government could monitor and regulate the inequities. Human resources is another area in which public-private partnership is increasingly evident. Historically governments across the world have attempted to regulate the flow of human resources from the public sector to the private sector in the form of compulsory service tenure, paying non-practice allowance, etc. Deficiency of human resources in the public sector has led to the government hiring private practitioners on contract in public hospitals.

### Contracting

Perhaps the most often cited form of public-private partnership, contracting is further categorized into 'contracting out' and 'contracting in'. *Contracting out* refers to a situation in which private providers receive a budget to provide certain services and manage a government health unit. The parties agree on guidelines about the quantity, quality and duration of the contract. Contracting out is used when the public facilities have a low utilization level, are difficult to manage due to systemic deficiencies, are in remote and inaccessible areas, and need to increase community involvement. Contracting out allows different levels of authority, responsibility and flexibility to be assigned to the private partner.

- Option 1: government transfers the physical infrastructure, equipment, budget and personnel of a health unit to the selected agency.
- Option 2: government transfers physical infrastructure, equipment and budget to the agency and, within government norms, gives it freedom to recruit personnel.
- Option 3: government transfers physical infrastructure, equipment and budget, and gives the agency freedom to use its own service delivery model without following prescribed patterns.
- Option 4: government transfers the physical infrastructure, equipment and budget, and gives the selected agency freedom to have its own personnel and service delivery models, to expand types of services provided, and to introduce user-fees in order to recover some proportion of costs.

*Contracting in* is a form of outsourcing non-clinical or support services to private contractors. Contracting in is undertaken in secondary and tertiary hospitals for services such as maintenance of buildings, utilities, housekeeping, canteen, kitchen, pharmacy and medicine stores, diagnostic facilities, transport, security and communications. Hospitals are given the freedom to choose the services to be given to contractors. It is assumed that in many hospitals contracting-in conserves resources, improves efficiency and supplies better quality services. Contracting in services leads to surplus human resources that can be transferred to other health units to fill vacant positions, if any. Resentment of employees and interference of trade unions are among the major obstacles to this process. Contracting in is useful when the efficiency level of services has to be improved, when scarce resources have to be conserved, when costs must be cut, and when trying out innovative delivery methods.

## *Franchising*

Franchising is a business model in which sale of a product or service is given as an exclusive right to a local entrepreneur (franchisee) to conduct the business in a delimited territory in a prescribed manner as per mutual agreement. Typically the franchiser has developed a value for the product or service in the form of either brand-building or exclusivity. The franchisee merely acts as a sales-point with incentives built into the agreement. The franchisees contribute resources of their own to set up the service outlet or clinic and pay membership to franchiser. Franchising is a useful mode when the health care demands of people are enormous but when the government is not in a position to meet these demands or when efforts to revitalize the infrastructure are time-consuming and slow. It is also a useful mode if the resources required to expand public health infrastructure are enormous or if the vast network of private hospitals can be tapped to improve quality standards of the private sector and provide quality care at affordable prices. The franchiser increases the demand for new services by marketing them through outreach activities (advertising and promotion) and by training the provider to market the services directly to potential clients (Montagu 2002).

In *partial franchising*, a franchisee enters into an agreement to provide a basket of services in lieu of payment of a fee or commissions from sale of services. The franchisee may also provide many other services that are not part of the contract. As this system is not revenue-sharing, there is no incentive to a franchiser to improve performance through promotional activities. Partial franchising is not a public-private partnership but suggests relevant experiences.

Under *full franchising*, a franchisee provides services defined by the franchiser; expansion of the range of services depends on mutual agreement. Full franchising is complex and requires detailed agreement on financial terms, subsidies, guaranteed caseload, quality of services and competition.

*Branded clinics* are subsidiary outlets of larger establishments (health services providers) that use the brand value of the parent organization. Branded clinics are more sustainable because of their ability to generate more income than social franchising units. Branded clinics are useful when the services to be provided need high visibility.

## *Social marketing*

Social marketing refers to donor-funded programs designed to meet unmet demand for health products, making them accessible to needy populations, typically with the support of multimedia communication campaigns. All social marketing programs have three things in common: a social goal, a methodology inspired by commercial marketing, and some dependency on donor funding with an objective towards changing behaviors and increasing access to needed health products. The product-based social marketing approach has two variations – the NGO-based model and the manufacturer's model (Armand 2003). In the former model, NGOs aim at maximizing the number of users consistent with their social goals; they seek to market their own brands that are designed to meet the needs and wants of specific target groups. For example, they reduce the price of products to make them affordable to the poorest users. The NGO often uses donated products and sells them at prices that only allow partial recovery of marketing and distribution costs. Common in countries with limited commercial presence or in those countries where contraceptives and other health products are expensive and poorly distributed, the NGO model depends on sustained donor funding and, in some cases, entails high operating costs. In contrast, the manufacturer's model comes with built-in product sustainability even without donor funding. Products are marketed at commercially viable prices through a manufacturer's existing distribution network, but they do not meet the needs of low-income or hard-to-reach populations.

Social marketing seeks to influence behaviors to benefit not the marketer but the target audience and society in general. This technique has been extensively used in health programs, especially for contraceptives and oral rehydration therapy, and is being used with more frequency for such diverse topics as drug abuse, heart disease and organ donation. Like commercial marketing, the primary focus is on the consumer – on learning what people want and need rather than trying to persuade them to buy some products. Social marketing is one of the earliest efforts at building public-private partnerships for marketing contraceptives. Government provides the subsidized contraceptives and finances both brand and point-of-purchase promotion schemes of selected marketing agencies. While using private sector techniques and partnerships with business, social marketing programs maintained close links with the public health sector for regulatory oversight and training staff (Ambegaokar and Lush 2004).

### *Joint venture organizations*

Joint ventures are launched with equity participation of government and the private sector. Proportions of equity and the nature of participation of each partner may vary from one venture to another. Joint ventures are mostly in building large-scale establishments or super-specialty ventures where government involvement is either not feasible or politically unsound.

### *Voucher schemes*

A voucher is a document that can be exchanged for defined goods or services as a token of payment. They are to be used within a specified period of time. The vouchers are then redeemed by accredited hospitals or certified clinics that provide a set of services (consultations, lab tests, surgical procedures, counseling, deliveries and drugs). The voucher system is a useful tool when cost-of-service is a major barrier to services, when the existing health facilities do not provide all types of services, when there is inadequate awareness about the need or features of the service, and when there is a need to generate demand for services – particularly among the poor and the disadvantaged.

### *Hospital autonomy or autonomous institutions (under MOU)*

When hospitals or health service establishments are given financial and administrative autonomy, it is presumed that flexibility in decision-making will lead to more efficiency, improved quality and greater accountability. Autonomy encourages a sense of ownership and involvement among the institution's workforce. It could also allow institutions to generate alternate sources of funds.

### *Mobilizing resources, technical expertise from corporate/ commercial sector*

With their resources, technical and managerial know-how, corporate enterprises can infuse professional expertise into public health institutions. Business and industry associations have long played significant roles in the form of corporate social responsibility. Recently they have become more visible in advocacy efforts, in pooling resources to introduce new schemes, and in adopting, managing and maintaining public health institutions.

### *Collaborating with professional associations*

Support of professional bodies such as local medical associations is sought to help in launching mass programs for immunization, pulse polio, cataract operations and health camps. They may also be involved in self-regulation, setting standard protocols, establishing quality assurance systems, encouraging ethical practices and providing programs of accreditation, training and Continuing Medical Education (CME).

### *Build, operate and transfer*

Build, operate and transfer (BOT) models have been successful in infrastructural development throughout the world. BOT requires part-financing of projects by the government, financial guarantees when needed, subsidized land at prime locations and assurance of reasonable returns on investment. These models are increasingly used to build large hospitals and to ensure quality services at reasonable rates to the poor. As a model for partnership BOT is used when large numbers of service delivery centers (hospitals, labs, diagnostic centers) have to be constructed within a short span of time but when the resources to do so are not immediately available.

### *Donations and philanthropic contributions*

While philanthropists have long contributed cash to the health sector, governments lack a formal mechanism to mobilize and utilize private donations for improving the local health situation. Recently, however, efforts have been made to create simple, transparent institutional mechanisms to encourage donations and to mobilize resources from wealthy members of the community.

*Involvement of social groups and community based organizations*

Long involved in immunization campaigns, health camps, information and education campaigns, social clubs and citizen groups such as Rotary bring their own expertise, organizational capacity and resources in providing health care services. Likewise local self-help groups and cooperative societies mobilize community resources that can be effectively used to procure drugs, emergency transport services, maternal and child care services, and HIV/AIDS care and support.

Different models of public/private partnership are useful at different times and under different circumstances. Donations by local industrial houses or philanthropists, businesses or corporate involvement, introduction of user-fees, and implementation of insurance schemes are methods to augment resources. 'Contracting out' is used when health facilities are underutilized or non-functional while 'contracting in' is used to improve the quality of services or to improve the accessibility to high-technology services or improve efficiency. Contractual appointment of staff aims to reduce the negative impact of vacant positions. Voucher schemes and community-based health insurance are invoked to reduce the adverse effects of health care costs on poor patients and improve equity in the health system. While some partnerships are of limited duration or for one-time activities, others are long-term. The thrust of partnerships also varies. Some focus on service delivery, some augment resources and infrastructure, others seek organizational and systemic improvement and yet others conduct simple advocacy activities.

The success or failure of these innovations depends on several factors. Systemic changes need to be brought about in order to ensure that partnerships are successful, sustainable and equitable. These changes are broadly categorized as:

1   capacity of the partners;
2   advocacy or positive image;
3   accreditation (standardization); and
4   regulation through monitoring and control.

The complexity involved in successfully implementing a partnership model can be illustrated with the example of 'contracting'. Among all the models, contracting has been the most common form of partnership. While other models are being tried in many countries, their lessons are yet to be documented. Given the widespread use of contracting as a method of public-private partnership, it is pertinent to examine the issues and lessons learned under this model.

## Contracting as a public-private partnership model

A primary objective of health sector reforms in many countries since the mid-1980s has been a smaller role for the government in health care. The strategies include creating competition among the providers through competitive contracting, expanding access to services through subsidizing private providers, and encouraging the rich to use private services so that government can focus on the poor. These strategies have gradually shifted toward contracting out services to the private sector. The reason for this gradual shift had been increasing disillusionment with the model of exclusive state provision of social services. Downsizing the government was one possible option (Bennett *et al.* 1997). Contracting (both 'out' and 'in') as a management tool in health sector reforms was adopted across all types of public health systems, whether the tax-based system (UK and New Zealand); social insurance (Germany and the Netherlands); vertically integrated (Denmark) or fragmented (the US). Functions of finance and delivery and the provider–purchaser split have been delineated (Ashton *et al.* 2004). According to Bennett and Mills (1998), contracting was a strategy for removing government from the 'coalface' of service delivery. Although contracting had been widely used for civil construction, equipment supply and maintenance, this strategy under the guise of new public management moved into areas where it was previously unknown.

'Contracting' refers to a situation in which private providers receive a budget from government for providing certain services. Government pays the private sector to deliver services that it used to deliver itself. The relationship between the government and the private sector is contained in a contract – a written agreement enforceable by law. In general, the private partner uses its own staff and resources but governments can also provide specialized facilities, equipment and additional inputs as appropriate. The two parties agree on some or all of the following: quantity, quality, price and duration of the contract (World Bank 2004).

According to Ashton *et al.* (2004), the benefits of contracting in the health system are to:

1   stimulate focus on quantity, quality and costs of care;
2   make service provision competitive and thus increase operational efficiency;
3   increase consumer choice by expanding the service base that had not been early expanded by the public system;
4   improve resource efficiency by encouraging prioritization of services provided; and
5   improve the accountability of providers in their use of public funds.

A classical definition of the verb 'to contract' assumes that it is a 'voluntary agreement' between two or more parties (Allen 1995). Risks are presumed to be equally shared among all partners signing the contract. According to Campbell and Harris (1993), the parties to a contract determine all its terms at the time that they agree to it. Such an agreement assumes that the judgments of the partners are correct about the nature of the world at the time of the agreement and about the way the world will develop during the time of performance.

Conceptually, contracts can be divided into two fundamental types: classical and relational (Macneil 1978; Campbell 1996). According to Allen (2002), partners in a classical contract have the freedom of contract (i.e. choice of partner; terms of the contract; settlement of disputes). It is a discrete transaction in which the identity of the partners does not matter. All possible future transactions, including contingencies and risks, are written and agreed in advance. All future matters are specified at the outset. Neo-institutional economists also call this model 'complete' or 'comprehensive'. However, many analysts argue that the classical form of contract is not always the most appropriate model for long-term contractual relationships.

A contrasting model is the 'relational' contract in which partners do not plan or specify their contractual relationships completely or in advance, disputes are often resolved without resorting to actual terms of the agreement, and contracts are treated as relationships over time rather than discrete exchanges. In relational contracts trust, faith and commitments are regarded as critical. Williamson (1985 cited in Allen 2002) presumes that classical contracts generally do not occur due to high transaction costs. Given the high transaction costs in the case of health care, contracts are unlikely to be complete (Bartlett 1991; Roberts 1993; Ashton 1998; Croxson 1999). Table 1.3 describes the main differences between relational and classical contracts.

At the operational level, there are many types of contracts and contract elements. At one extreme on a continuum is the British system of contracting for health services; the other extreme is the American system of contracting. In the UK, the public sector contracts internally, within the public health system, to general practitioners who act as 'gatekeepers' to the health system on behalf of

*Table 1.3* Classical and relational contract models

| Classical contract | Relational contract |
|---|---|
| Discreteness of the partners; partners need not know each other. | Non-discreteness, partnerships are unique and non-transferable. |
| Partnerships begin quickly through clear formal agreement and are terminated quickly by performance criteria. | Commencement and termination of contracts is likely to be gradual and not determined by a formal contract agreement. |
| All elements of the contract are specified and are measurable. | Contracts do not specify or measure all elements. |
| Trust is not crucial; opportunistic behavior could be handled as per agreement. | Opportunistic behavior is possible, but trust is more important for relationship to work. |
| Risk elements are clear and allocated in the contract. | All risk elements cannot be foreseen and an agreement is not necessarily binding. |
| No adjustments in contracts once it commences. | Extensive post-commencement planning and adjustment are likely. |

Source: Macneil 1978.

beneficiaries (patients). In contrast, in the US the government purchases a large portion of 'public' health services from private sector providers, both for-profit and not-for-profit, as in Medicaid and Medicare (Abramson 1999).

Bennett and Mills (1998) describe the stages of the contracting process:

- *Deciding whether to contract and which services to contract*, understanding what is to be achieved through contracting, priority-setting between services, relative costs of in-house provision versus cost by the contractors, and defining a package of services to be contracted.
- *Identification of the contractor and tendering process*, including advertising the contract, process of selecting the contractor (both in competitive and non-competitive contracts), and managing the tendering process.
- *Design of contract*, including issues such as the type of contract (lease, operating contract only, franchise), complete or incomplete contract, form of payment, quality specification, length of contract, specification of units of contracted service, etc.
- *Drafting of legal clauses in the contract*, including exit options, handling of grievances and settlement of disputes if any, etc.
- *Implementing the contract*, including transferring service location to the contractor, making adjustment to public sector service delivery, paying the contractor in a timely manner, etc.
- *Monitoring or auditing contractors*, which includes a strong management information system to collect and analyze information on the quality of service, beneficiary profile, costs of care, benefits and health outcomes to the community over a period of time.
- *Implementing sanctions for non-performance*, a range of possible sanctions for non-performance (as per the contract clauses) like verbal warnings, reduction of payment, non payment, legal proceedings, or even termination and ensuring that sanctions are implemented.
- *Evaluating and analyzing the implications of contracts* on the public health system as a whole or in parts.

According to Williamson (1987 cited in Bennett and Mills 1998), the ease of managing a contract depends on the following attributes:

- the ease with which features of the service can be defined and measured as well as specified in advance (in clinical care contracts it is difficult to specify fully exactly what services the contractor needs provide);
- the degree of asset specificity (which may allow or discourage contractors to cut corners or exhibit opportunistic behavior);
- the ease and the cost of gathering information about performance and hence monitoring the contractor's performance (for some clinical services it is difficult, even retrospectively, to judge the quality of contractor performance);
- identifying the technology and complexity involved in the production of services (primary, secondary or tertiary care; high or low technology, etc.).

The more complex a service being contracted, the more difficult it may be to specify the contract in advance;

- the nature of the contractor (not-for-profit providers may act with less guile than for-profit providers);
- the relative capability of contracting partners to absorb risk (central government or larger private partners are better able to absorb risks than local government or smaller private partners);
- the number of providers in the market and hence the likely degree of competition.

Services exhibiting different combinations of these characteristics require different approaches to contracting, and each different approach requires a different combination of capacities in both public and private sectors.

## Issues and challenges for private sector partnerships in the health sector

Abramson (1999) doubts that contracting evolves from strategic thinking by government. Rather contracting responds to the particular needs of a country at a particular time. Policy-makers, health authorities and NGOs consider several issues before negotiating and implementing a contract. Critical issues in the contracting form of public-private partnership include: what is the overall objective or purpose of the contract? How results-oriented is the contract? What gains or health outcomes are expected? how flexible is the purchaser (the public sector)? What kinds of incentives are in place? How well does the contract integrate incentives such as organizational and managerial capacity of the partners in terms of accounting procedures, costing and pricing of the services, supervision, performance monitoring and a valid information system? Allen (1995) notes that the contents of a contract reflect the partner's respective power, market share, expertise in the field and attitude toward risk-taking.

### Level of decision-making

Abramson (1999) and Brinkerhoff (1999) both observe that the extent to which a country's health system is decentralized shapes the contract process as well as outcomes. Key issues are the level (central, state or local government) at which contract negotiations take place and the guidelines to negotiate a contract that allow for local adaptation. Complete centralization leads to insensitivity to local conditions whereas decentralization of contract negotiations makes it difficult to monitor results. With local autonomy where decision-making is decentralized, partnerships can be formed more easily and operate more efficiently. Ideally under a federal framework, contract negotiations should occur at local level rather than have the local level simply implement a federal agreement.

## Design

Every contract should have explicitly stated key provisions on performance specifications and methods of monitoring, enforcement, dispute resolution and pricing. In legally binding documents these provisions should be carefully drafted in such a way that, if disputes arise in future, they withstand the scrutiny of the court. When courts look at contractual documents, they must be able to ascertain the parties' intentions at the time of their contractual agreement (Allen 1995).

- *Performance specification*: there must be clarity about services to be provided, description of actual tasks being performed, standard to which they should be performed, and their timing. Clarity is required about inputs, throughputs, outputs and outcomes of services. The inputs are staff, buildings, equipment and consumables. Outputs constitute the services provided to the target beneficiaries or activities performed (number of outpatient consultations, inpatient admissions). Outcomes are the impact of services on the beneficiary population in the form of intended objectives of the contract (e.g., reduced morbidity). The throughput or standard of care is to be measured in the form of quality of services, which is further divided into quality of outcome and quality of processes. Quality of outcomes is difficult to define in the contract other than indicators such as patient views. Quality of processes is an issue concerned with the organizations and the management of the providers. Indicators include waiting time, staff behavior, staff qualifications, and rational use of drugs or diagnostics.
- *Monitoring of performance*: monitoring is easier when the contract has been written clearly. Compliance with medical audits or peer review are frequently used monitoring mechanisms.
- *Pricing*: contacts should be able to state clearly the method used in pricing services.
- *Enforcement*: apart from specifying incentives for better performance, contracts need to state the exact circumstances in which a party is entitled to terminate the contract and to make clear that such termination will allow of the party to receive damages to compensate for its losses caused by the breach of contract.
- *Dispute resolution*: the contract should mention whether provision for referring disputes to a suitably qualified arbitrator rather than letting them languish in court. It is unnecessary for the written documents to set out what could happen in every contingency.

It is difficult to design a commercial contract in health services due to a number of limitations. First, it is necessary to have detailed information on the aims, priorities and requirements of the contract. Second, it is difficult to specify the standard of performance required because health services are complex. Third, a detailed commercial contract is unlikely to be sufficiently flexible to deal with contingencies. Finally the, transaction costs of writing such contracts are likely to be higher.

Abramson (2001) argued that in order to ensure accountability for the use of public funds through contracts, there is an immediate need to develop monitoring indicators and to improve the information system. Prior to assigning performance indicators under the contract, the purchaser (public sector) should clearly delineate the objectives of the contract. Indicators need to be objective, easy to measure, and applicable only those areas in which the contractor has some role to play. Objectives of the purchaser through the contract may be to increase efficiency, to enlarge the scope of services and the beneficiary population, or even to improve the quality of services. If the objective is to reduce expenditure and cut costs, then data need to be available on actual costs prior to and after the contract period. Such baseline data could easily construct the performance indicators needed for evaluation. There is also a need to specify those who will be responsible for supervision and evaluation as well as the periodicity in which evaluations will be conducted. As a rule of thumb, the more demanding the monitoring requirements are, the greater the administrative costs will be (Abramson 1999).

Knowles and Leighton (1997) suggest that internal consultations are needed about what indicators are to be used for measuring performance. It is also possible to weight the different performance indicators. Relative measures (rates and ratios) are more preferable than absolute terms. All measures should be based on empirical foundations, set through baselines, benchmarks and targets agreed by both the purchaser and the provider. Definitions of services are needed as well as linkage between monitoring, performance and release of payments. Abramson (1999) lists various performance indicators such as volume of services to be provided, timing and availability of services, coverage population, range of services, quality of services through end-user surveys, medication errors, staff qualifications, absenteeism, waiting-time for patient admission, percentage of cases referred to higher level health facilities and financial measurements such as cash flow, expenses and revenues.

### Costing and pricing

In order to understand the benefits of contracting services to the private sector, it is in the interest of the purchaser (the public sector) to know the costs of service delivery. Before agreeing on the price, each partner should estimate the unit cost of the services to be provided under the contract. On the basis of a demand analysis, the government then estimates the volume of services to be offered to the beneficiary population covered under the contract. While determining the unit costs, both partners need to be clear whether there would be cross-subsidies to the private partner from the public sector. The private partner needs to ensure that its costs can be covered by a contract, but it is not obliged to share its cost-estimates with the government. Pricing strategy could exempt a target population, set user-fees on a sliding scale or offer other types of subsidies. A gamut of pricing options is available ranging from cost-recovery mechanisms to exemption policies that provide services free of charge (Abramson 1999).

Apart from the cost of services and their delivery, contracting may include the costs of finding and selecting appropriate providers, of designing and negotiating contracts, of monitoring and enforcing the contracts, and of avoiding or resolving disputes between purchasers and providers (Williamson 1985). The costs associated with these activities are likely to vary greatly depending upon the contracting process, the type of service, and the nature of the relationship between purchasers and providers (Ashton *et al.* 2004). Administrative costs are the costs of contract management and supervision. Contracts in which payments are closely linked to contractor performance tend to incur higher administrative costs than outright subsidies or block grants; however, they contain mechanisms that ensure greater efficiency and higher quality in the long term.

*Funding and payment*

Performance of a contract is closely linked to the method of resource allocation and how the contractor is paid. Purchasers (the public sector) can pay for services in a variety of ways: either individually or in combination, per case, per day, per person, per year, or per the type of service (Wouters 1998). The payment mechanism may also vary. When the price of a package of services is negotiated before the services are rendered, the method is called 'prospective payment'. One prospective payment method is capitation, another is global budgeting. Prospective payments act as an incentive to the provider, who assumes greater financial risk, to employ greater efficiency. When payment is determined during or after the time in which the service is provided, it is considered a 'retrospective payment' or 'cost-based reimbursement'. Fee-for-service is the most common kind of retrospective payment (Maceira 1998).

Global payments through a predetermined budget based on population estimates for a geographical area may promote efficiency because such payments are not linked to volume or to the level of care actually provided; they encourage providers to conduct health promotion and disease prevention activities associated with primary care. This allows a provider to treat illnesses earlier at an appropriate level of care and thereby to control costs. A global payment mechanism may, however, undermine the quality of care. Because the provider receives payment regardless of the number or level of services delivered, there is an incentive to under-treat patients. And, perceiving a lack of quality, the population may cease to solicit needed health care. In case-based payment, since the provider is paid per person or per case treated, it is in the provider's interest to compete for clients, in part by offering high quality services that attract as many patients as possible. Because case-based payment is fixed per case, it encourages efficient use of resources. However, in order to minimize costs, the providers may fail to provide all the procedures associated with a particular diagnosis (Abramson 1999).

The ability of the public sector to purchase services and to pay bills during the contract must also be considered. Many NGOs with government contracts depend on timely payment for their financial survival. While some health care NGOs charge user-fees to patients (many others do not), the revenue from such fees is not sufficient to support an NGO for an extended period of time. Thus, a significant delay in payment from the government has a deleterious effect on an NGO's cash-flow and prevents it from carrying out the services to which it is contractually committed. An important consideration when deciding on a public sector contract is the degree to which the contracts and the contractors will be affected if the government fails to do its part to ensure proper handling of payments (Smith and Lipsky 1993).

Based on the experience of seeking private investment in building hospitals in Canada, Auerbach (2002) identified three disadvantages that must be overcome to justify any form of public-private partnership. One of the justifications for seeking private partnership to build hospitals under joint ventures is that the investment capital is available from private sources that is not available from government. But, according to Auerbach, such decisions are political in nature and self-inflicted in their outcomes. The choice is especially difficult to comprehend when it leads to higher rather than lower costs to taxpayers. When government decides to undertake a public project for public purposes but chooses to have it financed by the private sector, the private sector must borrow money for the same project at a higher cost than the public sector, unless the government in one way or another reduces the risk to the lender to such a degree that, either through guarantees or subsidies, the loan becomes, in effect, risk-free to the lender and completely equivalent to lending directly to the government. Indeed, if the lender lends at a risk-free rate, this negates the argument that government is getting value for money by transferring risk to the private sector. The market would say the opposite – that the risk of default is zero because the government bears the risk of failure, cost increases and so forth. Private financing of capital costs is more expensive.

Auerbach further argues that contracts with the private sector typically do not specify how much profit can be earned because such a specification would cap the incentive to earn as much as possible while still meeting the terms of the contract. In a partnership contract, a rational private sector partner will want to accept risk transfers from the public sector in the initial stages and negotiate for financial compensation for accepting them at a later stage. But if things go badly on essential health services that involve public safety, the government may not have an alternative service supplier. At this stage, the government will be in a poor negotiating position to sanction a supplier who demanded additional funds or time or who provided lower than expected levels of service or outcomes poorer than those agreed in the contract. Can the government afford to put the contractor into bankruptcy? Would it be willing to take over the service?

### Regulation and monitoring

Regulation of the health sector is one of the major responsibilities of the government and revolves around three key functions: accreditation, enforcement of national treatment protocols and standards, and quality assurance. Accreditation is the first step towards engaging the private sector. Accreditation specifies the basic requirements that a health care provider must meet in order to be considered for a contract. Requirements may vary depending on the type of contract (Bouchet and Abramson 1998). However, governments often do not explicitly state the quality standards, clinical norms, drug protocols and other regulatory measures in the contract.

### Information systems

For any contract arrangement to succeed, it is essential to have performance indicators that get monitored periodically. Well-designed information systems are critical to the success of a contract in operation. Bennett and Mills (1998) describe the requirements for an information system that will assist in decision-making on awarding contracts and the supervision thereof. While health ministries keep records on epidemiological and administrative information, very few countries have created the formats and records needed to monitor NGO contract compliance.

### Trust and perception

Trust is one of the most critical issues for the success of a partnership. Despite the overwhelming presence of the private sector, government often fails to recognize its contribution. In the context of contracting, trust is primarily based on expectations (Sako 1992). There is 'contractual trust' (expectations that partners will keep their promises) and 'goodwill trust' (mutual expectations of open commitment to each other). While both imply the absence of opportunistic behavior, 'goodwill trust' is particular to relational contracts as opposed to classical contracts. A third type of trust – 'competence trust' – refers to expectations that one party will competently carry out tasks whose technicalities are beyond the capabilities of the other party (Allen 2002).

The presence or absence of trust could be due to cultural factors. For many people the term 'private sector' has long meant only commercial enterprises and, in developing countries like India, commercial enterprises have traditionally been 'suspect' as exploitative and interested only in profit maximization by any means. This image explains the lack of trust or even opposition from advocacy groups about the notion of 'public-private partnership'. Non-governmental development organizations are overtly uncomfortable or even contradict anyone classifying them in the 'private sector'.

### Incentives and risks

While contracts should state financial and non-financial incentives to all partners, the risks involved for the partners are often not stated explicitly. In contracting services, the government as purchaser is supposed to distribute the risks and responsibilities between itself and the private provider (Walsh 1995). The terms and conditions, the price levels set, administrative costs, and the costs of supervision determine the distribution of risk. The higher the risk, the higher the level of compensation sought by the provider. But, if the provider underestimates the cost of services, it may encounter financial risk because it may not be reimbursed for all the costs incurred.

Different payment mechanisms distribute risk differently between purchasers and contractors. In fee-for-service, when charges are fixed for each type of services, the provider receives this rate for each service rendered; the purchaser therefore assumes the greater share of financial risk. Under a prospective payment system, which pays the provider a set amount per person enrolled in the health plan (whatever the services rendered), financial risk is transferred to the provider. In case-based payment, risk is shared by both provider and purchaser because a fixed amount is paid for all services related to a specific illness (Abramson 1999).

### Capacity of partners

Two primary conditions are required for any public-private partnership to succeed: capacity and willingness. Before any partnership contract is implemented, each partner needs to adopt for itself organizational and management systems, technical competence, and skilled staff to manage the contract. These competencies relate to reporting relationships, financial and accounting systems, internal communications, job profiles with clear division of labor, documentation and information systems, monitoring and supervision, etc. Collectively these competences represent the capacity of the organization to undertake an activity.

The capacity of an organization has internal and external dimensions. Internal capacity indicates organizational and managerial systems such as human resources, finance and information systems while external factors, particularly in the case of public sector organizations, include concurrent policies, management practices, rules and regulations, formal and informal power relationships, and the legal context of the contract, all of which may influence a particular task (Bennett and Mills 1998). In any partnership where more than one organization is involved in the performance of a task, a network of different organizations is responsible for implementing the task. Often one particular organization is central but the capacity of each organization in this network is relevant to the overall performance of the task (Hildebrand and Grindle 1994).

## Note

1 'A contract is a legally binding written agreement between two or more parties that specifies something provided (such as products or services) and something received in return (usually payment for the products or services' (Annigeri *et al.* 2004: 5).

# 2 Health systems and health care in India

## India's public health system and service delivery

During the six decades after independence, the infrastructure for India's public delivery of health services grew substantially and the health of its population improved. Periodic efforts were made to improve the capacity of the system to deliver health care services to all sections of the population. But despite the impressive progress, deficiencies exist in the overall performance of the public health system. Regional disparities are evident in terms of health infrastructure, morbidity status and socio-demographic imbalances in outcomes. The health system is characterized by inefficiency, low quality, inequities and poor accessibility.

India has one of the world's largest networks of health centres and hospitals under a public health system. At the beginning of the twenty-first century,[1] there

*Table 2.1* Growth in health infrastructure in India

| Indicator | 1951–1952 | 2005–2006 | Remarks |
| --- | --- | --- | --- |
| Population | 361 million | 1,027 million | Census data |
| Primary health centers | 725 | 22,669 | |
| Allopathic hospitals | 2,694 | 15,393 | Both public and private sectors |
| Allopathic beds | – | 683,545 | Both public and private sectors |
| All beds | 117,178 | 914,543 | |
| Doctors (allopathic) | 61,800 | 660,801 | Registered at Medical Council of India |
| Doctors (Indian systems) | – | 724,823 | Ayurveda, Unani and Homeopathy |
| Nurses | 16,550 | 908,962 | General Nursing Midwives only |
| Five-year plan budgets (millions of rupees) | 653 (First plan) | 589,203 (Tenth plan) | Includes health, family welfare, Indian systems plus homeopathy |
| Medical colleges | 30 | 262 | |

are 3,222 community health centers, about 3,500 urban family welfare centers, 22,638 dispensaries, 22,669 primary health centers and 142,655 sub-centers. In addition there were 15,393 secondary and tertiary allopathic hospitals in both public and private sectors with 914,543 beds. Table 2.1 sketches the progress since 1951 in creating health infrastructure in India.

India's progress over the decades has been impressive. Life expectancy has increased while rates of birth, death and infant mortality have declined. Significant progress has been made in the control of communicable diseases like smallpox, polio and malaria. But achievements have not been uniform across all sections of society or across different regions in the country. Disparities between rural–urban, low–high income groups and various social strata continue to plague the health system, and there are significant inter-state and intra-state disparities in terms of health indicators. States like Kerala and Tamil Nadu are comparable to middle-income countries while the BIMARU states (Bihar, Madhya Pradesh, Rajasthan, Uttar Pradesh) resemble the least developed countries. Table 2.2 displays these disparities.

## Causes and consequences of the failing public sector

Various factors constrain the effectiveness of India's public health system. In addition to meager resource and budgetary allocations, there are inherent organizational and managerial deficiencies. Limited resources are inequitably allocated towards tertiary care services, thus starving the primary care level. Lack of staff, medicine and supplies as well as inadequate equipment has forced the poor and the impoverished to seek health services from the private sector. Private out-of-pocket expenditures in India are high, estimated to be 86 percent of all health expenditures. Out-of-pocket payments are debilitating for the poor and vulnerable sections of the population. Studies have documented the extent of economic stress on the poor. While the provision of services through the public sector has been slowly undermined, deliberate as well as inadvertent government policies favor the rapid but unregulated growth of the private sector.

Despite the significant progress in health status and the creation of a vast network of institutions, the public health system has been unable to deliver health care services at desirable levels of quality and efficiency. Studies indicate that the average utilization level of government health institutions in rural areas is less than 25 percent. Many reasons are cited to explain the poor performance of the public sector. The critical problems afflicting public sector health systems are broadly categorized as:

- Inability to address emerging diseases and the epidemiological transition.
- Inadequate financial resource commitments, including inequitable budgetary allocation.
- Structural and managerial inefficiencies, including management of health personnel.
- Unregulated growth of the private health sector and its consequences.

Table 2.2 Regional imbalances in health indicators

| Indicator | Low performance states | | | Higher performance states | | | All India |
|---|---|---|---|---|---|---|---|
| | Bihar | Uttar Pradesh | Madhya Pradesh | Maharashtra | Kerala | Tamil Nadu | |
| Per capita health expenditure[1] (in rupees, 2001–2002) | | | | | | | |
| In public sector | 92 | 84 | 132 | 196 | 240 | 202 | 207 |
| In private sector | 687 | 1,040 | 733 | 815 | 1,618 | 644 | 790 |
| Maternal mortality rate[2] (per 100,000 births) | 371 | 707 | 498 | 135 | 195 | 76 | 408 |
| Female life expectancy at birth[3] (1998–2002) | 59.5 | 58.5 | 56.7 | 67.4 | 75.9 | 66.3 | 63.3 |
| Population per allopathic bed[4] (2002) | 3,029 | 2,647 | 5,582 | 920 | 325 | 1,135 | 1503 |
| Net public sector subsidies by percentage of beneficiary[5] | | | | | | | |
| Poorest quintile (20%) | 4.1 | 10.2 | 8.8 | 18.0 | 19.7 | 19.9 | 10.2 |
| Richest quintile (20%) | 50.3 | 39.0 | 37. | 16.8 | 21.9 | 14.8 | 31.0 |
| Deliveries assisted by health personnel[6] (2005–2006) | 30.9 | 29.2 | 37.1 | 70.7 | 99.7 | 93.2 | 48.3 |

Notes
1 National Health Accounts, India 2001–2002;
2 NRHM data centre (2001–2003);
3 CBHI Health information India 2005;
4 Health Information India 2004;
5 World Bank 2001;
6 NFHS-3 Facts Sheets (2006).

- Poor mobilization of the community as critical stakeholders in the health sector, including local bodies, NGOs and the private sector.

## Epidemiological transition

With 17 percent of world's population, India globally accounts for 23 percent of child deaths, 20 percent of maternal deaths, 30 percent of TB cases, 68 percent of leprosy cases and the largest number of HIV cases. The burden of communicable diseases, non-communicable diseases and injuries account for 50, 33 and 17 percent respectively in India compared to 18, 64 and 18 percent respectively in China (1998 data, Misra *et al.* 2003). Women in reproductive age groups and children below five years constitute the most vulnerable groups in the society. Malnutrition, anemia and pregnancy-related complications (including maternal mortality) are high in India. At 707 deaths per 100,000 births, maternal mortality in Uttar Pradesh is worse than many African countries. India's disease burden accounts for 269 million disability adjusted life-years (DALYs) lost (23 percent of global DALYs).

The high prevalence of sexually transmitted diseases in India makes its population vulnerable to HIV infection. By 2015 the number of AIDS cases is estimated to be three times more than the current level, entailing a corresponding increase in the prevalence level of TB of about 8.5 million cases. Control of communicable diseases is hindered by poor surveillance systems, delayed response, limited involvement of local bodies and inadequate budgetary allocations. While the effort to control communicable diseases is stretching the limits of public health system, the rapidly rising burden of non-communicable diseases (NCD) poses a severe challenge to the health system. Projections in India for 2020 indicate that NCDs will increase to 57 percent from 33 percent in 1998. This epidemiological transition and the increased vulnerability to NCDs generate great economic costs, particularly on the poor who need specialized clinical attention, prolonged care and expensive treatment. Cardiovascular diseases and diabetes will more than double; cancers will rise by a quarter. Mental health affects about 6.5 percent of Indians, a figure that is expected to increase due to stress from disruptions in income, unemployment and lack of social support systems.

## Financing and resource constraints

The single most important reason for the poor status of India's public health system is argued to be inadequate budgetary allocations by government towards the health sector. Public spending on health has remained stagnant at around 1 percent of GDP compared to the global average of 5.5 percent. The states, which bear up to 90 percent of the public health spending, have their funds largely committed to salaries, leaving little room for essential drugs, supplies and maintenance of existing services. Disparity in the allocation of resources between the primary and tertiary care systems seriously impairs the equity and efficiency of the public health system.

Another inequity in the public health system relates to who benefits from the public health funding. The poorest quintile of the population receives only 10 percent of public subsidies on health care while the richest quintile gets about one-third (Mahal *et al.* 2002). According to a World Bank report (2001) India has one of the world's highest levels of private out-of-pocket financing – 87 percent. Out-of-pocket expenses at the point of service are about 85 percent (Kulkarni 2003). A significant proportion of the resources spent by the people end up in the unorganized private sector.

Such financing has a debilitating effect on the poor who are disproportionately disadvantaged by disease because of limited access to adequate medical services. Hospitalization or chronic illnesses often leads to liquidation of assets or indebtedness. In the 1986–1996 decade, the number of poor not seeking treatment due to financial reasons increased from 15 percent to 24 percent in rural areas and from 10 percent to 21 percent in urban areas (Selvaraju and Annigeri 2001). Over 40 percent of hospitalized patients borrow money or sell assets to cover expenses, and 35 percent of hospitalized Indians fall below the poverty line because of hospital expenses. Approximately 300 million people or 29 percent of the Indian population lives in poverty, and it is estimated that every year out-of-pocket medical costs push 2.2 percent of the population below the poverty line (Mahal *et al.* 2002).

Without a regular national health accounts system, it is not known to how much is spent on what and by whom. Public spending is driven more by historical precedent than by evidence or need. In the absence of systematic evaluation, cost-effectiveness of interventions does not factor into decisions about new strategies or budget allocations. The system of releasing funds is fraught with uncertainties and budget cuts imposed are often arbitrary. The present system of budgeting may be sufficient for accounting and ensuring expenditure control but it is not useful for policy shifts towards partnerships. In sum, India's systems of health financing are archaic and need to be overhauled (NMCH 2005).

## Organizational and managerial challenges

Over successive plan periods, the government created many public institutions of health care delivery in the form of community health centers, primary health centers and health sub-centers as well as referral institutions like district hospitals, teaching hospitals and research institutions. Expansion of these facilities, however, has been without appropriate attention to institutional capacity, resource allocation, quality and performance standards, management systems and better governance. As a result public health care has become a structurally complex and endemically inefficient system.

Despite significant increases in trained health personnel, there are critical shortages in almost all categories of health staff in rural areas. Many public health centers are not fully functional due to shortages of staff, drugs and equipment. Prolonged delays in recruitment, corruption and political interference in postings and transfers, inadequate incentives, career stagnation, unfavorable working conditions, high workload and poor supervision have all contributed to low morale, absenteeism, unionization and poor performance among health workers. HRD policies are needed for recruitment, posting, promotion and transfer, incentives, training and professional development. The demoralization that exists among the workforce must be countered by enhancing professional and career opportunities (Venkat Raman 2002).

The availability and quality of human resources in the health sector is another significant concern. Current human resources (doctors, nurses, midwives) fall short of the international norm of 2.5 per 1,000 population. There are shortages in specialties such as anesthesia, ophthalmology, gynecology, skilled nursing and paramedical resources such as pharmacists and laboratory technicians in health facilities. Lack of faculty has been a major impediment in expanding medical colleges and opening new ones. There is concern about the low quality of instruction and poor skill acquisition as well as general neglect of community medicine in private medical colleges. And little attention has been paid to training community-based health providers.

## Mobilization of community resources

Though health is constitutionally a responsibility of the states, health policy is often guided from the center. Historically, plans for health services are based on the overall health objectives of a state rather than on an assessment of community needs. Many states are strapped for resources as mobilization of local resources for improving the quality of health services in public health institutions has not been successful. User-fees – one of the initiatives to mobilize resources – generate little revenue in India. In government health facilities, state-level cost-recovery rates (revenue as a percentage of total expenditure) show that Kerala (15.86), Punjab (10.87) and Haryana (9.51) are better performing states compared to Himachal Pradesh (0.67), Rajasthan (0.92) and Orissa (0.96) (Kulkarni 2003). Initiatives such as hospital autonomy through Rogi Kalyan Samitis (RKS) are restricted to only a few states although the National Rural Health Mission has advised the states to institutionalize RKS. While involvement of non-governmental organizations is increasingly part of health services delivery in the public sector, many of these health services revolve around family welfare programs or preventive services. As a result, health institutions at the level of primary care are regarded as family planning units. While disease prevention and health promotion activities are important, the provision of curative health services at the level of primary care has steadily deteriorated.

## The private health sector in India

The growth of the private sector has coincided with fiscal constraints on the government and their negative consequences on the ability of government health centers to deliver services. Impetus for the rapid growth of the private sector inadvertently came from government policies that urged the private sector to offer specialty services, thus paving the way for a spate of public subsidies.

Other factors facilitating the growth of the private sector are the decline in public expenditures on health, particularly for capital investment; rising incomes that increase the ability as well as the willingness to pay for health services; popular perceptions about better quality in the private sector; and an unfettered regulatory environment. While information on the extent of the private sector in health care delivery is incomplete, various sources offer different estimates. In 1947 the private sector in India provided 8 percent of health care facilities (World Bank 2004). Today 93 percent of all hospitals, 64 percent of beds, 85 percent of doctors, 80 percent of outpatients and 57 percent of inpatients are in the private sector (World Bank 2001).

## Taxonomy of the private sector

Broadly the private health sector consists of 'for-profit' and 'not-for-profit' agents, groups or organizations. Diversity in the composition of the private sector ranges from individuals (either solo or group practice), polyclinics, nursing homes, diagnostic centers, pathology laboratories, pharmacy shops, stand-alone specialist services, trusts and corporate firms – not to mention the unqualified providers (quacks). Each addresses different segments of the market. Individual practitioners from various systems of medicine provide the bulk of medical care in the for-profit health sector. The not-for-profit sector is hetero-geneous for there is no clear definition about what precisely constitutes a not-for-profit organization.

The private sector in health care is dominant in all the sub-markets – medical education and training, medical technology and diagnostics, manufacture and sale of pharmaceuticals, hospital construction and ancillary services, and the provision of medical services. An important subset of providers is the large number of informal providers – quacks (one in almost every village), bone-setters, traditional healers and traditional birth attendants. A survey in three dis-tricts of Andhra Pradesh found one 'quack' for every 2,000 inhabitants (Rao *et al.* 1997).

## Size and structure

It is estimated that the private health market in India is worth 710 billion rupees plus another 310 billion rupees if the pharmaceutical industry is included. By 2012 the health care market in India is projected to be 1,560 billion rupees plus another 390 billion rupees if the health insurance market is added (CII-McKin-sey Report 2004). By 2012 it is also estimated that India will require an addi-tional 750,000 beds, 520,000 more doctors and an overall investment of 1.5 trillion rupees, four-fifths of which is projected as the share of the private sector.

Analysis of the 57th Round of the National Sample Survey shows that in 2001–2002 an estimated 1.3 million private health care providers or enterprises with 2.2 million employees were providing health care services in India. Most of these are own-account enterprises (OAEs) that number over 80 percent of the

*Table 2.3* Health institutions in Indian states (percent)

| State | Non-profit sector | For-profit sector |
|---|---|---|
| Andhra Pradesh | 0.26 | 99.74 |
| Bihar | 0.18 | 99.82 |
| Gujarat | 0.76 | 99.24 |
| Himachal Pradesh | 15.23 | 84.77 |
| Haryana | 3.90 | 96.10 |
| Jharkhand | 0.05 | 99.95 |
| Karnataka | 1.05 | 98.95 |
| Kerala | 1.68 | 98.32 |
| Madhya Pradesh | 0.47 | 99.53 |
| Maharshtra | 2.40 | 97.60 |
| Orissa | 0.23 | 99.77 |
| Punjab | 4.47 | 95.53 |
| Rajasthan | 1.46 | 98.54 |
| Tamil Nadu | 2.90 | 97.10 |
| Uttar Pradesh | 0.46 | 99.54 |
| West Bengal | 1.82 | 98.18 |

Source: NCMH Report 2005.

total health facilities in the country. OAEs are typically run by an individual or a household business that provides health services without hiring additional workers on a regular basis. The 2.2 million health workers include skilled, semi-skilled and unskilled providers. The individual providers in the private sector range from *dais* (traditional midwives) and faith-healers through paramedical staff to specialized doctors. Although less than 1 percent of India's total work-force, they account for over 56 percent of the workforce in the health sector. The remaining 44 percent is engaged in health establishments. More than one million OAEs are health facilities with a solo practitioners; another 75,000 hire one or more workers on a temporary basis. In rural India, one-third of these individual practitioners have no registration of any kind (NCMH 2005). In 2002, of the 691,470 registered practitioners of Indian systems of medicine (Ayurveda, Unani, Tibbi) and homeopathy, most are solo practitioners in the private sector.

On the other hand, health establishments in the country numbered roughly 230,000 but accounted for less than one-fifth of all health providers. Establishments are those enterprises that hire at least one worker on a regular basis. Contrary to the popular belief that the private sector in India is predominantly urban, over 92 percent of OAEs and 7 percent of establishments are in rural areas. Of the health establishments, 85 per cent have fewer than 25 beds; the average number of beds is ten, within a range from five to over 700. Tertiary care institutions that provide specialty and super-specialty care comprise only 2 percent of the all private institutions; corporate hospitals constitute less than 1 percent.

Because of its heterogeneity in terms of organizational structure, pattern of funding, ownership, nature of services and changing character, the scattered and disorganized not-for-profit sector does not fit into one typology. The not-for-profit health sector accounts for barely 1 percent of all health establishments. The spread of the non-profit sector in health varies greatly among the different states. For example, 43 percent of health establishments in Uttaranchal are non-profit, followed by Punjab at 15 percent. However, the presence of non-profit health establishments in states like Bihar, Goa, Jharkand and Karnataka is negligible, accounting for less than 1 percent of the total. The percentage of villages with any NGO presence ranges from 1 percent in Uttar Pradesh to 34 percent in Maharashtra. In India as a whole, about 10 percent of villages have some type of NGO (Mahal *et al.* 2000).

## 'Not-for-profit sector'

Most non-profit health establishments are registered as societies or trusts under central and state laws. Until the 1960s most of these non-profit health establishments were hospital-based but, over the years, they have expanded to include community-based health service providers. Most non-profit providers are engaged in advocacy, health education, health promotion, traditional and indigenous medicine and research activities, although some of them actually provide clinical care. Since 1960 the government has actively engaged the NGO sector in health schemes and programs. Successive plan documents and various expert groups have argued the need for, and importance of, NGOs in the provision of health services to the community through subsidies and grants-in-aid.

Contributions by NGOs in the health sector, particularly in disease control programs, HIV/AIDS, reproductive health, birth control and community health, are large. Recognizing the contributions, the ninth Five-Year Plan (1997–2002) anticipated the transfer of a number of public sector facilities (particularly primary health centers) to NGOs. Yet the percentage of non-profit NGOs in health sector remains low. It is estimated that 7,000 NGOs work in health care. Non-profit hospitals are estimated to make up 10 percent of all hospitals with approximately 13 percent of all beds in India (GOI 1988). Of all private hospitals, 17 percent were not-for-profit with 42 percent of all private beds.

The non-profit private sector is heterogeneous in terms of ownership, motives, sources of funds and geographical location. Ownership of non-profit organizations ranges from solo individuals through faith-based organizations to initiatives for corporate social responsibility. Motives range from missionary zeal to creating political constituents. Sources of funds include user-fees, government grants-in-aid and donations. Most non-profit organizations provide primary care services plus a few at secondary and tertiary level. Located in urban and semi-urban areas, most of these organizations establish themselves in places where infrastructure is already present.

The report of the National Commission on Macroeconomics and Health suggests that, contrary to the for-profit sector, public subsidies to NGOs have produced substantial social gains. For example, under the blindness control program, the not-for-profit sector performed almost one-third of the four million cataract surgeries in a year. However, due to the rising costs and the uncertainty of grants-in-aid, the proportion of free services in the non-profit establishments is decreasing while user-fees have been increasing. In order to counter this trend, NGOs engage in differential pricing by charging higher amounts to well-off patients and then provide free care or subsidized rates for the poor.

The not-for-profit sector has its own constraints and limitations. The issue of sustainability is central to their existence. In order to achieve appreciable and sustainable results, NGOs have to make long-term commitments to the community. They frequently face difficulties such as shortage of trained staff, high turnover of middle-level workers and dependency on donor agencies. Numerous trust hospitals have become more commercial in their operations, hence altering their character from a charitable institution to a private for-profit corporate image.

Berman and Dave (1994) found that not-for-profit hospitals are able to achieve efficiencies due to low wages of employees by using contract workers, utilizing specialist services on an honorary basis, prescribing generic drugs and emphasizing referrals as well as limited use of expensive technology. As a result, the average total expenditure per hospitalization in a charitable institution is less than in for-profit hospitals. The cost per hospital bed per day in the not-for-profit sector is low, but both the forty-second and fifty-second rounds of the National Sample Survey Organization showed increasingly low utilization of charitable institutions for outpatient care. Limited numbers of NGOs are involved in health and family welfare in rural areas, most of which had weak financial management and low technical capacity (Misra *et al.* 2003).

State differentials indicate the private sector's propensity to set up practices and facilities in the more advanced states. Only 12 percent of hospitals in Himachal Pradesh are in the private sector compared to 95 percent in Kerala. Contrary to commonly held views, private hospitals are relatively less urban-biased than the public hospitals. About 31 percent of private sector hospitals and 29 percent of private beds are in rural areas compared to 25 percent of public sector hospitals and 10 percent of public beds.

## Private sector characteristics

In 2005 the National Commission on Macroeconomics and Health conducted a survey of qualified providers in eight districts in India. The survey covered 83 towns, 80 blocks and 9,987 villages with a total population of 21 million. The data indicate that the ratio between the public and private sectors is 60:40 in rural areas and 10:90 in urban areas. The higher percentage of public facilities in rural areas is due to public sector sub-centers. Proprietors run 91 percent of the facilities, 86 percent of which are small outpatient clinics with one or two beds. Two-thirds of health facilities and four-fifths of beds are in urban areas. Three-quarters of all specialists are in the private sector (61 percent of anes-thetists, 78 percent of cardiologists, 85 percent of general physicians, 73 percent of gynecologists and surgeons), a majority of whom practice in hospitals with over 30 beds.

In terms of services, almost half of hematology and urine tests and one-third of angiographies are conducted in the public sector. There is substantial infusion of diagnostic technology, largely by the private sector – CT scan, MRI machines, ultrasound and Doppler machines. In the provision of dental, ENT and orthopedic services as well as treatment of non-communicable diseases such as myocardial infarction, cancer chemotherapy, mental health, medical termination of pregnancy and hysterectomies, the private sector accounts for almost three-fourths of the total caseload. Average bed occupancy in the private sector is 44 percent compared to 62 percent in the public sector. Occupancy in the private sector is highest in establishments under 30 beds (64 percent) and declines in establishments with more beds (24 percent in hospitals with more than 75 beds).

In terms of costs of care, payment in the private sector is predominantly fee-for-service paid out-of-pocket by patients. There is huge variation in the prices charged for similar services. For example, caesarean sections range between 3,500 and 50,000 rupees. Prices are lower in rural areas but far higher in places where capacity to pay is more or inputs costs are greater. The private sector actively engages in providing treatment for acute care as well.

While comparing the performance of the private and public sectors, the survey found that the deployment of medical equipment requires less time in the private sector than in the public sector for procurement and commissioning (three months compared to 18 months). Breakdowns are fewer in the private sector while medical equipment is better utilized in terms of investigations per machine, number of investigations per staff and unit cost per investigation. The private sector achieves these results by employing an optimal number of staff, working more hours and delivering reports sooner. Private doctors and technicians annually conduct more investigations per machine than in the public sector. The unit cost of ultrasound services in a private hospital is 60 percent that of a public hospital and 70 percent that of private diagnostic centers. The price of MRI is 12 times higher in public hospitals than in private ones. Tables 2.4 and 2.5 sketch the characteristics of the private sector reported in the survey.

## Private sector behavior and regulation

The behavior of the private health sector and its consequences are often debated. Behavior in the private health sector depends on the interplay of complex factors such as the nature of financing and repayment, types of technology employed, input costs, quality control, public expectations and perceptions, regulatory framework and social values that determine how equitable, efficient, safe and accessible they could be. In the absence of regulations governing location, standards or pricing, private facilities operate in marketplaces and residential colonies with freedom to provide any kind of services, of whatever quality and cost, which varies from facility to facility. Caused by proliferation of medical equipment and technologies in urban areas, excess capacities have led to both excessive and irrational use of technologies. Over-prescribing and subjecting

*Table 2.4* Diagnostics and national disease control programs

| Equipment in health facilities | Percentage in private sector |
|---|---|
| Hematology | 54 |
| X-ray | 85 |
| ECG | 88 |
| CT scan | 90 |
| MRI | 92 |
| *National health programs* | |
| Malaria | 55 |
| Tuberculosis | 47 |
| Acute Respiratory Infections | 53 |
| Medical Termination of Pregnancy | 78 |
| Deliveries | 38 |
| Caesarians | 59 |
| Cataract/eye care | 75 |
| Acute Myocardial Infraction | 71 |

Source: NCMH Report, 2005.

*Table 2.5* Cost of care (in rupees)

| Service | Private facilities | Public facilities | Private:public ratio of cost |
|---|---|---|---|
| Normal delivery | 472–1,573 | 0–128 | 18.3 |
| Caesarean section | 1,792–4,647 | 50–250 | 24.3 |
| Major surgery | 1,638–5,975 | 0–711 | 20.8 |
| ECG | 56–115 | 0–55 | 3.6 |
| X-ray | 68–123 | 0–143 | 2.2 |
| Blood test | 30–59 | 0–19 | 5.1 |

Source: NCMH Report, 2005.

patients to unnecessary diagnostic investigations characterize the private sector. The private sector tends to hire staff at low wages and to discharge patients earlier than medically advisable in order to obtain a quick turnover of patients (Baru 1998).

There is a nexus between private medical practitioners and pharmacy shops, some of which are owned by the doctors. Private clinics depend on referrals by quacks who act as procuring agents in exchange for a commission. Fee-splitting occurs between diagnostic centers and referring doctors as well as when traditional practitioners practice allopathic medicine. These unqualified practitioners enjoy close rapport with the local community and are accessible at all times to provide treatment for ailments, including antibiotics that give quick relief. But their poor knowledge and lack of training have caused substantial morbidity.

Prices in the private sector are high as pricing is largely determined by the market costs of inputs like land, buildings, equipment, labor and capital.

However, government subsidies to the private sector such as free land or excise waivers have not lowered the prices. Private sector prices are also influenced by three factors: the experience of the treating physician, technology and location. It has been observed that, due to low occupancy of beds, the private sector attempts to cut costs by appointing unqualified personnel at low wages, selling drugs and earning commissions from diagnostic laboratories for every case referred. The private sector promotes the perception that equates the use of sophisticated technology as 'good' quality and value for money. The perception that quality is expensive is primarily due to underutilization of facilities in the private sector. As a result the private sector 'pushes' irrational diagnoses and then justifies it by arguing that otherwise the consumer protection act would fault them for wrong diagnoses. The motivation to continue this practice will remain as long as payments are based on fee-for-service because every visit and every additional investigation generate revenue for the provider.

The consequences of such behavior by the for-profit sector are disastrous for the poor. The fifty-second round of the National Sample Survey found that in Bihar the costs of medical treatment push 35 percent of those hospitalized into poverty compared to 16 percent in Kerala. In Bihar 90 percent of service delivery is in the private sector compared to about 60 percent in Kerala. Recently patients, advocacy groups, consumer federations and the general public have begun to demand that the private sector should be made accountable in terms of location, quality and cost of care.

The NCMH (2005) noted that 'Although beer bars and pan shops require a license for establishing and running these stores in India, health facilities-whether consultation chambers run by doctors or a big private hospital-do not require a license'. The mushrooming of the private health sector without a regulatory structure is a cause for concern. Only around half of India's health establishments are registered under the Medical Practitioners Act; another 8 percent are registered under other laws (usually the Societies Act, the Shops and Establishments Act, and the Local Bodies Act). State-wise analysis reveals that in Assam only one-quarter of health facilities appear to be registered, followed by Orissa where over half the establishments lack registration. At the other end of the spectrum, smaller states like Goa and Uttaranchal have a negligible number of unregistered health establishments (2 and 7 percent, respectively).

## Health sector reforms

The endemic challenges in public health systems have long been documented. Inequities in the private health sector and malfunctioning in the public health system exacerbate the impoverishment of India's poor as they seek health care. As budgetary constraints erode the capacity of the public health system, governments and policy-makers are exploring alternative policy options and strategies not only to improve the efficiency, performance and quality of the public health system but also to enhance the equity, accountability and affordability of the private health sector. The government's Five-Year Plans repeatedly emphasize the need to reform the health sector. In the last decade, bilateral and multilateral development organizations have advocated significant reform in the health sector. The World Bank (2001: 12, 14) emphasized the importance of reforming India's health sector:

> Now is the time to carry out radical experiments in India's health sector, particularly since the status quo is leading to a dead end. Now is the opportunity for governments to reform the way they work. But it is evident that there is no single strategy that would be best option. The proposed reforms are not cheap, but the cost of not reforming is even greater.

Health sector reform is defined as 'a sustained, purposeful change to improve the efficiency, equity and effectiveness of the health sector' (Berman 1995). The World Health Organization (1977) defined health sector reform as:

> a sustained process of fundamental change in policy and institutional arrangements of the health sector, usually guided by the government. The process lays down a set of policy measures covering the four main core functions of the health system, namely governance, provision, finance and resource generation. It is designed to improve the functioning and performance of the health sector and ultimately the health status of the people.

Health sector reform includes a deliberate effort to change the role of the public sector in terms of providing, financing, purchasing and regulating health care. As a result, health sector reform entails changes in the roles of other organizations and institutions involved in the delivery of health services (Abramson 1999). But there is no universal strategy for health sector reform. Depending on its needs and problems, every country adopts its own forms of reform.

Thomason (2002) classifies three types of health reforms in developing countries:

- Changes in financing methods include user-charges, community financing, insurance, stimulating private sector growth and increased resources to health sector.
- Changes in health system organization and management include decentralization, contracting out services and reviewing the public-private mix.
- Public sector reforms per se include downsizing the public sector, productivity improvement, introduction of competition, improving geographic coverage and increasing the role of local government.

After reviewing recent experience with health sector reforms in Latin American countries, Abrantes (2003) suggests that reforms are necessitated by tight fiscal constraints and public pressure. The common approach resembles the 'marketization' of health organizations undertaken in several OECD countries. These provide greater autonomy for managers in public hospitals, allow public hospitals to raise and retain resources without reducing funds already earmarked in state budgets, allow them to compete with the private sector for patients, and establish new accountability systems. These reforms are being implemented at national, regional and local levels with varying degrees of difficulties and success.

Globally the genesis of health reform is traced to the early 1980s when many countries, faced with fiscal constraints, imposed severe budgetary cuts on the public health system. Guided by the IMF and the World Bank, countries sought to stabilize the deteriorating health systems through alternative funding mechanisms. By the mid-1990s, the focus of reforms shifted to sectoral development programs. The concerns of users and the involvement of other stakeholders of the system became predominant. Decentralization, use of private provision of health services and an emphasis on governance, accountability and regulatory issues became critical.

The World Development Report (1993), which provided the impetus for reforms in many developing countries, proposed reduction of government expenditures on tertiary facilities, imposition of user-fees on affluent patients who use government hospitals and services, financing and implementing a package of public health interventions and improving the management of public health services through measures such as decentralization and contracting out. The report also recommended deliberate changes in government spending on health in order to benefit the poor. Recently, health sector reform has become a central theme in many developmental forums. Initiatives such as the Commission on Macroeconomics and Health, the Millennium Development Goals and the emergence of international financing mechanisms like the Global Fund on AIDS, have prompted financial and institutional reforms in the health sector.

Approaches to health reform in India are recommended in various documents such as the Five-Year Plans, World Bank papers, India Health Report and the National Commission on Macroeconomics and Health. Apart from several common recommendations for health reform, each document underlines the importance of collaborating with the private sector and of creating facilitating conditions in fostering partnership with the private sector. Given the overwhelming presence of the private sector in health care, state governments in India have been exploring the policy option of creating partnerships with the private sector in order to meet the growing health care needs of the population. The private health sector is regarded as easily accessible, better managed and more efficient than its public counterpart. It is assumed that collaboration through public-private partnerships will improve equity, efficiency, quality, accessibility and accountability of the entire health system.

The eighth Five-Year Plan (1992–1997) revoked the concept of free medical care and recommended user-fees, even at nominal amounts, for health services. User-charges are levied on patients above the poverty line for diagnostic and curative services offered in health institutions while highly subsidized or free care was ensured for the needy. The ninth Five Year Plan (1997–2002) urged the reorganization of health services to bring about greater efficiency and effectiveness and to enable the population to obtain optimum care at affordable cost. The tenth Five-Year Plan (2002–2007) recognized that health sector reforms must address issues of equity and devise a targeting mechanism by which people below poverty line can obtain ready access to subsidized health services. It emphasized organizational and management reforms, structural integration in the health ministry, a fully functional health information system including surveillance, and improved regulation to ensure quality standards in clinical care. Also, for the first time, the tenth plan envisioned the need for private sector participation in the delivery of health services to the needy and underserved sections of the population. The tenth Five-Year Plan reflects the broad vision enunciated in the 2002 National Health Policy.

In 2001, the World Bank argued convincingly the need for and merits of various approaches to health sector reforms. According to this report, there are four major objectives:

- making the health system more pro-poor, gender-sensitive and client-friendly;
- increasing health spending by developing health-financing systems;
- harnessing the private health sector's energy and countering its failures;
- emphasizing quality, efficiency and accountability of health services in both public and private sectors.

The Commission on Macroeconomics and Health, which was set up at the behest of the World Health Organization, suggested various options for health sector reforms in India. After critically reviewing the diverse experiences of India's health system, the report recommended various reforms. The commission focused on the burden of disease, better management of the public sector, financing care (including drugs and medical technology) and human resources. While emphasizing the need to strengthen the regulatory framework, the commission reviewed the merits and demerits of public-private partnership.

While there is a consensus that the health sector requires radical reforms, perspectives on the content of reforms range from 'marketization' to complete government provision of health services. Proposals include increased resource allocation and mobilization of funds, strengthening organizational and managerial capacity, decentralization of management of health institutions, enhancing the quality, efficiency and accountability of both the public and the private health sectors, and collaborating with the private sector to harness its potential and counter its failures. Several state governments in India have initiated health sector reforms in which partnership with the private sector has emerged as a significant avenue. As elsewhere in the world, however, there is a growing realization in India that, given their respective strengths and weaknesses, neither the public sector alone nor the private sector alone can solely service the health system.

## Note

1 Data from National Health Profile India (2006). http://cbhidghs.nic.in/cbhi/book/ (accessed March 25, 2008).

# 3 Public-private partnerships in India

## Case studies of public-private partnership in India

Since 1992 the importance of private sector involvement in the delivery of health services has been highlighted in successive plan documents, committee and commission reports of the central government and by bilateral and multilateral donor agencies. During the past decade, several state governments in India have experimented with encouraging private sector involvement in health care. In the initial stages, the most common forms of private sector involvement have been to establish medical colleges, build super-specialty hospitals through tax concessions and subsidized land, to waive taxes or provide concessions for the import of medical equipment, to outsource ancillary services in hospitals, to procure medicine and drugs through private vendors, to computerize medical records and to engage ambulance operators.

Governments have only recently begun to involve the private sector in delivering health care services to the poor and underserved sections of society. This chapter reviews the initiatives for private sector collaboration in various Indian states during the past decade. Although the roles of the central and state governments in their policy initiatives are not clearly delineated, the central government is expected to play a catalytic role by developing standards and mechanisms for quality control of public and private providers, developing capabilities in professional associations, launching social franchising models in states, building technical capacities for implementation, responding to requests for technical assistance from states, providing budget heads and mechanisms for the flow of funds, dialoguing with stakeholders for policy development, creating user-friendly websites about policy strategies and disseminating information about operational models. In turn, the states are supposed to identify specific programmatic needs to map the private sector, to design specific partnership details, to develop standards for interim accreditation, to improve capacities of government to monitor and regulate the private sector, and to build capacity at district level.

For example, the central government has provided guidelines for public/private partnerships in national disease control programs like the Revised National Tuberculosis Control Program (RNTCP) and Reproductive and Child

Health (RCH) under the 2005–2012 National Rural Health Mission (NRHM). During the past decade, both the central and the state governments have initiated PPP arrangements. Efforts are underway to replicate successful partnerships between public, private and voluntary groups in the delivery of services at primary, secondary and tertiary levels of health care. While most of these initiatives involve collaboration between the public sector and the private sector, several could be bracketed under government grant-in-aid schemes.

Based on 16 in-depth case studies, this chapter analyzes recent policy initiatives for public-private partnerships in the health sector of nine states of India. Some of these states have hosted health systems development projects funded by the World Bank; others participate in the sector investment program of the European Commission for Health and Family Welfare. The case studies span continua in terms of rural/urban/tribal mix; for-profit and not-for-profit partners; primary care versus specialty care services; clinical services and non-clinical support services; stationary and mobile health facilities; and financial issues ranging from community insurance schemes to contractual ancillary services. After briefly describing the highlights of each case, this chapter explores patterns among them across nine themes, then identifies policy implications that are detailed more fully in the next chapter. Table 3.1 provides a list of the 16 case studies.

### SMS hospital, Jaipur (life line fluid store (LLFS) and CT scan and MRI facility)

Initially LLFS operated through an arrangement between manufacturers and contractors. Products of manufacturers were sold on consignment, and the manufacturers were paid fortnightly on the basis of sales. The nexus between the contractor and the drug manufacturer caused a monopoly so the SMS hospital committee decided to determine the list of items to be sold and to negotiate their sale price. Instead of a tendering process, 'lowest-price certificates' from the manufacturers are used. Shortages of medicine (which are to be provided by the hospital) mean that the contractor has to deal with irate patients.

Apart from the usual pressures from the administration and from local politicians (such as free distribution of medicine or to stock a particular type of medicine) the private contractor has experienced computer breakdowns, shortages of medicine and erratic supply of electricity. The hospital-provided computer is secondhand and its frequent breakdowns compound the problems in maintaining records of daily operations. The contract for CT/MRI screening was allotted to a private contractor after enormous public resistance by political groups in the state. Operations began only after a lengthy legal case between the hospital and the contractor. Therefore, from its beginning, the facility has been under scrutiny by the media that highlight minor incidents. The contractor feels that the hospital administration is almost hostile towards his operations.

To compound these problems, staff employed by both contractors report grievances directly to the hospital's medical superintendent, aggravating the

*Table 3.1* List of case studies

| Health facility or Partnership | Location | Scope of services |
|---|---|---|
| Sawai Man Singh Hospital | Jaipur, Rajasthan (state capital) | Outsourcing radiological services (CT/MRI) and hospital pharmacy |
| Arpana Swasthya Kendra | Molarbund, Delhi (slum community) | Maternity health services including immunization |
| Uttaranchal Mobile Hospital and Research Centre | Bhimtal, Uttaranchal (hilly region) | Clinical and diagnostic services through health camps by mobile vans |
| Rajiv Gandhi Super-specialty Hospital | Raichur, Karnataka (rural district) | Provision of super-specialty clinical care services |
| Management of Primary Health Centers by Karuna Trust | Karnataka (rural) | Provision of round-the-clock primary care services and management of PHCs |
| Yeshasvini Healthcare scheme | Karnataka (state-wide) | Provision of surgical care through subsidized health insurance |
| Karnataka Integrated Tele-health and Telemedicine Project | Chamarajanagar, Karnataka (rural tribal district hospital) | Tele-diagnosis and consultation for coronary care; emergency support |
| Rogi Kalyan Samiti in Jaya Prakash Hospital* | Bhopal, Madhya Pradesh (state capital) | Hospital autonomy to augment resources and better manage services |
| Mahavir Trust Hospital (Revised National TB Control Program) | Hyderabad, Andhra Pradesh (state capital) | Provision of drugs, disease surveillance through networking with private sector |
| Andhra Pradesh Urban Slum Health Care Project | Adilabad, Andhra Pradesh (rural district) | Improve institutional deliveries, immunization, and provide reproductive health services |
| Arogya Raksha Scheme | Ranga Reddy, Andhra Pradesh (semi-urban district) | Low cost insurance for accidents and hospitalization; promote birth control. |
| Emergency Ambulance Service | Theni, Tamil Nadu (tribal district) | 24-hour emergency ambulance services |
| Mobile (Boat) Health Services | The Sunderbans, West Bengal (Gangetic delta) | Health clinics from mobile boats for people in remote islands |
| Bhaga Jatin Hospital | Kolkatta, West Bengal (state capital) | Contracting-out catering, laundry and cleaning services |
| Shamlaji Hospital (Community Health Centre) | Sabarkantha, Gujarat (tribal district) | Inpatient admissions, referrals, CHC management, and emergency services |
| Chiranjeevi Yojana | Himmatnagar (Sabarkantha district headquarters) | Reduce maternal and infant mortality; increase institutional deliveries |

Note
* An initiative for hospital autonomy within the context of decentralized local government in Bhopal.

problem for the contractors. However, if the contractors have problems or grievances, no mechanism exists to resolve them. Since SMS is a teaching hospital,
the facility is often booked for students and faculty so the contractor operates at
a loss. The quantity of services is not sufficient for the contractor to make sufficient income from the contract.

On their part, patients complain that the contractual clause for providing free
services to BPL families has made them to 'run from pillar to post' among many
authorities in order to prove that they are BPL beneficiaries. There is no single
'window' or authority to verify the BPL beneficiaries. Consequently most of
them queue at the medical superintendent's office. Although otherwise cooperative, the medical superintendent is always preoccupied so, depending up on his
'mood', he may either grant or deny BPL benefits. Patients also complain that
the staff at the CT/MRI facility recycle films or use inferior quality films or
smaller-sized films to save costs – and that they give priority to paying patients.

Outsourcing of radiological diagnostic services has become a common form
of private sector involvement in the tertiary care hospitals in India. Despite the
shortcomings such models are likely to be scaled up in the country.

### Municipal Corporation of Delhi (MCD) and Arpana Swasthya Kendra (ASK), Delhi

Conceptualized and approved by a few officials in the Municipal Corporation of
Delhi (MCD), the project is identified more as one of individuals than of the
establishment. (As one informant said, 'the motive is not beyond suspect'.) The
health staff unions of the MCD opposed this initiative and continue to regard it
as a move towards privatization of MCD health facilities. MCD has not provided a medical officer at the health facility for overall coordination and supervision. Zonal health officials are not enthusiastic about reporting on the NGO's
management of the facility.

Although unhappy with certain aspects of the services such as user-fees,
patients invariably agree that the voluntary health care center is better than any
government hospital. However, without sufficient avenues to generate resources,
the financial sustainability of the private partner is not clear. When the project
director is eventually transferred from her current position, the acceptability of
continuing with the same private agency will become doubtful. In the long-run,
the role of the public staff unions will be critical. This is a situation in which, if
the leadership leaves, the entire project may be sidelined or perhaps deliberately
negatively targeted.

### Uttaranchal mobile hospital and research centre (UMHRC), Bhimtal

UMHRC is a technology demonstration project made a reality by enthusiastic
and committed individuals. Topographically the region is a challenge for mobile
services due to its hilly terrain, the poor network of roads, frequent landslides
and road blockages during the rainy season. But long-term commitment by part-

ners – other than the Government of Uttaranchal – is unlikely. Two of the part-ners (the Government of India's Technology Information Forecasting and Assessment Council and the privately endowed Birla Institute for Scientific Research) are not health sector organizations so their interest in the project is likely to wane over time. However, since this project provides one of the better alternatives for access to health care by the population, it may not be easy to wind up. Yet the region does not have a well developed private sector in health care that could be coopted for expanding or even continuing such a scheme. The scheme does not have referral linkage with either the private sector or public hospitals for specialist services. Therefore, the patients cannot access a complete cycle of clinical services.

The standard practice of one camp per site per month is not only insufficient but also generates enormous work for the visiting team. The frequency and dura-tion of the camps are among the main concerns of the beneficiaries. Members of the mobile clinics, especially women members, have to remain on the camp trail for periods exceeding 15 days at a stretch, with which they find it difficult to cope. Furthermore, not having been trained or briefed about community health or public health matters, medical staff had to learn on the job.

Sustainable finance is also a problem. The user-fees collected over three years total 1.3 million rupees or less than one-tenth of expenditures during the same period. Therefore, user-fees are not sufficient to sustain the project if government funding stops. Likewise, there is no clarity on the responsibilities of each partner; staff are unable to identify the agency to which they should report in case of grievances. Given a widespread feeling that the supervising coordina-tor from the implementing agency has an autocratic style, there are demands for more transparency about administrative decisions. Lack of experience in the health sector by the implementing agency has been an impediment too. While overall a valuable initiative, it would be difficult to sustain such projects without more partners willing to manage mobile service delivery.

### *Rajiv Gandhi super-specialty hospital, Raichur*

Because northern Karnataka lacked super-specialty care, its inhabitants traveled to Hyderabad or Bangalore for specialist services but long distances caused great hardship for the poor. With a 600-million rupee loan from OPEC, the Government of Karnataka built the Rajiv Gandhi super-specialty hospital and staffed it with appropriate personnel. However, due to the economic backward-ness of the region, the hospital could not retain sufficient specialists – even from government cadres – so, despite an investment of such magnitude, the hospital was almost idle. The Government of Karnataka then transferred the management and operation of the hospital to a private agency. Apollo Hospital Enterprises Limited was considered suitable under a negotiated agreement that reserves 40 percent of inpatient beds for patients below the poverty line. During the first year of the partnership, many poor patients claiming free care came to the Rajiv Gandhi hospital for specialist services. There was no mechanism to verify their claims for such benefits. Subsequently the contract was amended so that patients in the BPL category must be referred by a government hospital or clinic before being considered eligible for services.

The duration of the agreement and financial commitments between the partners are crucial issues. The initial agreement between the Government of Karnataka and Apollo Hospital Enterprises Ltd is for ten years but extendable for another decade. Contracts for such long periods have merits and demerits. For a private for-profit organization, long contract periods make better sense, especially in an underdeveloped region. However, by relying too much on services provided by a private partner, the government runs the risk of not making efforts to develop its own infrastructure or to manage it better. Long contractual periods make for a better business model, especially in an underdeveloped region.

The agreement anticipates that the hospital will not generate a profit for the initial three years, during which period the government will bear all expenses (losses) and even for subsequent years. Such an arrangement provides little motivation for the private partner to deploy resources efficiently and optimally. Of course, from the fourth year onwards, the hospital is expected to generate a surplus. However, in case losses continue, the hospital still receives an annual service charge calculated at 3 percent of turnover plus reimbursement of all expenses. Profits would be divided 70:30 between the government and the private partner.

The counter-guarantee to reimburse losses is a government decision loaded with risk. A questionable component of the agreement is the amount of funds invested by the government in the partnership. The government agreed to meet a monthly revenue expenditure of ten million rupees in addition to capital expenditures for medicine and medical equipment plus a one-time grant of 95 million rupees for re-equipping the hospital and another 110 million rupees for administrative expenditures. Infusion of such large financial resources is likely to continue. In 2004 the Rajiv Gandhi hospital incurred a loss of 23 million rupees.

Verification of patients eligible for free services – whether through BPL cards or other documents – has been a major concern for the government as well as hospital authorities. There is pressure by political interests recommending people for free services, even if they are not eligible. The proposal to appoint an officer to verify BPL cards in order to avoid fraud depends on the integrity of the officer. Reports indicate that patients treated in the Above Poverty Line category often get converted into Below Poverty Line patients through the connivance of others within and outside the hospital.

### Management of primary health centers by Karuna Trust, Karnataka

Under the leadership of Dr. H. Sudarshan, the Karuna Trust had envisioned its operation of one model primary health center in every district of Karnataka. The trust was experienced with an excellent reputation for providing health services. The state government asked whether it would consider 'adopting' the management of several PHCs on an experimental basis. Sensing a challenge, the Trust undertook the partnership but, during the initial stage, it met hostile reactions from many quarters including government health staff, local political leaders, community members and even the media.

Rumors were circulated that the government intended to transfer the management with an ultimate aim to privatize all PHCs and, furthermore, that the 'adopted' PHCs would charge patients for any health service. At first, protests from local people prevented the NGO from taking possession of the PHC buildings. It required considerable efforts by the chairman of the trust, a well respected figure in the state, to persuade the community to let the trust demonstrate its care for the people. The PHC staff too displayed great sensitivity to negate the apprehensions of the community. Today community support for the trust is very high. As an important lesson for community-level public-private partnerships, the foundation for success depends on acceptability by the stakeholders and, more importantly, treating the beneficiaries as stakeholders.

The success of Karuna Trust in managing the PHCs on an experimental basis provided the ground on which the state government promulgated a policy on public-private partnerships. However, this partnership is fraught with complexities. About one-quarter (27 percent) of operational expenses are borne by trust funds, i.e. donations. Because most NGOs are not as endowed at the Karuna Trust, the sustainability of such a mode of financing is untenable for replication of this model. Without user-fees or any additional revenue, incentives for improving services become difficult.

Another major concern in this partnership has been the delay in releasing the payments of government grants. On one occasion, the grants were not released for over a year. The NGO survived on its own funds but other NGOs are unlikely to survive such a delay in payment. Even if an NGO charged user-fees, it would be difficult to survive for such a prolonged period without government grants. There are also serious problems of staff turnover and irregular power supply. However, the NGO has considerable autonomy to incorporate additional services or to conduct innovative experiments like using indigenous systems of medicine, community health insurance, outreach services and round-the-clock emergency care.

### Karnataka Integrated Telemedicine and Tele-health project, Chamarajanagar district

Karnataka Integrated Telemedicine and Tele-health (KITTH) began as an experimental project to provide super-specialist health care in a remote rural location using Information Communication Technology (ICT). The objective is to allow the poor to receive specialty clinical advice at a local public hospital rather than traveling long distances and incurring great expense. To allow clinical experts to interact and to examine the medical records of patients remotely in real time, digitalized information had to be transmitted to the clinical experts who in turn could interact with both the local doctors and patients through audiovisual devices. The system required a set of doctors who could perform preliminary diagnoses and conduct radiological procedures plus a set of telecom and IT professionals who could convert the medical records of the patients (X-rays, scan images, etc.) into digital form. Only when surgical intervention was needed would the patient travel to a specialist hospital. The complex tasks being performed under this partnership require close coordination between the partners.

An impact study conducted in 2005 indicated that patients who used this service have saved an average of 81 percent of costs. Despite the obvious benefits, many issues confront such pilot projects. One such issue relates to financing and resource implications. As a first step in the project a coronary care unit was established in a district public hospital with the help of Narayana Hrudayalaya (NH). The government used considerable resources to upgrade the technology in the district hospital, including investment in emergency power supply, equipment for satellite linkage and audiovisual recording devices. Doctors had to be trained in the new equipment that was installed, and close coordination with district hospital doctors was also required. Local doctors received short-term training at NH on cardiology and at the Indian Space Research Organization (ISRO) on telemedicine.

The high initial costs prompted criticism as does the frequent need to upgrade technologies for hardware, software and communications like bandwidth optimization, servers, software and video-conferencing systems. While relatively easier to demonstrate in an experimental manner, large-scale replication of the system would strain public resources. Capital expenditures to establish ground facilities and satellite links could be borne by the states for pilot projects but a nationwide operational network of at least 3,000 nodes could only be operationally sustained if it were largely self-reliant. For this technology must become affordable, doctors and other auxiliary personnel must be trained and compensated adequately, and costing of services needs to be carefully worked out to ensure that fee charged from the patients is truly affordable.

The pilot project does not reflect the present cost of technical services provided by ISRO. If ISRO were to charge tariffs for its services, the cost of care would increase and user-charges would be required. Fear of increased fees may limit enthusiasm for the project. The current public-private partnership has benefited people in the region but the cost-effectiveness of a nationwide system is questionable.

### Yeshasvini health insurance scheme, Karnataka

Without the initiative and perseverance of a few individuals, this scheme for community-based health insurance would not have succeeded. But however innovative, such a scheme is vulnerable because, when the concerned individuals show no further motivation or if they are excluded from the decision-making hierarchy, dynamism is lost and the scheme loses its support. Stakeholders regard the scheme as an individual enterprise rather than an institutionalized system. Yeshasvini's success required the personal dynamism and motivation of Dr. Devi Shetty to conceptualize and design the scheme through his hospital's resources, the enthusiastic support of the then Secretary of the Co-operatives Department to lend administrative approval, and the political wisdom of the then Chief Minister of Karnataka to launch this scheme. Most of the hospitals participating in the scheme were personally contacted and empanelled by Dr. Shetty. Despite the spectacular success of this low-cost, mass-enrolled community-based health insurance scheme, many challenges remain to be addressed in this partnership.

First, initial estimates for premiums were based on an assumption that less than 1 percent of incidence of cardiac surgeries would be needed each year. It was unclear, however, whether the agency took into account the morbidity status of the population or the proportion of patients who would require surgery. As a result, the premium calculated at only five rupees per person in the first year was increased to ten rupees in the second year of the scheme. Such changes in the rates created a sense of apprehension among the bureaucracy as well as the beneficiaries. This is borne out by the fact that the government, which paid equal contribution for every member enrolled in the first year of the scheme, changed its finance to a consolidated sum in the second year.

Another issue relates to the volume of membership, and the manner in which members had been enrolled. The scheme is open only to members of agricultural cooperative societies and, apart from the member and his/her spouse, only two children were eligible for benefits. A large membership is critical for the cost-efficiency of any scheme of pooled risk. By the first quarter of 2005, nearly one-quarter of the ten million members of cooperative societies in Karnataka were registered under the scheme. Even then, in many families only one member was registered, a fact that suggests that people are not yet fully aware of the scheme. In order to keep the administrative overheads to the minimum, the government arranged for post offices to collect the insurance premiums and to issue membership cards.

Though the members appreciate the scheme, there are complaints that the membership is compulsory rather than an option. The need for everyone to be a member of the scheme is grounded on the logic that, if the membership were voluntary, only the sick would enroll, thus leading to adverse selection and eventual bankruptcy of the scheme. Most members regard the scheme as a government scheme – a perception that, in the opinion of some, is a blessing in disguise. If the scheme had been identified as a private sector initiative, there would have been little enthusiasm among members of the cooperative societies.

Enrolment of private hospitals and a professional body to manage the funds of the Yeshasvini Trust were other challenges faced while implementing the scheme. Despite low occupancy rates, most private hospitals were unwilling to participate in the scheme. It took the persuasive power of Dr. Shetty who personally traveled to private hospitals in the state in order to solicit their participation in the network. To prevent misuse of the scheme, safeguards have been built into the system. There is a lengthy pre-authorization stage and claims take a long time to process.

A central tenet of any viable community-based health insurance program is not only a large membership base but also a capacity to become self-financed.

Subsidies from the Karnataka state government violated this cardinal principle at the beginning of the scheme. But by the end of two years of operation, Yeshasvini had provided free medical consultations to approximately 85,000 farmers of whom 23,500 had various types of surgery while 1,700 had had heart operations. The scheme covers a significant percentage of the target population with potential to cover more. Its major drawback is that poor farmers are not covered for all health related issues but only those for outpatient care and all expenses connected with surgery. The items not covered (diagnostic tests and medicine) continue to be a heavy burden on poor families, often causing or reinforcing rural indebtedness.

The principal secretary of the state department of cooperatives is extremely important for the continuation of the scheme. The reputation and personal initiative of Dr. Shetty had been critical for initiating the scheme, but Narayana Hrudayalaya then began another rural health insurance scheme so its interest in Yeshasvini could wane over time. The governing council of the trust has not met for quite some while to review the functioning of the community insurance scheme.

### Rogi Kalyan Samiti (RKS), Jaya Prakash Narayan hospital, Bhopal

Rogi Kalyan Samiti (literally Patient Welfare Committee) is a form of hospital autonomy through decentralization of hospital management. The idea of hospital autonomy was raised in 1995 by the then District Collector of Indore during a potential but averted epidemic of the plague. Over the years decentralized management of government hospitals has become popular and is now accepted for countrywide implementation under the current National Rural Health Mission. The objectives are to augment hospital resources through levying user-charges, renting out space in hospital premises, improving hospital services and patient amenities, purchasing drugs and supplies in case of emergencies, maintaining hospital premises, and monitoring and improving the overall quality of hospital care. An RKS can purchase vehicles (particularly ambulances), train doctors and paramedical staff, dispose of bio-medical waste and ensure nutritious food and medicine for patients below the poverty line. It also authorizes free services for BPL, ex-army and physically handicapped patients. As a registered society, its members are from NGOs, local government, elected representatives and officials who oversee the functioning and management of the local health institution (whether hospital, community health center, clinic, etc.).

Strictly speaking, RKS is not a public-private partnership but rather a public-public partnership. The differences between RKS and other forms of hospital autonomy are:

•   RKS can generate revenue through user-charges, donations and/or by renting premises and it retains control of the revenue generated instead of remitting it to the government treasury. This provides an incentive for hospital administrators who can prudently use the resources to improve the overall quality of services.

- Unlike other hospital committees, RKS has extensive representation from the local community, civic bodies and other stakeholders.
- RKS makes the hospital improve its managerial capacity in terms of generating and managing financial resources (compared to expenditure control in the past), better accounting systems, documentation through management information systems (MIS) and accountability in service provision.

To be more successful, however, hospital administrators feel that RKS should be free from interference by other departments in its day-to-day functioning. It should be free to take any decision by itself for the betterment of health services. Staff members say that the decision to form an RKS should have been based on wider consultations within the hospital rather than on an administrative fiat from the government. Evidently the capacity of the hospital to undertake this new form of management had not been assessed before the RKS was implemented. Despite these limitations RKS has been replicated in several states in India in secondary and tertiary care units and has become an important initiative under the National Rural Health Mission.

### *Mahavir Trust hospital, revised national tuberculosis control program, Hyderabad*

This partnership is a rare situation where in a public health program the private sector took the initiative to collaborate within itself. After three years of operation and international recognition, the government initiated a formal collaboration. The Government of India launched the Revised National Tuberculosis Control Program (RNTCP) in 1993 with its DOTS strategy – directly observed treatment short-term. Dr. K.J.R. Murthy, a senior chest specialist at the private charitable Mahavir Trust hospital, saw that involvement of the private sector – more specifically, of private individual practitioners – is critical if the RNTCP program is to succeed. According to him, most patients seek treatment in the private sector but most private facilities do not follow national guidelines for either diagnosis or treatment.

Under Dr. Murthy the trust hospital reached out to the private practitioners to sensitize them about RNTCP and to develop a collaborative model. For this purpose the trust hospital began to liaise between the government and the individual practitioners. Private practitioners were encouraged to refer cases of suspected TB to the trust hospital with an assurance that they would continue to be the patients' primary care-givers. Practitioners were encouraged to use their private clinics as DOTS centers and to be supplied free drugs from the government that they could administer to their patients. This collaboration benefited everyone. Patients accessed drugs at locations in their neighborhoods, doctors did not lose their patients and in fact improved their 'reputation', and the government was able to reach larger numbers of patients. This collaboration was called a 'public-private mix' or the PPM model, and became a popular success.

However, the success of this model was not without its challenges. According to Dr. Murthy, collaboration was an historical accident. At the inception of the project, when he and his team of doctors visited local private practitioners to persuade them to refer symptomatic cases to Mahavir hospital, there was widespread suspicion. Fearing loss of their patients to the larger hospital, private practitioners at first refused to collaborate. They had to be assured that they would not lose patients.

It was also difficult to obtain funds. A prestigious local institution for public management education provided a conduit to facilitate funding to the Mahavir Trust hospital from international development agencies. Until 1998, the trust hospital managed this collaboration on its own. From 1998 to 2001 the World Health Organization funded the project. And in 2002 the Mahavir Trust hospital signed a Memorandum of Understanding with the District Tuberculosis Control Society. Since then, the hospital has handled one tuberculosis 'unit' or a population of approximately 500,000.

From 15 private doctors in the first year of collaboration, the Trust has enlisted 320 private practitioners (210 allopathic doctors, 110 others) to participate in the scheme. The MOU is renewed every two years. By collaborating in this scheme, the hospital initially ran the risk of being viewed as a TB hospital, an image potentially detrimental to the financial health of the hospital. Other medical professionals at Mahavir hospital did not take kindly to the hospital undertaking this scheme. While the hospital trustees supported the initiative, nonetheless this collaboration had to sustain itself. The TB clinic employs 13 staff members, some on the hospital staff and others on contract. Four paramedical staff visits each DOTS center thrice weekly to check on drug adherence of defaulters and to make home visits.

Among the serious concerns is how private practitioners continue to obtain chest radiographs (in which they often have a financial incentive) for most patients prior to referral. It causes needless expenditure by patients as well as risks occasional failure to refer TB carriers whose radiographs are not interpreted as consistent with TB. Informal discussions with local practitioners indicate that only patients who are unable to pay for treatment are referred, which means that those who could afford treatment are retained by private doctors for financial gain. The trust hospital's involvement in the project derives from the continued enthusiasm of certain individuals. Were they to leave, the sustainability of the project would be questionable. The staff employed for this project express some unhappiness about discriminatory treatment, but the project continues to receive support from the trust itself because the project has received wide attention. It has helped the hospital to gain significant goodwill that it would be loathe to risk losing.

### Emergency ambulance services, Theni district, Tamil Nadu

Theni district is a well endowed district in Tamil Nadu but, compared to the state average, its maternal mortality rate is high. One of the main causes of high maternal mortality is attributed to the lack of adequate transport facilities to convey pregnant women to health institutions for childbirth. To redress this problem the Government of Tamil Nadu introduced a scheme of ambulances to transport pregnant women needing institutional delivery. The ambulances were allocated to an NGO called Seva Nilayam that, in turn, engaged a local self-help group to operate, maintain and sustain the scheme. This scheme is part of a World Bank health system development project.

Various problems have confounded the scheme. Initially the goal was to operate five ambulances through four NGOs. However, two NGOs later withdrew because the government no longer gave them grants. Ambulances are not to be used for any purpose other than transporting pregnant women for deliveries. Beyond supplying the vehicles and a one-time grant, government provides no other support. No paramedical staff are employed to accompany the ambulance. While drivers have cell-phones for rapid communication, the rural areas sometimes have connectivity problems.

The two ambulances allotted to Seva Nilayam are supposedly self-sustaining through user-fees at 5 rupees per kilometer. It was expected that each ambulance would log about 5,000 km every month, thus generating revenue of 25,000 rupees plus another 3,000 rupees through donations. Overall expenditures were estimated at 23,000 rupees (two nurses at 2,000 rupees per month, two drivers at 2,000 rupees per month and other expenses such as fuel and maintenance at approximately 15,000 rupees). The monthly surplus would then be used for maintaining an office, communication expenses, etc. All these calculations are specious. How the expected revenue was calculated or the quantum of emergencies needing ambulance conveyance was estimated is unknown. Given the escalating costs of petrol, it seems counterproductive to restrict services only to pregnancy-related transport and still expect sufficient profit. During the first 22 months of the project, monthly income was 16,240 rupees while monthly expenditure (for the first 16 months) was around 24,000 rupees. As a result the project was not self-sustaining.

Seva Nilayam operates another parallel transport program in the Theni district called the Emergency Accident Relief Centre for which the government also provided a vehicle. This project provides immediate first-aid and medical help to accident victims on site and transports them to the nearest government hospital. Seva Nilayam sought permission to use this ambulance for other emergency purposes – such as snake-bites, heart patients and antenatal women in dangerous condition – but was strictly directed to use this ambulance for no purpose other than road accidents.

Daily operations reveal many improvisations that contradict the Memorandum of Understanding. Instead of the specified rate of five rupees per kilometer, drivers charge eight rupees plus an extra sum for driver's allowance and cleaning charges. The ambulance has been used for transporting all kinds of items, including corpses. Despite regulations, the vehicles do not halt overnight at the nearest government health center. The popularity of the ambulance is low; local inhabitants know the telephone numbers for auto-rickshaws but not for the emergency ambulance. Drivers' salaries are 3,000 per month (not 2,000 as per the MOU). All these deviations point to the unrealistic contract clauses in the MOU that deprive the private sector of incentives and lead to perverse practices. There is also the problem of monitoring. Government officials rarely visit the facility to monitor its services, and accounts, logbooks and patient records are poorly maintained. Despite these limitations this kind of project has potential. Those who have utilized its services vouch their readiness to use the ambulance again due both to the exorbitant charges levied by the private ambulances and to concerns about safety.

### Urban slum health care project, Adilabad, Andhra Pradesh

Many Indian states are rapidly urbanizing with large proportions of their popula-tions living in slums. Slum dwellers are more vulnerable to health problems and rely for health services either on the expensive professional private sector or non-professional quacks. Economic deprivation often forces them to seek ser-vices from the latter. In 1999, the Government of Andhra Pradesh launched an urban slum health care project aimed at providing good quality health care ser-vices to the urban poor, including preventive, reproductive and child health services.

With a grant-in-aid from the government backed by World Bank funds, private agencies in the private sector have been hired to provide a package of health services to a designated slum area. Between 2000 and 2002 the Govern-ment of India provided about 90 percent of project funds with the balance from the state. Since then the State Health and Family Welfare Department has been funding the entire scheme. The government provides the premises, equipment and operational expenses including salaries for the staff, drugs and supplies. NGOs are selected on a competitive basis by a district committee chaired by the District Collector. Currently there are 192 Urban Health Centers in 74 munici-palities of 21 districts, each covering approximately 20,000 slum dwellers. The project also involves the women's forum (mahila aarogya sangham) and local self-help groups that are useful for community mobilization, behavioral change and health education.

During the initial years of the scheme, it was difficult to identify NGOs willing to be partners in the scheme. Because it was an extension of the World Bank's India Population Project, many NGOs considered the scheme to be only temporary. There were also reports that NGOs were formed only in order to receive grants under this scheme, with many politicians opening their own NGOs. Some NGOs wanted to use this scheme in other areas. Despite these initial concerns, the project over the years evolved clear benchmarks for targets, performance indicators and institutionalized the system of managing and moni-toring the functioning of the scheme. There is also a grading system to rate the performance of the NGO in achieving the targets. To retain its contract, an NGO must perform to a minimum grade point in the evaluation.

The Urban Health Centers in Andhra Pradesh are run with government funds. Without government support, NGOs could not operate a health center so sustainability depends on funds from a single source. As long as the government continues to fund the NGOs through grants-in-aid, the scheme is sustainable.

### *Arogya Raksha Scheme, Ranga Reddy district, Andhra Pradesh*

The state government introduced the Arogya Raksha Scheme (ARS) in 1999 with an objective of providing hospitalization benefits and personal accident benefits to persons below the poverty line who had been sterilized in any government health institution. The scheme also sought to protect the survival of two children of the insured for a five-year period. It was assumed that around 200,000 families would enroll during the first year so based on a five-year premium of 75 rupees per insured family the scheme required the government to pay 15 million rupees to the insurance agency.

A public company called New India Assurance agreed to manage the funds; services would be provided by government hospitals registered with the scheme. Eligibility was restricted to BPL cardholders who had undergone a family planning operation, with coverage for a maximum of two children. The benefits include free treatment as an inpatient at any designated hospital up to a maximum of 2,000 rupees per hospitalization and 4,000 rupees per year. Non-hospitalization services are not covered in the scheme. In case of death or disability, a maximum compensation of 10,000 rupees would be paid to his/her child if under five years of age.

To provide clinical services to the members of the scheme, the government envisioned one private hospital per mandal (development block). About 500 private hospitals and nursing homes were identified as member hospitals for the scheme. The insurance company empanelled the hospitals. MOUs were signed with private nursing homes for clinical services in exchange for subsequent reimbursement. At the time of sterilization in a government hospital, all eligible members were issued certificates that were to be shown whenever availing hospital services. After five years the benefits would terminate.

ARS is a low-cost, low-value insurance scheme with many restrictive clauses to prevent misuse of the scheme. However, there are serious concerns related to the scheme and its eventual closure. The scheme operated under too many conditions. The documentation required for each condition meant that the administrative costs for each episode were very high. The number of private nursing homes chosen could have been based on the membership density rather than a diktat to have one hospital per mandal. Some hospitals with only a handful of beneficiaries seemed uninterested in providing such low-value services that needed such stringent administrative verification and documentation for reimbursement. On site reports indicate that many hospitals did not attend to insured patients. Despite repeated complaints to the district health office, no action was taken. And delay was reported in reimbursements by the insurance company.

The role of the public sector insurance company raises even more serious questions. Over a two-year period the state government paid the company a total of 30 million rupees to manage the program. However, the company reimbursed claims worth less than ten million rupees. Although allegedly the 'willing partner' in the scheme, the response of one of the managers of New India Assurance reflected the prevailing attitude:

> The company does not have any interest in taking such kind of schemes because the company cannot spend time and resources on making records and claims for a small number of certificates. Also, we do not count it as an insurance scheme because all the certificates were provided by the government. There was no other mode of collection of premiums from any other party.

The role of the government also raises serious doubts because there had been no monitoring or supervision or audit of the funds handled by the insurance company. When complaints appeared that empanelled private hospitals were not providing services to insured members of the scheme, no action was taken against those hospitals. The status of the 20 million rupees is not known other than as a profit for the insurance company. Local health officials want the scheme to be revived because it has potential benefits for the poor, but no one in authority was willing to comment. The scheme closed in 2004.

### Mobile health service in the Sunderbans, North 24 Parganas district, West Bengal

With its creeks, lagoons, islets, backwaters, marshy forests and wild animals, the Sunderbans are among the most challenging regions on earth. Providing basic amenities in the area is not only uneconomical but logistically challenging so the region remains backward. Morbidity is high due to lack of health services. The public health system's primary health centers – many built over 50 years ago – do not function because of shortage of staff. The region's hostile terrain as well as its backwardness discourages the public health staff posted there. In 1998, within the World Bank's health systems development project, the state government of West Bengal began to explore the possibility of engaging NGOs to provide mobile (boat-based) health services in the region. Five NGOs were identified to provide such mobile services.

In 1999 the state government engaged the Southern Health Improvement Samity (SHIS) to undertake, on an experimental basis, the task of providing mobile (launch-based) health services in four villages of South 24 Parganas. Since then mobile health services cover 192 villages in two districts of the state. Currently the NGO provides mobile health services for 81 villages in the North 24 Parganas district, covering a population of over 300,000. The state government provides a financial grant for the maintenance of boats, salaries for personnel and operational costs. The mobile health clinic receives monthly supplies of medicine for free distribution. The MOU spells out a number of activities plus a detailed work-plan to accomplish these objectives. All services are to be free. Many observers have commended the project for its innovativeness and for serving the poor. The project had since been reviewed by independent evaluators who recommended that is be continued.

Notwithstanding the rightly deserved praise, several issues need clarification. Having functioned in the region for a long time, the NGO has a high profile reputation. Funding has not been a major constraint. Yet despite the advantages of engaging this particular NGO, no long-term contract has been signed. The longest duration of a contract has been 19 months. The current MOU (in 2006) is for only nine months. Discussions with beneficiaries found that women are unhappy with the NGO, but their husbands pressured them to say 'good things' about its service. The women found numerous faults with the services including user-fees, irregular camps, lack of transport during emergencies, non-availability of medicine, etc. In particular they complained that, despite a large budget specifically for transporting emergency patients, ambulances are not available.

It is not clear why such contrasting images exist. A link between the short contracts and this feedback is possible but uncertain. On user-fees, many beneficiaries said that the NGO charges five rupees for registration at every health camp (some say monthly) although the MOU does not authorize any cost recovery. The number of camps conducted also requires clarification because the NGO claims to organize an average of 300 health camps every month. Given only two launches and seven doctors, very little time could be devoted to each camp if that claim is correct.

Despite these questions, mobile health services seem the best method to provide health care in a fragmented area. However, due to the complicated logistics required, the project is unlike to remain operational without external funding. Yet government funding seems uncertain and lacks continuity. While mobile health services may be the best alternative, the strategy of maintaining defunct Primary Health Centers needs radical review. The adoption and management of remote PHCs and rural hospitals could be another option even while continuing to fund the mobile health clinics.

### Contracting catering, laundry, cleaning services, Bagha Jatin hospital, Kolkata

Outsourcing ancillary services was one of the earliest forms of private sector involvement in public hospitals. Such contracts are often categorized under public-private partnership, yet whether the arrangement should be called PPP is debatable. With funding from the World Bank, the Government of West Bengal launched a health systems development project in 1996. The project sought to infuse efficiency in secondary and tertiary hospitals in the state. Non-clinical ancillary services were identified as those that could be contracted out to the private sector in order to improve both efficiency and the quality of hospital services as well as to allow hospital managers to concentrate on patient care. The state government also promulgated a policy for public-private partnerships in the health sector with clear guidelines.

One hospital where the private sector has been engaged to provide non-clinical support services is Bagha Jatin, a 100-bed hospital in Kolkata. Cleaning, catering and laundry services have been contracted after a competitive tender-based selection process. Cleaning and catering services are provided by individual contractors while an agency handles the laundry. Cleaning was outsourced at a fixed monthly rate. Contracts for catering and laundry are based on volume. While cleaning and catering have a long history, the laundry service was recently contracted out. The hospital appears to be satisfied with the services provided but the contractors for cleaning and catering are very dissatisfied with their contracts. In fact the contractor for cleaning and scavenging refused to meet the research team to explain his concerns. Because the cleaning services have been secured at a very low rate (24,000 rupees monthly for salaries to all staff plus cleaning materials), the average monthly remuneration of 1,300 rupees per employee is below the state minimum wage.

The catering contractor supplies all three meals according to dietary requirements at a daily rate of 27 rupees (recently raised to 28.5 rupees). On average the contractor supplies only 30 meals per day. A rough calculation indicates that the contractor, after all his expenses, makes a marginal profit from this contract. The fact that a 100-bed hospital with a 60 percent occupancy rate only needs 30 meals per day suggests that the catering services are primarily used by BPL patients or that the quality of food is not high enough for everyone. The rate for each meal is fixed by the state government's finance department, a decision that could have been left to hospital managers rather than exercised by a central agency. The finance department could have set a ceiling and asked the respective public hospitals to negotiate better rates. The hospital management would then feel responsible about supervising the catering contractor. Currently, if a contractor pleads for an upward revision of the rates, the hospital on its own cannot oblige.

The laundry service has been recently contracted out but the cost-benefit to the contractor is yet to be fully understood. A rate of 7.45 rupees per kilogram of soiled linen was fixed, but it is not evident whether there has been any calculation of costs or a break-even point for profit. In terms of sustainability, cleaning and catering could be sustained due to cost-savings for the hospital – provided a commensurate number of permanent hospital staff are no longer on the payroll. But, to maintain the quality of services, an upward revision of the rates is essential. However, no contract includes a clause allowing such upward revision or specifying incentives linked to performance.

### Shamlaji hospital (community health center), Sabarkantha district, Gujarat

Engaging the private sector to run secondary health centres is not common. One such partnership currently in operation in the state of Gujarat is a Community Health Centre (CHC) at Shamlaji – therefore popularly called Shamlaji hospital – in the tribal area of Sabarkanta district. During the first two years after its construction in 2000 the government tried to run the hospital but failed. In 2002 the 30-bed health center was transferred to an NGO called the All India Movement for Seva (AIMS). The hospital is supposed to serve a population of 100,000 people in 80 villages. The choice of NGO was not based on a competitive process. Rather the NGO asked if it could adopt and manage a government health facility. A policy for such participation from the private sector had already been approved by the state government with eligibility conditions clearly laid out.

Selection of the partner NGO was made according to strict conditions. A minimum bank balance is required to bid for the services but applicant NGOs need not submit security deposits. District administrators supervise and monitor the partnership while an advisory committee comprised of eminent citizens and local representatives provides operational direction to the NGO. Based on an administrative decision, the Community Health Centre was transferred to the NGO for two years on an experimental basis, extendable beyond that period after review and mutual consultation. The government equipped the hospital with all the facilities normally in a CHC. The government also provided grants-in aid to pay salaries to staff and to purchase medicine and supplies. Staffing is the responsibility of the NGO within the staffing norms for a normal CHC. About 3,000 out-patients and 900 inpatients are treated monthly with user-fees charged on select services. By all accounts the hospital has been functioning well and serving the tribal population.

The main force behind the success of this experiment is the initiative and the vision of Dr. Haren Joshi, a 65-year-old cardiovascular surgeon who returned from the US. He observed that the area lacked any kind of health services. The area is poorly developed and therefore government hospital staff would not remain in the region. Furthermore, economic backwardness of the region inhibited the private sector. When transferred to the NGO, the CHC was in disrepair and poorly maintained with very few patients seeking services. During the first few months after the transfer, patients were not willing to come to the hospital for fear of user-fees and due to a rumor that the hospital had been 'sold' to a private doctor. The hospital had to conduct outreach services to win the confidence of people in the region. Being located on a major highway, the hospital provides care for victims of road accidents. It also provides medico-legal services and organizes specialist care camps.

The partnership is sustainable although entrenched fears about privatization need to be overcome. At present, all stakeholders commend the functioning of the health centre. The steady rise in the number of patients over the past three years is a positive sign. However, the health centre's financial sustainability depends on government funds. With the resources meant for a CHC, the government has been getting more services than a CHC normally provides. It is, in the words of one respondent, 'a good deal'.

## Chiranjeevi Yojana, Sabarkantha district, Gujarat

Among all the partnerships documented, Chiranjeevi Yojana in the Gujarat is unique. The scheme has many objectives. Public hospitals in the state lack clinical specialists, notably gynecologists. Institutional deliveries are rare while infant and maternal mortality rates are high in districts that are populated by tribes or exceptionally arid. A major cause of high morbidity in these districts is lack of access to specialized services by indigent members of the community, especially for obstetric complications. The Chiranjeevi scheme facilitates safe childbirth for women in families below the poverty line without any cost to them.

Under the scheme private practitioners affiliated with a recognized health facility deliver babies for beneficiaries of the scheme at a consolidated sum of 1,795 rupees per delivery in their clinics or at 659 rupees per delivery in a government facility. Once empanelled, each doctor is paid an advance of 15,000 rupees. A private doctor may exit at any time after settling the accounts or may renew empanelment after 100 deliveries. The doctors were enrolled after meeting with the Indian Federation of Gynecologists as well with the Indian Medical Association. In the tribal district of Sabarkantha, 46 gynecologists enrolled under this scheme. Of the 7,536 deliveries recorded in the district, 1,505 deliveries were through the Chiranjeevi scheme.

However, the private doctors expressed dissatisfaction because the case-fee is too low to conduct caesarean deliveries. The honorarium includes the cost of all tests, medicine, supplies and expenses. But, after deducting a sum of 250 rupees paid as an incentive to the patient and the health worker who brought the patient to the clinic, a doctor actually receives only 1,545 rupees or 409 rupees, depending on the delivery site. Unfortunately the scheme seems to have attracted private practitioners primarily because of its honorarium. The original objectives of reducing infant and mortality rates and of facilitating institutional birth deliveries are not mentioned. Also, awareness among the potential beneficiaries is low while documentation and reimbursement take considerable time and energy.

Sustainability of the scheme depends on continued government funding. Critics ask why the state government cannot spend a similar amount to improve delivery rooms and maternity wards in public hospitals. They also note that only complicated cases go for institutional delivery under this scheme, thus leading to an adverse selection of cases and diminishing the incentives to the private doctors. Categorization of patients is also a problem. Private hospitals do not have mechanisms to verify BPL patients but they do not turn away any patient for lack of a certificate. At discharge, however, confrontation is almost inevitable because patients without cards are charged normal rates – even though they then claim to belong to the BPL category. Both patients and doctors lack clarity about the scheme.

Yet the scheme is a success story. Newspapers report that among the 11,151 deliveries conducted under Chiranjeevi in the five districts covered by the scheme, no maternal death occurred. The state government plans to introduce the scheme throughout the state and proposes to increase both overall funding and the honorarium paid to the health worker. Partnerships that began in pilot districts have been extended across the entire state of Gujarat – and several other states have adopted this scheme.

## Patterns of public-private partnership in India

The 16 case studies are analyzed on the basis of type of partnership, locational logic, objectives and scope of services, benefits for target populations, responsibilities of partners, selection of private sector partners, capacity to monitor performance, payment mechanisms and operational concerns.

### *Types of partnerships*

Types of partnerships include contracting (both contracting-in and contracting-out), performance management, technology demonstrations, voucher schemes, community-based health insurance and hospital autonomy. Tables 3.2 and 3.3 reveal that contracting is the predominant PPP model in India. However, several innovative initiatives are being piloted in parts of the country. The private partners engaged in the partnership vary from individuals (entrepreneurs or doctors) through NGOs at different scales of operations to private corporate hospitals. Of the 16 partnerships and 19 contracts examined, only eight partners were NGOs (including a non-profit research institute), three individual entrepreneurs, two private companies, one public sector company, several individual physicians, two large private hospitals and a large corporate hospital. In addition, two autonomous Government of India agencies were involved in partnerships.

Some partnerships deal with simple contracts (laundry, catering, cleaning); others are more complex with many stakeholders and their respective responsibilities. For example, Karnataka's Yeshasvini health insurance scheme involves the Department of Co-operatives (with its own hierarchy of functionaries), the Yeshasvini Trust, many private local hospitals, a corporate Third Party Administrator and beneficiaries with their eligibility conditions. Other than the Yeshasvini scheme, the principal partner in all partnerships is the state Department of Health and Family Welfare. In most partnerships, the contract has been engaged directly by the ministry although in some projects the contracts were signed on a decentralized basis by the local hospital committee.

In terms of monetary value, the least valued contracts are in providing catering services (at a rate of 27 rupees per meal for about 30 meals daily) and cleaning and scavenging services (24,000 rupees per month) for Bhaga Jatin hospital, Kolkata. The most expensive partnership is the Rajiv Gandhi super-specialty hospital in Raichur. Concerning duration, the Chiranjeevi scheme in Gujarat is the newest (since December 2005). Other 'contracting out' partnerships (lifeline fluid store in Jaipur's SMS hospital; PHC Management by Karuna Trust in Karnataka) are nearly a decade old.

No pattern was observed in terms of the chronology of a partnership or geographical region. Nine partnership contracts are based in hospitals or health centers while the remaining seven are either community-based or outreach services. Some private partners have worked in the health sector field for a long time (Karuna Trust; SHIS in the Sunderbans; Apollo Hospital). One partner had no prior experience in health care at all (Birla Institute of Scientific Research, Uttaranchal).

Table 3.2 Types of partnership and partners

| Partnership | Type of partnership | Public partner | Private partner | Initiation |
|---|---|---|---|---|
| SMS Hospital – CT Scan and MRI Facility (Jaipur) | Contracting a private entrepreneur to provide super specialty radiological diagnostic services | Hospital Committee (Rajasthan Medicare Relief Society), SMS Hospital, Jaipur | Vardhman Scanning and Imaging Private Ltd., Jaipur (commercial partner) | 2004 |
| SMS Hospital – Life-Line Fluid Store (Jaipur) | Contracting in hospital drug store to supply quality drugs and other supplies at cheaper rate to patients | Hospital Committee (Rajasthan Medicare Relief Society), SMS Hospital | An independent drug store owner (commercial partner) | 1996 |
| Municipal Corp. Delhi – Arpana Swasthya Kendra (Delhi) | Adoption and management of health center (contracting out management) | Municipal Corporation of Delhi, Government of National Capital Territory (Delhi) | Arpana Trust, Madhuban, Haryana (non-profit NGO) | July 2003 |
| Uttaranchal Mobile Hospital and Research Centre (Bhimtal) | Technology Demonstration project – collaboration (joint venture through a trust) to run mobile health clinics | Department of Health and Family Welfare, Government of Uttaranchal, and Technology Information Forecasting Assessment Council, Department of Science and Technology, Government of India | Birla Institute of Scientific Research, Bhimtal, Uttaranchal (private educational research institute) | October 2002 |
| Rajiv Gandhi super-specialty hospital (Raichur) | Management contract (contracting out; elements of a joint venture) | Department of Health and Family Welfare, Government of Karnataka | Apollo Hospitals Enterprises Limited, Hyderabad (commercial partner) | October 2001 |
| Management of Primary Health Centers (Karnataka) | Contracting out (an NGO is contracted to manage PHCs and provide all PHC services) | Department of Health and Family Welfare, Government of Karnataka | Karuna Trust, Bangalore (non-profit NGO) | April 1996; formal since 2000 |
| Karnataka Integrated Telemedicine and Tele-health project, Chamarajanagar District hospital. | Experimental collaboration (joint venture) as a technology demonstration project | Department of Health and Family Welfare, Government of Karnataka District Hospital; Indian Space Research Organization, Government of India | Narayana Hrudalaya hospital (a private commercial hospital), Bangalore | April 2002 |

| | | | | |
|---|---|---|---|---|
| Yeshasvini Health Insurance Scheme (Karnataka) | Co-operative health insurance managed through a trust (community-based health insurance) | Department of Cooperatives, Government of Karnataka | Narayana Hrudayalya (private hospital) in Bangalore; Family Health Plan Ltd. (Apollo Hospitals Enterprises Limited Hyderabad); network of 160 private hospitals in Karnataka | November 2002 |
| Rogi Kalyan Samiti (RKS), Jaya Prakash Hospital (Bhopal) | Hospital Autonomy (decentralization of hospital management through local governance and by public participation through Patient Welfare Committee); case of a 'public–public partnership' | Department of Health, Government of Madhya Pradesh & JP Hospital (district general hospital), Bhopal | RKS (Patient Welfare Committee) is a registered non-profit society with members from citizen groups, private donors, local government, and health officials | November 1995 |
| Revised National Tuberculosis Control Program (RNTCP), (Hyderabad) | Collaboration for disease surveillance and treatment under national health program; also called 'public–private mix' | District Tuberculosis Control Society, Directorate of Health Services, Government of Andhra Pradesh | Mahavir Trust hospital, Hyderabad (a private sector for-profit hospital) and private medical practitioners and/or nursing homes | 1995 |
| Emergency Ambulance Services, Theni district (Tamil Nadu) | Performance contract for the provision of emergency ambulance services in the region. Ambulances are owned by the government. | Directorate of Health Services, Government of Tamil Nadu | The Seva Nilayam Society in association with Ryder-Cheshire foundation (local non-profit NGOs) | December 2002 |
| Urban Slum health care project, Adilabad (Andhra Pradesh) | Contracting in (performance contract with grant in aid, but with out any public premises being handed over to the private partner) | Commissioner of Family Welfare, Government of Andhra Pradesh, (under World Bank-funded IPP-VIII project – currently linked with the RCH-II project) | Social Action for Integrated Development Services (SAIDS), Adilabad district (a local non-profit NGO) | 2001 |
| Arogya Raksha Scheme, Ranga Reddy district (Andhra Pradesh) | Health Insurance scheme based on voucher (or service eligibility certificate). Funded by the government, operational management by the profit oriented public sector company and service delivery by private health service providers | Department of Health and Family Welfare, Government of Andhra Pradesh and New India Assurance Company (a public sector for-profit insurance company) | Private clinics and/or hospitals, one in each development block | March 1999 (no longer operating) |

Table 3.2 continued

| Partnership | Type of partnership | Public partner | Private partner | Initiation |
|---|---|---|---|---|
| Mobile Health Services in the Sunderbans, North 24 Parganas district (West Bengal) | Performance contract under grant-in-aid (contracting in); private provider received no public property or premises | Department of Health and Family Welfare, Government of West Bengal (project funds from the World Bank) | Southern Health Improvement Samity (SHIS) (non-profit NGO) | February 1999 |
| Contracting in catering, cleaning and laundry, Bagha Jatin hospital (Kolkata) | Conventional outsourcing of non-clinical support services in a hospital | Department of Health and Family Welfare, Government of West Bengal | Three commercial entrepreneurs (two individual contractors and one private company) | 2002 Catering and cleaning; 2005 Laundry |
| Shamlaji Community Health Centre, Sabarkantha district (Gujarat) | Contracting out (NGO contracted to adopt and manage a CHC and provide all CHC level services) through grant-in-aid on pilot basis | Department of Health and Family Welfare, Government of Gujarat | All India Movement for Seva (AIMS) (non-profit NGO) | June 2002 |
| Chiranjeevi Yojana, Sabarkantha district (Gujarat) | Contracting in by enrolling private practitioners to provide emergency care; case-based remuneration; no public premises or properties given to the private sector | Department of Health and Family Welfare, Government of Gujarat | Gynecologists based in private clinics, nursing homes and/or public hospitals | December 2005 |

Table 3.3 Classification of partnership types

| Type | Case | Overall scope of services | Private partner(s) |
|---|---|---|---|
| Conventional contracting in | SMS Hospital, Jaipur | Radiological diagnostics (CT Scan, MRI) | Private company |
| | | Drugs and medical supplies store | Individual entrepreneur |
| | Bhaga Jatin Hospital, Kolkata | Catering and kitchen services | Individual entrepreneur |
| | | Cleaning and scavenging services | Individual entrepreneur |
| | | Laundry services | Private company |
| Performance management contracts | Arpana Swasthya Kendra, Delhi | Management of a maternity health center | Non-profit NGO |
| | Karuna Trust, Karnataka | Management of Primary Health Centers (PHC) | Non-profit NGO |
| | Shamlaji Hospital, Sabarkantha District, Gujarat | Management of a Community Health Center (CHC) | Non-profit NGO |
| | Rajiv Gandhi hospital, Raichur, Karnataka | Super-specialty clinical care services | Large corporate hospital |
| Contracting out | Urban Slum Health Care Project, Adilabad, Andhra Pradesh | Providing maternity and child care and reproductive and child health services | Non-profit NGO |
| | Chiranjeevi Yojana, Sabarkantha District, Gujarat | Enrolment of the private obstetricians and gynecologists for conducting deliveries | More than 45 individual private doctors |
| | Emergency Ambulance Services, Theni District, Tamil Nadu | Providing transport for emergency cases | Non-profit NGOs (2) |
| | Mobile Health Services the Sunderbans, West Bengal | Providing mobile (boat-based) health services | Non-profit NGO |
| Technology demonstration project (collaborative partnership) | Uttaranchal Mobile Hospital and Research Centre, Bhimtal | Mobile health vans delivering diagnostic and health care services | Non-profit research institute |
| | Karnataka Integrated Telemedicine and Tele-health project, Karnataka | Tele consultation and in patient services for cardiac and other specialist care | Large private hospital |
| Community health insurance | Yeshasvini Health Insurance Scheme, Karnataka | Health insurance to the members of farmers cooperatives | Large private hospital; corporate third party administrator; over 160 private hospitals |
| Voucher scheme | Arogya Raksha Scheme, Andhra Pradesh | Hospitalization services to those who had undergone sterilization after two children | Public sector company |
| Hospital autonomy | Rogi Kalyan Samiti, JP Hospital Bhopal | Decentralized management of hospital and improve the quality of care | One clinic per block State-run district hospital |
| Public-private mix | RNTCP, Mahavir Trust Hospital, Hyderabad | Surveillance and treatment of TB patients, under disease control program | Large private hospital; private doctors; nursing homes |

*Objectives*

The objective of each partnership is to protect the poor from costs associated with acute illness. This goal has been pursued by facilitating improved access to institutional deliveries, providing protection to infants and expectant mothers, ensuring access to affordable or free services, enabling the telecommunication technology, ensuring specialists on contract and providing economic subsidy to the cost of care by community based health insurance. The objectives of the partnership projects become more apparent when the background to the partnership is examined. Most partnerships seek to provide basic primary care or community health services, but four of them provide super-specialty clinical services. Two other partnerships supply non-clinical support services.

The circumstances that lead government to seek private partnership are varied. In only three partnerships had the government resorted to open tenders and a bidding process. In most of the partnerships, the government and the private partner consulted each other before venturing into partnership. As evident in the following three examples, the charisma, the leadership and the vision of both private partners and public officials were significant.

- For Arpana Swasthya Kendra in Delhi, a maternity health center was the last building to be constructed with funds from the World Bank's IPP-VIII project. However, due to insufficient staff, the building lay idle. An NGO in the slum community where the health center had been built approached the IPP-VIII project director with a request to allow it to manage the health center. The project director recommended the proposal to an MCD standing committee that, after deliberation, approved the transfer of management control to the NGO under a contract.

- In Karnataka's Yeshasvini insurance scheme, Dr. Devi Shetty – founder-director of a well known heart hospital, Narayana Hrudayalaya, and already a popular figure for his pioneering work on low-cost cardiac surgeries and charity – was invited to endorse a milk product at a function organized by the Karnataka Milk Federation (KMF), a cooperative society with over two million members. During the function Dr. Shetty offered to provide services to all KMF members if each paid a monthly fee of five rupees. His proposal was transmitted to the state government through the then Secretary of the Department of Co-operatives, which not only approved it but agree to contribute half of the subscription for each enrolled member. Dr. Shetty and his staff provided most of the planning and initial implementation before the Yeshasvini Trust undertook this responsibility. To make the services available to beneficiaries throughout Karnataka, Dr. Shetty used his personal contacts and persuasive skills to attract private hospitals all over the state into a network of service providers. Dr. Shetty later played a similar role in establishing a coronary care unit in the Chamarajanagar district hospital for the Karnataka Integrated Telemedicine and Tele-health Project.

- For adoption and management of Primary Health Centers (PHCs) in Karnataka, the Honorary Secretary of the Karuna Trust – Dr. Sudarshan – was critical. The initial suggestion to manage a PHC came from the Karnataka Government during one of its periodic meetings with NGOs. After consulting at various levels (including local village-elected representatives), the Karuna Trust submitted a proposal that the state cabinet formally approved. The success of this experimental project lead government to issue a formal policy in 2000 that invited private sector organizations to manage PHCs under Memoranda of Understanding.

Similarly initiatives of people like Colonel Pant (retired) for the Uttaranchal mobile health clinic, Dr. K.J.R. Murthy for the DOTS/TB-control program at Hyderabad's Mahavir Trust hospital, Mr. M.A. Wohab for the boat-based mobile health services in West Bengal's Sunderbans, and Dr. Haren Joshi in Gujarat's Shamlaji Hospital have inspired partnership initiatives in the delivery of health services to the poor. Policy pronouncements by the government alone are not sufficient for PPP initiatives. Visionary leaders, trust-based relationships and mutual benefits are important for any private sector partnership.

Mutually compelling circumstances provide yet another critical factor for the establishment of a partnership. Northern Karnataka is an economically backward, drought-prone region with a large proportion of its population living below the poverty line, many of whom are Muslims. People in the region travel long distances to Bangalore or Hyderabad for specialist medical care. Therefore, the Government of Karnataka built the Rajiv Gandhi super-speciality hospital – popularly called the OPEC hospital due to being funded by a soft loan from the Organization of Petroleum Exporting Countries – in Raichur. The government initially attempted to run the hospital but found that specialist doctors could not be retained in such a difficult area. Despite the investment of more than 600 million rupees, the hospital lay basically unused. At the same time, a corporate chain of hospitals based in Hyderabad – Apollo Hospitals Enterprises, Ltd – had been seeking to establish its own hospital in the region but was wary about construction costs. The dilemmas of the Government of Karnataka and of Apollo Hospitals fit well together for establishing this partnership of mutual benefit. Through this partnership, the government can provide free services to the poor while Apollo Hospitals is able to establish its business operations without having to invest in buildings or other infrastructural needs. Because the corporate hospital is able to pay its staff well, it retains the specialists, which the government was unable to do.

Sometimes partnerships are based on the need for technological innovation with an objective to optimize synergy between information and communication technologies and medical technology. In Karnataka's Integrated Telemedicine and Tele-health Project, the initiative for providing tele-linkage came from the Indian Space Research Organization (ISRO) while medical expertise was offered by Narayana Hrudayalaya (NH). As an experimental pilot project, NH set up a coronary care unit in the Chamarajanagar district hospital to support the work of the physicians already working there. The linkage between coronary care units at a private hospital and at a public hospital through telecommunications is the unique feature of this project.

Contrary to the typical outsourcing model, many states have invited the private sector and NGOs to provide primary clinical care services on a selective basis. They experimented on a pilot basis to explore how to overcome inefficiencies in the delivery of health services by the public sector. In Karnataka and West Bengal, policies were framed after learning lessons from pilot projects. In Rajasthan and Gujarat, policy was introduced without pilot projects. In Tamil Nadu and Andhra Pradesh, using the private sector in the provision of health services has long been encouraged, especially by industrial houses. In Delhi, the success of Arpana Swasthya Kendra may lead to more innovations in the system.

### Target populations

In terms of geographical area, the partnership projects range from metropolitan cities to hilly regions and remote islands. Of the 16 partnership projects, five are city-based; the rest are in rural and tribal regions. Six partnerships provide services to geographical areas with difficult terrain. Five projects operate throughout the respective states. Table 3.4 illustrates the location, target population and special benefits to the poor in each partnership project.

Partnerships have well-defined beneficiary groups. Each focuses respectively on women, children and the poor as beneficiaries. Some projects reach the poor almost on their doorsteps while others are static with special privileges to the target population. Some projects provide clinical services; others are indirectly related to clinical services via insurance, service vouchers, etc. The primary focus of the services is to help the people below the poverty line (BPL). All but one partnership focus on initiatives that earmark services for the poor. In most of the partnership agreements, special clauses provide privileges or concessions to BPL beneficiaries.

However, identification of actual beneficiaries versus those excluded from a subsidy is of critical concern. No uniform procedures have been adopted to verify the status of beneficiaries. At times verification of BPL patients is left to the discretion of hospital managers. In other cases, BPL beneficiaries must bring their identify papers (BPL card or ration card). Such identity papers are easy to obtain, yet there is no mechanism to verify whether they are authentic or if the patients actually belong in the BPL category. While it may be prudent to leave the verification of BPL patients to the facility managers, they face pressures to grant favors, especially if the services are expensive. Sometimes, as reported at Jaipur's SMS hospital, interpretation of the BPL category by hospital administrators may be whimsical. But other partnerships have better systems to verify the antecedents of the putative BPL patients such as where patients must obtain a citation from the local government hospital. In projects where there are two types of service (with or without user-fee for non-BPL and BPL patients respec-

Table 3.4 Location, target population and services for the poor

| Partnership project | Location and target population | Specification of services to the poor |
|---|---|---|
| SMS Hospital, CT Scan and MRI Facility (Jaipur) | Large tertiary hospital in the state capital; beneficiaries from all of Rajasthan plus from neighboring states | Free for BPL patients, patients above 70 years, and freedom fighters (approximately 20% of patients); pre-negotiated contracted rate for other patients |
| SMS Hospital (Life Line Fluid Store – LLFS) | Ditto | LLFS drugs are less expensive than in the market. Provision of 20% services to the poor is not clear |
| Municipal Corporation of Delhi (MCD) and Arpana Swasthya Kendra (Delhi) | Urban slum resettlement colony in Delhi; over 25,000 population, primarily migrants | OPD card is ten rupees (user-fee) for all patients; services include specialist consultation. MCD supplies medicine free to all patients. Lab tests, ANCs and immunization free for the poor. Free surgeries for select poor patients in private hospitals with subsidized emergency transport |
| Uttaranchal Mobile Hospital and Research Centre (Bhimtal) | Six districts in western Uttaranchal; target population is dispersed in the hilly region; 70% of the state population lives below the poverty line | Services free for patients with BPL cards, including outpatient department consultations, radiological diagnostics and pathological tests |
| Rajiv Gandhi Super-specialty hospital (Raichur) | Hospital provides super-specialty services to drought-prone northern Karnataka with its large BPL population; people travel far for specialist medical treatment; hospital is the region's only super-specialty hospital | Free out-patient services to BPL patients; 40% of beds are reserved for BPL patients with costs reimbursed by the government. BPL patients admitted only on referral from a PHC or CHC; special officers verify BPL category patients. The hospital also treats patients under the Yeshasvini scheme |
| Management of Primary Health Centers (Karnataka) | Two remote rural/tribal districts in Karnataka characterized by low literacy, poverty, malnutrition, high diarrhoeal diseases and high infant mortality | All patients are provided free health services for diagnosis, treatment and drugs. No user-charges reported in this partnership |
| Karnataka Integrated Telemedicine and Tele-health project (Chamarajanagar District hospital) | Services are meant for the people in Charmaraja Nagar is an economically backward rural tribal district populated mainly by poor farmers; the district had no facility for coronary care | Free diagnostics, medicines and treatment for BPL patients and Yeshasvini card-holders. Others are charged nominal user-fee (Rs. 30 for ECG, Rs.100 per day bed charges, Rs 40 for X-ray). Government reimburses the cost of services to BPL patients via quarterly advances; free medicine |

*Table 3.4* continued

| Partnership project | Location and target population | Specification of services to the poor |
|---|---|---|
| Yeshasvini Health Insurance Scheme (Karnataka) | Approximately 2.2 million farmers from Karnataka's cooperative societies enrolled – including families, ten million members | Scheme is principally targeted on poor farmers (members of agricultural cooperative societies); members are issued insurance cards |
| Rogi Kalyan Samiti (RKS), JP Hospital (Bhopal) | All patients of this district general hospital in the city of Bhopal, capital of Madhya Pradesh | Services free for BPL patients, former defense personnel and physically handicapped patients; others pay nominal user-fees for all services |
| Mahavir Trust Hospital (Hyderabad) | City of Hyderabad with a catchment area of 500,000 people (standard size of a 'unit' under RNTCP); target population is a mix of rural and urban beneficiaries | The entire program is under a national TB-control program (RNTCP); no charges are levied on any patient so no specific concessions for the poor |
| Emergency Ambulance Services, Theni (Tamil Nadu) | Two development blocks of Theni district, a tribal region with high infant and maternal mortality, low rates of institutional delivery, and poor transport facilities | 10% of the cases are to be provided free ambulance services but who are eligible is unclear; others pay five rupees per kilometer for the service (actually eight rupees per kilometer) |
| Urban Slum Health Care project, Adilabad district, (Andhra Pradesh) | APUSH covers 74 municipalities in 21 districts of the state with 192 UHCs in operation. Each UHC covers ± 20,000 slum dwellers; this project is run by an NGO providing services to 15,000 townspeople | Free services for only women and children in an urban slum community; no user-charges but, to use the services, a woman should be a member of the health group |
| Arogya Raksha Scheme, Ranga Reddy District (Andhra Pradesh) | BPL card-holders who have been sterilized (with only two children under five years of age); services in any government hospital; beneficiaries presumed to number 200,000 per year | Target beneficiaries are restricted to those below poverty line with only one or two children. A certificate of sterilization in a government hospital attested by an Auxiliary Nurse Midwife is a prerequisite to obtain services |
| Mobile Health Services in the Sunderbans (West Bengal) | North 24-Parganas district of West Bengal (81 villages with a population of 305,085) is characterized by difficult terrain, high morbidity, economic backwardness and lack of access to health care services | No explicit statement about specific benefits for poor patients; the entire population in the socially and economically backward region need health care services |

| Catering, cleaning and laundry services in Bhaga Jatin Hospital (Kolkatta) Shamlaji hospital, (Community Health Center), Sabarkantha District (Gujarat) | 100-bed government hospital in Kolkata with over 50,000 outpatients and 1,000 inpatients annually. Sabarkantha, a predominantly tribal district in Gujarat, has a population of over 100,000 in 80 villages; health facilities are scarce in the region. Hospital received 27,110 outpatients and 4,309 inpatients | BPL (free bed) patients are supplied free meals; all others pay 50% of the charges. Rs.27 per day per person for three meals. Private partner cannot charge user-fees for immunization, sterilization, children referred under ICDS program, maternal and child health services, TB/leprosy and other national disease control programs, or for diagnosis and treatment of the poor. User-fees for others on select services |
| Chiranjeevi Yojana scheme (Gujarat) | Five economically backward tribal districts in Gujarat, on a pilot basis (since extended throughout the state). Total population in the five districts is 9.97 million | Free services for BPL women. Scheme primarily targeted on pregnant BPL women; certificate of eligibility through BPL card or a certificate from a village official. ANC registration in a government facility is a requisite for availing this scheme |

tively), there have been confrontations between hospital managers and beneficiaries. Wherever the government had agreed to reimburse the services provided to the BPL patients (in contrast to budget support through grants-in-aid), the agreement document does not clearly spell out a verification mechanism.

### Services

Partnership agreements cover a wide range of services including outpatient consultation, inpatient admissions, outreach services, radiological diagnostics, ambulances, medical stores, ancillary services, super-specialty care, tele-consultation, tuberculosis treatment, reproductive and child health, etc. Many have support services as well. Five partnership projects restrict activities to specific services – radiological services at SMS hospital, cardiac care in the Karnataka Telemedicine project, TB treatment through the Mahavir Trust hospital, pregnancy-related ambulance transport in Theni, and institutional delivery for childbirth in the Chiranjeevi scheme. Several other partnership projects limit patients to a narrow range of services. In the Yeshasvini scheme, patients are not allowed any medical treatment (inpatient admission) that does not lead to surgery; also, only two unmarried children plus the spouse of a cooperative society member are allowed membership. This project clearly delineates categories of exclusion. Appendix 3.1 lists the respective services provided by institutions engaged in partnership projects.

### Selection criteria

Less than half of project partners were selected through a competitive process of open tender and bidding. In most projects either the state government or the private sector took the initiative to contact the other sector and to initiate collaboration. Since most partnerships were not based on a competitive process, eligibility conditions were either unclear or tailored to ensure that the choice of the specific private partner would withstand administrative scrutiny. Some states chose private sector partners on the basis of their prior experience. Based on pilot projects, the governments of Karnataka, West Bengal and Gujarat drafted a policy on public-private partnerships. Other states such as Rajasthan and Tamil Nadu formulated their policies well before any experience with partnerships.

The evidence indicates that a competitive process of selecting the private sector partner is less effective than an invited or consultative partnership. Among projects where partners were chosen on a competitive basis, private contractors are either unhappy or have been unable to perform for their own benefit. All these partners are private individuals or private-for-profit agencies. Only the partner in Andhra Pradesh's urban health scheme in Adilabad (who was selected on a competitive basis) is performing without complaints. The problem may possibly be that, while competing to win a contract, a private competitor's primary concern is to showcase a very low cost per unit of service – because the government invariably chooses the lowest bid in a tendering process. While economical for the government in the short run, the contractor over the long term expects some concessions or upward revision of tariffs. In the absence of the latter, the contractor is unlikely to deliver services at the initial level of enthusiasm.

These findings point to the type of policy that governments should adopt. It may be a legal requirement for the government to choose the private partner on the basis of a transparent, competitive and objective process, and such an approach may be useful for commercial projects. But in the service sector where the priority is to reach the poor, a similar approach may not be the best option. The documented success of several partnership projects indicates the importance of prior negotiations with potential partners. For both administrative legality and political acceptance, prior negotiations are preferable and these could be made more transparent by using a committee structure with members from government plus eminent persons.

In partnership projects, the criteria for eligibility by the private sector include certain minimum qualifications such as prior experience, minimum cash reserves and familiarity with the region. In both case studies at Jaipur's SMS hospital, the financial conditions were stringent. The private agents who won the contracts had to deposit large amounts of security money (two million rupees per radiological machine; 40,000 rupees for the drugstore). Conditions also related to the deadlines within which the contractors had to implement their agreements, failing which there was a stiff monetary penalty. No other partnerships required such huge security deposits nor imposed such financial penalties for delays in implementation. In any partnership, by definition, equality among the partners is essential for success. In Rajasthan the state government is the dominant partner, a feature absent in all other partnership projects. Although governments always provide the funds, the contractual terms do not reflect dominance by the state.

In many projects, state bureaucrats selected the private partner through a committee process. In all the case studies except Uttaranchal's mobile health clinic, Tamil Nadu's ambulance service and West Bengal's Bhaga Jatin hospital, the partners had prior experience with the health sector. There is no particular pattern to indicate that those without prior experience in health sector do badly in the execution of projects, but all partnerships projects required the contractors to be registered.

### Commitments of partners

In most partnership projects the public sector provides the infrastructure and, in some cases, the government also supplies fuel for transport vehicles or its equivalent budget. The Yeshasvini health insurance scheme was initially run from the premises of Narayana Hrudayalaya, but then the office of the Yeshasvini Trust was transferred to government premises.

Most projects delineate the responsibilities of private partners. A common theme is the provision of agreed services to a target population of BPL beneficiaries. Other themes are the provision of uninterrupted services, employment of qualified staff, maintenance of equipment and premises, payments of tariffs, rentals and taxes, and submission of periodic accounts and reports. Some partnership agreements entail more specific responsibilities. In Rajasthan's SMS hospital, if the CT scan and MRI equipment breaks down, it is the responsibility of the private partner to arrange alternative services at the same cost as negotiated. Karnataka's Rajiv Gandhi hospital must provide free services during any natural calamity. Gujarat's Shamlaji hospital should cater for medico-legal cases and treat accident and trauma cases. In Uttaranchal the sites for the mobile health clinics are determined in consultation with the government. In West Bengal the private partner is expected to conduct a baseline survey of the health status of the population throughout the Sunderbans and encourage people to seek services from government health centers.

Most hospital-based services allow the private partner to extend services beyond the scope of the agreement after informing the government but the agency must also facilitate all national disease control programs plus immunization and family planning. Of critical concern in projects is how to monitor adherence to mutual commitments. Appendix 3.2 summarizes the commitments of each project's respective public and private partners. Private partners generally have the responsibility to verify BPL beneficiaries, except in Rajasthan's SMS hospital where hospital managers verify their bona-fides and in Karnataka's Rajiv Gandhi hospital where the government appoints a verification officer. Most projects identify BPL patients through BPL ration-cards although in certain schemes – Arogya Raksha, Yeshasvini, Chiranjeevi – beneficiaries must possess specific documents.

### Performance indicators

Most partnership agreements state guidelines and operational details but without indicators for performance or evaluation. In only three cases – Arpana Swasthya Kendra, Aroyga Raksha, the Sunderbans' mobile health scheme – are outcome indicators for the private partners explicitly stated. Other projects only briefly state the frequency of performance reviews or the committee responsible for monitoring them. In Jaipur's SMS hospital, the private partners submit weekly reports while the hospital authorities periodically conduct quality control checks. The drugstore also submits a monthly report on its inventory. The performance of both private partners is reviewed quarterly. Arpana Swasthya Kendra has no specific timeframe for assessing its performance but it is expected to achieve certain health outcome indicators in the community. Uttaranchal's mobile health clinic project does not specify performance indicators either but it has a quarterly review. In Raichur the agreement for the Rajiv Gandhi hospital contains no performance indicators but the Raichur District Collector is the immediate supervisory authority while a ten-member governing council biannually reviews the performance of the hospital.

The Memorandum of Understanding authorizing the Karuna Trust to manage PHCs has no specific performance indicators but includes several monitoring systems. Apart from a quarterly review by the district-level health officials, reviews are conducted by village health committees, women's groups and an internal monitoring committee. Chamarajanagar's KITTH project has only a quarterly performance review by representatives of the partners. However, the urban slum project in Andhra Pradesh not only has explicit evaluation parameters but also consolidates the data through a format that has a weighted score of 200 points. The indicators include service-related targets and health-related outcomes. Likewise, the mobile health services in the Sunderbans of West Bengal are measured through morality and morbidity indicators.

### Payment mechanisms

Partnership projects rely on two types of payment. The first category spans rates paid by patients in the form of user-fees and insurance premiums, but many partnership projects do not allow user-fees to be charged to beneficiaries. In primary care services, the impact of revenue from user-fees requires review as to whether they have been beneficial to the public health facility or the private partner. In Uttaranchal the revenue from user-fees collected by mobile health clinics over a three-year period is less than 10 percent of the expenditure incurred. Whether the revenue from user-fees is added to the grants received or to be accounted within the grants is unclear. In all other cases, the revenue from user-fees does not appear in financial statements. How user-fees will be counted and used is not stated in any partnership agreement except in Madhya Pradesh's Rogi Kalyan Samiti.

The second category of payments concerns grants-in-aid or budgetary support for which a private partner (whether individual or agency) agrees to provide services. Such categorization must be interpolated with the nature of services provided – whether specialist clinical or primary care. The tariffs are fixed either on the basis of tendering or mutually negotiated systems or else unilaterally fixed by government. Table 3.5 sketches this classification.

In projects where partners were chosen through competitive tenders, the rates are quoted by the private partner. In Jaipur's SMS hospital and Kolkata's Bhaga Jatin hospital, rates had been fixed based on tariffs quoted by the private partner. Although operated by an individual competitively chosen, the rates for medicine and supplies in the LLFS drugstore are determined by the hospital authorities. In Raichur's Rajiv Gandhi hospital, however, the tariffs were negotiated without a tender. The Memorandum of Understanding only specifies the proportion of free services to be provided to BPL patients, not the rates of services to non-BPL patients. The contract for Theni's emergency ambulance service states a rate of five rupees per kilometer – but, in practice, a higher rate is being charged.

Some partnerships in which the private partners were not competitively chosen do charge a user-fee but only after obtaining government permission. Almost all projects receive grants from the government for their operational expenses. Karnataka's Rajiv Gandhi hospital and the Yeshasvini scheme receive partial grants from the state government. In the Yeshasvini scheme, the rates for

*Table 3.5* Modes of tariffs and payment

| Nature of partnership | | Primary-care level | Specialist-care level |
|---|---|---|---|
| Competitive | User fee | Emergency Ambulance services (Theni) | CT Scan/MRI, SMS Hospital (Jaipur) LLFS drugstore, SMS hospital (Jaipur) Catering, Bhagajatin hospital (Kolkata) |
| | No user fee | *Urban Slum health project (Adilabad, Andhra Pradesh)* | |
| Non-Competitive | User fee | *Arpana Swasthya Kendra (Delhi)* *Mobile Health Clinic (Uttaranchal)* *Mobile health clinics (West Bengal)* *Shamlaji CHC (Gujarat)* | Rogi Kalyan Samiti (Bhopal) Rajiv Gandhi Hospital (Raichur) Yeshasvini Scheme (Karnataka) *KITTH, Chamarajanagar (Karnataka)* |
| | No user fee | *PHC management (Karnataka)* RNTCP, Mahavir Hospital (Hyderabad) *Chiranjeevi Yojana (Gujarat)* | |

Notes
Arogya Raksha does not fit these categories; *italics* represent projects with budgetary support (grants) from government.

each surgery or hospitalization may be considered to be user-fees charged by the private hospital to the trust – not directly to the patient. Only the Karuna Trust in Karnataka and the urban health scheme partner in Andhra Pradesh do not charge any fees. In no case are BPL patients charged any fee, although the discretion to determine BPL beneficiaries is left to the private partner.

Other issues not mentioned by any MOU are the user-fee rate and how the revenue will be used. Government grants to partnership projects have invariably paid for primary care services, which counters the claim that public-private partnerships have diverted government's attention toward specialist care services. Even in primary care, the argument that public-private partnership is a route to privatization does not hold because, without government grants, the private sector could not sustain operations at these locations. Therefore, government's responsibility is indispensable.

One burning issue in public-private partnerships relates to payment of the private partner by either grants-in-aid or another form of budgetary support. This issue concerns the timeliness and procedures involved in getting funds released. A common complaint in projects where the government provides financial support is that it does not release the payments in time. In one instance, a state government did not release a grant to its NGO partner for nearly 13 months. Fortunately the NGO was large with a long history and deep pockets so it was able to cope with the delay. For a smaller agency such a delay would have ensured closure.

Very few partner agencies reported having received their government grants on time. In Jaipur's SMS hospital both the private agencies are paid monthly. In Delhi the government provides no monetary support to Arpana Swasthya Kendra other than a monthly supply of medicine and the initial investment for equipment and furniture. In Karnataka's Rajiv Gandhi hospital, the state government funds not only equipment and infrastructure but also administrative expenses. There have been no complaints about delay in the release of funds although the budgetary support is large. However, the Karuna Trust complains about the irregular release of its grant-in-aid that is supposed to be released quarterly. After initial capital investment for equipment and connectivity, Chamarajanagar's cardiac care project has no explicit statement about regularity of payments other than that the state government will reimburse the costs incurred for BPL beneficiaries. In the Yeshasvini scheme, a professional Third Party Administrator is handling reimbursements to the private hospitals with no complaints to date.

Other partnerships have no financial transactions. Hyderabad's Mahavir Trust hospital employs a few staff for the RNTCP on its own funds. Other than the initial investment, there are no financial transactions between the NGO and the Government of Tamil Nadu for Theni's ambulance service. West Bengal's mobile health clinics in the Sunderbans receive four million rupees over the year, released quarterly, while the contractors at Bhagajatin hospital are paid monthly. Grants-in-aid are regularly released against the bills submitted monthly by Gujarat's Shamlaji hospital and Karnataka's Karuna Trust. These grants cover salaries and other operational expenditures. While the private agencies in the Chiranjeevi scheme are each advanced.15,000 rupees to pay the empanelled doctors, payment is such a sensitive issue that the private partner agencies underplay their difficulties. Partnership agreements often do not mention the timing of payments to the private agency or how the private agency would cope in the event of non-release of payments.

Most partnership projects lack explicit monetary incentives for the private partners. Incentives are rather indirect. In Jaipur's SMS hospital, the incentive for the CT scan and MRI operator is the high volume of patients at the hospital plus the freedom to provide services to outside patients at his own rate whenever the machines are idle. In the drugstore, the contractor's incentive takes the form of a 1 percent commission on total sales. Karnataka's Rajiv Gandhi hospital is the exceptional case. The government not only allocated enormous funds for capital investment and recurrent expenditures but also agreed to bail out the private partner in case of losses. Apart from meeting all expenses, the state government pays 3 percent of total expenses as a service fee. The agreement specifies that if the hospital makes a profit, then 30 percent of it would accrue to the private partner. Beyond all these conditions, the hospital management is allowed to use 60 percent of bed capacity to admit paying patients. The incentives in the Yeshasvini scheme are apparent, too, because previously underutilized private hospitals empanelled under the scheme could increase their bed occupancy rate while the Third Party Administrator is paid according to the number of claimants.

In Bhopal's Rogi Kalyan Samiti (RKS), the decentralization of authority acts as an incentive for hospital managers to improve hospital amenities, including quality of care. The user-fee collected can be used to purchase supplies or maintain equipment. Previously, all funds collected were sent to the government treasury so the hospital had to seek approval for all expenditures, however minor. Delay in the release of funds also led to frustration, deterioration in delivery of services and loss of motivation among the hospital managers. Hyderabad's Mahavir Trust hospital has no incentives for the private partners other than supplies of medicine, X-ray film and lab equipment. In the Arogya Raksha scheme of Andhra Pradesh, the monetary value of medical services on offer to the private hospitals and clinics empanelled under the scheme is no incentive compare to the administrative overheads required to process a case. On the other hand, the lump-sum received by the insurance company from the government under a presumptive calculation of 200,000 beneficiaries greatly exceeded the costs of any services rendered. The complicated system of registration and of access inhibited clients from applying or the hospitals from providing services so the insurance agency actually avoided enlisting clients or providing services to more beneficiaries.

For many NGOs, government grants sustain their existence. In the case of private for-profit partners, working with the government in one part of a state provides significant impetus to their future contracts with the government in other parts of the state. Interestingly state governments have been very circumspect about granting incentives to the non-profit private sector whereas concessions to the private-for-profit sector are frequent. The discrepancy may be due to better negotiating skills by the private sector or perhaps eagerness of the government to collaborate with the private for-profit sector. There may even be a philosophical approach of the not-for-profit agencies against such agreements with the government. It is widely accepted that for-profit agencies may negotiate financial details and profit margins to the most minute detail whereas a similar approach by a non-for-profit agency would be seen as inappropriate. Such difference is evident in Karnataka where the state government has contracted with Apollo Hospital Enterprises Ltd to run Raichur's Rajiv Gandhi hospital and with the Karuna Trust to manage several Primary Health Centers. While the Karuna Trust is given only 90 percent of the salary costs of the staff plus some minor materials, the Rajiv Gandhi hospital gets reimbursed for all its expenses plus a service fee. Furthermore, while Karuna Trust is expected to widen the scope of its services, services at the Rajiv Gandhi hospital are restricted to the agreement clauses.

In almost all the partnership projects where not-for-profit agencies are involved, the contract clauses do not specify explicit incentives. In all five cases of non-profit partners – Arpana Trust in Delhi, BISR in Uttaranchal, Karuna

Trust in Karnataka, SAID in Andhra Pradesh, SHIS in West Bengal, AIMS in Gujarat – none receives a monetary incentive or any form of performance-linked incentives. In fact, in the case of Arpana Trust, except for the building and a monthly quota of medicine, there is no support from the government.

### Sustainability and scalability

Because public-private partnership as a formal policy instrument is at a nascent stage, many state governments are still organizing themselves to engage the private sector. Some state governments have evolved a detailed policy framework based on pilot experiments. Other states continue to experiment without a clear policy. Tamil Nadu, for example, introduced PPP in the 1990s by inviting the corporate sector to manage primary health centers. After initial interest, however, this initiative was not sustained. Other than a government notification, no formal policy document has been developed.

A critical factor is the triggering mechanism for introducing public-private partnerships. In West Bengal, Karnataka, Andhra Pradesh and Gujarat where health sector reform projects had been initiated with funds from the World Bank, the states have separate Health Systems Development Project cells. The officials in these cells are well trained in PPP concepts and systems but their initiatives have to be complemented by legal, administrative and procedural modifications in the state health departments. The latter are not easy. Despite these limitations the officers are able to design systems such as tenders, policy guidelines, forms for financial transactions, performance monitoring, etc. However, officers trained in health sector reforms are often transferred and their successors are unable to understand or appreciate the systems developed by their predecessors. Sometimes the systems are followed without modification; sometimes they are abandoned. As a result, apart from the trained officials, lower-level functionaries are either unaware of or unskilled in handling the private sector agencies. District-level health functionaries may be unable to screen a budget proposal from a private agency, to understand their accounting procedures or to monitor the functioning of a private agency.

Similarly the private agency may not be able to understand the public bureaucratic system of functioning. Bureaucracy requires a great deal of documentation for checks and counter-checks with which the private sector, especially the non-profit NGOs, is unfamiliar. For example NGOs may not be able to calculate the unit-cost of their services or to follow accounting systems as detailed as those of a government agency. Such gaps in the systems and practices lead to a great deal of misunderstanding. The questions are whether the government has the flexibility to let the private sector use its own systems and procedures while managing the partnership, or whether the government should create detailed procedural guidelines for the private agencies to follow as per bureaucratic norms. There may be functionaries in both government and the private agency who are competent in managerial and technical skills so government officials must be trained for 'oversight' functions without being intrusive.

Replicating or scaling-up partnership projects is contextual and specific to the circumstances in which the partnership had originated. The relevant issues include relationships between leaders in the public and private sectors, the scope of services, the availability of a willing private provider, the geographical terrain, technical and managerial capacity of the partners and, most importantly, the perceived benefits and risks in such partnerships.

## Benefits and pitfalls of public-private partnerships

Specific public-private partnerships as institutional experiments seem to work well. However, attention must be paid to issues of leadership, managerial capacity, bureaucratic gamesmanship, perceived risks and benefits, incentives and payment systems.

### *Risks and vulnerabilities*

Perception of risk depends on two factors:

1   the rule-bound behavior of the partners with no scope to contravene the rules of the partnership (with strict disincentives for any deviance);
2   the notion of 'trust and relationship' between the partners.

Risks vary at different levels of health functionaries as well as the scope of services. At the policy level, the risks are political in nature. Popular sentiments (media, political parties, health action groups, staff unions, etc.) may prevent the government from making overt gestures towards the private sector, especially the for-profit sector. The prevalent assumption is that the private sector is primarily interested in profits so its image is that of an 'exploiter'. While an image makeover about the 'private sector' among India's middle class is evident, an unpopular image of the private sector remains a reality in rural India.

In the current context of liberalization, where public sector commercial activities are slowly being divested from the government control through disinvestment or privatization, there is a strong suspicion that the government may resort to similar steps in the health sector. This suspicion is strengthened because the government has not effectively regulated the asymmetrical growth of the private sector in health care. The private for-profit sector seems unable to convince others about its interest in the delivery of health services to underserved populations in association with the government. In reality, however, the private for-profit sector has shown little enthusiasm about primary level health services but there is great enthusiasm to 'collaborate' with the government in providing tertiary care services and in medical education – particularly setting up medical colleges. This pattern reinforces the image that the private for-profit sector collaborates with the government only if there are monetary benefits without having to face any risk. The case of the Rajiv Gandhi super-specialty hospital in northern Karnataka is a case in point.

Inclusion of non-profit organizations within the private sector confuses some people. Non-profit organizations are popularly perceived as 'givers', which is an advantageous image. A number of these organizations masquerade as charitable trusts, some of which are floated by political personalities. Cutting across the spectrum, political parties raise few doubts when governments engage NGOs. However, non-profit organizations are competent only to play limited roles such as providing inexpensive primary care services (e.g. Karuna Trust in Karnataka; Seva Nilayam in Tamil Nadu; Arpana Trust in Delhi; SHIS in West Bengal; SAIDS in Andhra Pradesh, etc.).

At the operational level, risks for partners are on many dimensions. These include financial risk, performance and accountability risks, risk of confrontation between stakeholders and risk of reputation for the private sector. While the for-profit private sector may well be capable of withstanding financial risks during project implementation, any error on the part of a not-for-profit agency could close it down. The accounting systems in not-for-profit agencies are rarely sophisticated, and any errors could lead to administrative strictures that may lead to unforeseen complications. The government agency may delay the release of funds until the error is rectified. A crisis of funds at this stage could stop services to the beneficiaries, further complicating the issue. Furthermore, any administrative stricture may lead to audit inspections by the government, thus denting the reputation of the agency and depriving it of opportunities to bid for additional projects.

Another problem relates to accountability for performance and service delivery. The government is ultimately responsible for the delivery of services so the private sector is seen as an agent of the government. If deficiencies occur in the private sector, responsibility for dereliction of services falls on government health officials. Coordination between the stakeholders is another area for potential conflict. Differences in personalities and their respective styles can jeopardize the functioning of the partnership. In both Jaipur's SMS hospital and Kolkatta's Bhaga Jatin hospital, fall-outs due to differences in personality were visible. On the other hand, the positive influence of personality was evident in Karnataka's Karuna Trust and the Yeshasvini scheme, in Delhi's Arpana Trust and in Gujarat's Shamlaji hospital.

In the case of SMS hospital, the risk of losing an enormous security deposit actually influenced the functioning of the scheme. Once the contract expires, whether another contractor with similar terms and conditions would be ready for such partnership is doubtful. In Raichur's Rajiv Gandhi hospital, if the Apollo corporate chain of hospitals does not function effectively, the alternatives available for the government are not evident. Yet if the partnership in Raichur is successful, it is not known whether the government would be willing to extend similar arrangements elsewhere. But if the project were unsuccessful, one could ask: 'if Apollo could not, who else could?'

Another risk concerns whether a partnership is based on each partner's rule-bound behavior or 'trust'. One substantiated hypothesis is that partnership projects run higher risks if the partners are chosen through a competitive tender process rather than through a selectively negotiated agreement. A competitive selection process does not automatically distinguish those who perform effectively from those who cannot. The partnership is based solely on the terms and conditions agreed by the partners without any prior contact between them. On the other hand, selection of partners on the basis of their prior track-records helps to identify effective partners and thus leads to a more judicious selection. Whether non-profit private agencies prefer partnership with government based on prior relationships or whether they prefer a competitive selection process requires analysis. In the projects documented in this study, some partnerships occurred after prior relationships while others occur after a competitive selection process. Other than the urban health scheme in Andhra Pradesh, all partnerships between government and not-for-profit organizations have been based on selection after prior contact.

### Relative autonomy of partners

One of the conditions for a true partnership is the relative autonomy of both partners in day-to-day operations as well as in overall management. Autonomy is characterized by the non-intrusiveness of the public sector partner (except its roles of funding, oversight and monitoring) and by the freedom of the private agency to take operational decisions without resorting to cumbersome bureaucratic approvals. Once a partnership agreement has been signed, each partner assumes its responsibilities without being constantly told about 'dos and don'ts'.

In almost all documented partnership projects, the autonomy of the private agency has not been compromised. In Raichur's Rajiv Gandhi hospital, the private sector has full independence in matters pertaining to clinical services while the governing body (or government) is the final authority for administrative and financial issues. In Jaipur's SMS hospital and Kolkata's Bhaga Jatin hospital, hospital authorities were seen as intrusive, but in no partnership projects is the government regarded as overbearing. However, the partnership agreements provide enormous scope for an active (interventionist) role by government agencies. Possibly government agencies lack either technical skills or willingness to take an active and intrusive role. If government officials would take a more active role in monitoring and supervising the partnership projects, a relevant question would be to ask what prevents these officials from taking a similar interest in monitoring the functioning of government hospitals and their functionaries.

In most projects the private partners are free to decide any additional services beyond those to be provided under the contract. They are also free to generate additional resources although, if user-fees are introduced, the private partners are required to obtain government permission. Apart from providing funds, the government plays a subtle role in dominating the partnerships. For example, in the Yeshasvini scheme, the government undertook the task of enrolling the members through the registrar's office and de facto controlled the project's viability. Similarly in the Chiranjeevi scheme, the government holds overall control of the entire project. However, some partnership projects could survive without any role by government. Raichur's Rajiv Gandhi hospital could become self-sustaining; Hyderabad's Mahavir Trust hospital needs no government help; and Theni's emergency ambulance could become self-sustaining if certain controls were removed.

There are also instances in which the private sector agency has influenced government. For example, the Arpana Trust sought the management of a health centre under the Municipal Corporation of Delhi; the Karuna Trust sought to manage Primary Health Centers in Karnataka; Narayana Hrudayalaya developed both the Yeshashvini scheme throughout Karnataka and the telemedicine project in Chamarajanagar; the Mahavir Trust hospital promoted a public-private mix in Hyderabad; and Southern Health Improvement Samity in West Bengal sponsored mobile health clinics in the Sunderbans. All these non-profit agencies have been influential in shaping their respective state governments' policy towards public-private partnerships in health. In summary, the often expressed fear about loss of autonomy by private organizations that work with the government is misplaced.

### *Service standards and quality of service*

One major gap in the partnership MOUs has been a lack of specific conditions related to the quality of services to be delivered to beneficiaries. In most projects, the importance of delivering quality services is stated but not in specific terms. Only the SMS hospital mentioned that the private agency is responsible for improper contrasts in CT/MRI images. While scope existed for defining the specific quality of services in the Memoranda of Understanding with the KITTH project, the Rajiv Gandhi hospital and the Yeshasvini scheme, none were stated in the agreement. Since a majority of the partnership projects delivered primary care services, quality issues in specific terms were evidently not considered.

### *Summary observations on policy implications*

Chapter 6 explores detailed policy inferences across 20 inter-related issues:

1  It is always not clear who initiated the policy option for public-private partnerships. However, states that experimented with partnership ideas before formalizing a policy seem to be more successful than states that promulgated a formal policy well before experimenting with it.
2  There is no uniform pattern to indicate which services are best provided through partnerships and which services are strictly off-limits for private partners.
3  Most successful 'hassle-free' partnerships have been with private non-profit organizations.
4  Contracting is the predominant form of partnership.

5   It is unclear whether the PPP policy option was guided by multilateral development funding agencies, compulsions of resource constraints, competitive bureaucracy or state intentions to innovate in health care delivery.

6   Policy pronouncements by the government alone are not sufficient to initiate partnerships. Social entrepreneurships, visionary leaders and relationships based on trust among the stakeholders (the bureaucracy and the private sector) are essential prerequisites for successful partnerships.

7   Some 'troubled' partnership initiatives have been caused by insufficient consultations with the facility level or field managers prior to finalizing the partnership contracts.

8   Pre-negotiated partnerships agreements based on detailed dialogue are more effective than competitive bidding in the choice of partners. Partnership initiatives by the bureaucracy have less success than partnerships initiated by the private partners.

9   The private non-profit sector is more likely to undertake partnerships at the primary care level than the for-profit sector, which is more likely to provide secondary and tertiary clinical care.

10   In almost all the partnerships, poor patients have been earmarked for special services.

11   User-fees are not uniform across the partnership projects. Wherever user-fees have been charged, the revenue generated is negligible.

12   Capacity of private partners and the bureaucracy to manage partnerships is underdeveloped. Known for their informal and flexible systems and organizational processes, private partners are uncomfortable with the rigid organizational and managerial processes and procedures of the public sector bureaucracy. Bureaucracy has yet to become conversant with the principles of New Public Management.

13   Successful public-private partnerships require a proactive and enterprising bureaucracy so current administrative systems and procedures must be modified or reformed.

14   Contract agreements (Memoranda of Understanding) must include performance indicators, supervision and monitoring, documentation and information system, incentives or penalties, dispute settlement mechanism, exit options and quality standards to be followed.

15   Pricing tariffs for services in both block grants and case-based reimbursement must be based on a survey of competitive rates. Mired in red-tape, the payment system is a major deterrent for public-private partnership initiatives.

16   Understanding risk assessment and risk sharing is at a nascent stage in this policy initiative.

17   Policy innovations like public-private partnerships are contextual. They cannot be uniform across all the regions or suitable under all political and administrative dispensations. Public-private partnerships are no substitute for provision of health services by the public sector through better governance.

18   Though the initiation of a public-private partnership can be an administrative decision, political support and community perception are critical. In

states where the private sector is prevalent, partnership initiatives are an alternative not necessarily because of competitive efficiency but to prevent further pauperization of the underserved and the poor.

19 Engaging the private sector is fraught with political risk. Given the government trend to transfer its responsibilities to the private sector, any collaboration with the private sector is perceived suspiciously. It is imperative to create sufficient political consensus as well as appropriate legal systems in order to delineate the scope for partnership. Likewise a policy shift towards public-private partnerships requires institutional systems within bureaucracy including trained personnel, procedural guidelines for resource management and financial systems, management information systems, supervision and monitoring.

20 Given limited evidence, it is too early to judge whether it is more effective to subsidize inputs (as in the Yeshasvini scheme) or to provide direct subsidies to the poor by purchasing the services from the private sector (as in the Chiranjeevi scheme). Likewise it is inappropriate to conclude that partnerships with the private sector have a catalytic effect on public sector health services (quality of care, accessibility, service utilization level and human resource performance).

## Appendices

*Appendix 3.1* Scope of services under partnerships

| Partnership project | Range of services under partnership |
| --- | --- |
| SMS Hospital, Jaipur (CT Scan & MRI Facility) | Radiological diagnostic services such as CT scan, X-ray, ECG, MRI Scan, and other services. The contracted rates under the partnership have been negotiated. |
| SMS Hospital (Life line fluid store – LLFS) | Supply of drugs and essential items such as IV fluid/emergency medicines at bulk rates. |
| Municipal Corporation of Delhi (MCD) (Arpana Swasthya Kendra), Delhi | Clinical services for outpatient consultation, lab tests, ante-natal checks, X-ray, ultrasound, etc.; referrals for emergency deliveries; specialist care in private hospitals; And mobile health clinic. Community-based public health activities including maternal and child health services and prevention and promotion activities. |
| Uttaranchal Mobile Hospital and Research Centre, Bhimtal | Out patient clinical consultation; radiological diagnosis, such as ultra sound, ECG, X-ray; lab test, including blood, urine and stool tests. |
| Rajiv Gandhi Super-specialty hospital, Raichur | 350-bed hospital. Outpatient clinical consultation; inpatient services, super-specialty services include CT scan, endoscopy, X-ray, Cardiology, Neurology, Oncology, Nephrology, Pediatrics, plastic surgery, etc. Round the clock emergency services, medical camps, and awareness campaigns. |

*Appendix 3.1* continued

| Partnership project | Range of services under partnership |
| --- | --- |
| Management of Primary Health Centers – Karuna Trust, Karnataka | Round the clock delivery of health services in the PHC. Outpatient consultation, diagnostics, ECG, X-ray, laboratory, immunization; national health programs, RCH program, and emergency care. The trust also provides inpatient services (20 beds), ambulance, eye clinic, dental clinic, and indigenous system of medicine, etc. |
| Karnataka Integrated Telemedicine and Tele-health project, District hospital, Chamarajanagar | Radiological diagnosis – X-ray, CT scan, MRI, ECG, histo-pathology, etc. Online tele-examination of medical diagnosis and follow up advice. Referral for advanced investigation or surgical care at the Narayana Hrudayalaya, Bangalore. Link between coronary care units of a public hospital and a private hospital. |
| Yeshasvini Health Insurance Scheme, Karnataka | 1,600 different types of surgeries costing up to a maximum of Rs.200,000 including cardiac by-pass surgery. Free outpatient consultation in any of the member hospitals. Cost of surgery, medicines, medical and diagnostic investigations covered. Treatment not leading to surgery is not covered. |
| Rogi Kalyan Samiti (RKS), JP Hospital, Bhopal | It is a 205-bed hospital with almost all specialties including radiological diagnosis, CT scan, etc. User charges used for augmenting quality of amenities and services. |
| Mahavir Trust Hospital, Hyderabad | Detection, diagnosis, counseling and treatment of TB patients; follow-up and reporting; health education, monitoring drug adherence; documentation. Initial treatment at the hospital, subsequently followed by private practitioners. |
| Emergency Ambulance Services, Theni District, Tamil Nadu | Provide round the clock transport services to emergency obstetric, cases and pregnant women for deliveries. First-aid and transport of accident victims. Provide outreach services in tribal areas. |
| Urban Slum Health Care project, Adilabad district, Andhra Pradesh | Antenatal check-ups, institutional deliveries, immunization of children, nutritional supplements, deliveries by trained attendants, care of abortions, respiratory tract infections, sexually transmitted infections, neo-natal care, birth control (family planning). Community mobilization, disease surveillance, health education, and outreach activities. |
| Arogya Raksha Scheme, Andhra Pradesh | Free hospitalization charges (as inpatient up to a maximum of Rs.2000 per |

| | |
|---|---|
| | hospitalization, and Rs.4,000 for all treatments in a year). Accident compensation of Rs.10,000 (due to death), to be compensated to one of the children less than five years old. |
| Mobile Health Services in Sunderbans, West Bengal | Mobile health clinics providing out-patient consultation, diagnostic services (X-ray, ECG, lab investigations); ante-natal and post-natal checkups; well-baby clinics; family planning, immunization; TB control, transportation of emergency cases; specialist health camps (obstetrics, pediatrics, gynecology, ophthalmology, etc.). One camp per village per week. |
| Contracting out non-clinical support services, Baghajatin hospital, Kolkata | Kitchen and dietary services providing three meals a day, provided on request from patients. Cleaning, scavenging work in the hospital premises (wards and offices). Two mechanized laundry units to wash and disinfect hospital linen. |
| Shamlaji hospital, (Community Health Centre), Sabarkantha District, Gujarat | 30-bed hospital; outpatient services; inpatient admissions; 24-hour emergency care; radiological diagnostics; laboratory; minor surgeries; specialist services on gynecology, obstetrics, cardiology, STI; ANC and family welfare services; eye care. National health programs; ambulance; accidents and injuries; medical camps; and outreach program. |
| Chiranjeevi Yojana, Sabarkantha district, Gujarat | Conduct of deliveries (normal and complicated) and medication for a predetermined fee, either in private clinics or in government hospitals. Conveyance for pregnant women. Honorarium to the health worker. |

*Appendix 3.2* Commitments of public and private partners

| Partnership project | Responsibilities of public sector partner | Responsibilities of the private sector partner |
| --- | --- | --- |
| SMS Hospital, Jaipur (CT Scan & MRI Facility) | Infrastructure, in the form subsidized space; water and electricity connection, access to other common facilities like cafeteria, staff room, and other amenities. Responsibility to verify the BPL beneficiaries. Addressing any patient complaints; supervision of the quality of services, patient feedback, and ensuring uninterrupted services. Formal monitoring and performance management. | Round the clock service, free service to 20% patients, under of BPL category. If machine is out of order, onus to provide at own cost under the approved rate; upgrade machines after four years. Installation of machine, after due civil and electrical works; adequate staff and their salary. Insurance against damages, theft, etc. Weekly submission of accounts; monthly remission of rent, electricity, water etc. Maintenance of records; access of the facility to students and faculty for research. |
| SMS Hospital (Life line fluid store – LLFS) | Space, infrastructure, access to amenities and purchase of medicines in bulk and fixing the sale price of drugs and supplies is the responsibility of the hospital authority. Supervision and monitoring of the services. | Round the clock provision of services; free drugs to 20% of the patients; appointment of the staff, inventory control, and record keeping; payment of rent, electricity and water charges; monthly reports to the hospital; cash collections to be deposited daily. |
| Municipal Corporation of Delhi (MCD) (Arpana Swasthya Kendra), Delhi | Rent free building with adequate equipments and furniture to run a health center; monthly quota of medicines and supplies (worth Rs.35,000); payment of taxes, and levies; training to health workers; supervision and monitoring of activities, services and health outcome targets. | Provision of all agreed health services, achievement of targets and health outcomes, as per the MOU; organize health camps; appoint and manage staff, their salaries, their benefits; maintenance of building. All documents, reports service related software be turned over to MCD. |
| Uttaranchal mobile hospital and research centre, (UMHRC) Bhimtal | Budget support (50% from govt. of Uttranchal, 50% from TIFAC); and providing fully equipped van. UMHRC trust appoints a lady medical officer and support staff on contract; the other doctor and the radiologist on government deputation. Trust supervises the performance. | BISR as the implementing agency to organize and conduct mobile health camps in 15 sites in two different routes once in a month; determine BPL beneficiaries; appointment of the project coordinator; purchase of medicines and other supplies; maintenance of accounts (of user fee collected), records and reports. |

| | | |
|---|---|---|
| Rajiv Gandhi Super-specialty hospital, Raichur | Hospital building, staff quarters, access road, power, water connection, other amenities, and infrastructure. For the first few years bear operational expenditure in addition to capital expenditure, as one time grant and for re-equipping the hospital. Pay service charges in case of no-profit. Appoint officers to verify BPL patients; supervision and monitoring of performance. | Installation, operation and maintenance of building, all facilities, equipments and support services; provide round the clock services, employ qualified staff, purchase and maintenance of equipments and building, pay electricity, water tariffs and taxes. Maintain separate accounts of funds generated to be duly audited; maintain all records of services rendered to BPL patients; extend services during natural calamities; report to the district commissioner. |
| Management of Primary Health Centers, Karnataka | Handover PHC building; provide equipments and supplies; salary for the staff (75% to 90%) appointed by the NGO (within PHC staffing norms). Water, electricity charges are reimbursed. Reimbursement of contingency and building maintenance (Rs.25,000 per annum); drugs and supplies (Rs.75,000 per annum); fuel (100 litres per month). | Appointment of all the staff at PHC and at sub-centers as per staffing norms and own service conditions. Provide curative, preventive and health promotion activities; outreach services and any other services that is possible; maintenance of buildings and equipments; provide round the clock services; maintain adequate stock of medicines; provide services and drugs to all patients free of cost. |
| Karnataka Integrated Telemedicine and Tele-health project, Chamarajanagar District hospital | Provide rent free space in the district hospital, equipments, power supply, infrastructure and amenities; staff salary and cost of VSAT connectivity. Pay the cost of treatment for BPL patients in advance as well as training of staff for the first five years. ISRO provides free tele-link, satellite connectivity for live video/audio/ image transmission through VSAT, but charges for leasing transmission (telecom) equipment. After five years, state govt. to bear the entire cost. | Narayana Hrudalaya created cardiac care unit, appointed and trained the staff (two doctors and other staff trained in coronary care and telemedicine) and manages the unit in the district hospital. Free tele-consultation to patients below BPL, and charges nominal (pre negotiated) rates to other patients; pay salaries of specialist consultants who are associated with the project. |

*Appendix 3.2* continued

| Partnership project | Responsibilities of public sector partner | Responsibilities of the private sector partner |
|---|---|---|
| Yeshasvini Health Insurance Scheme, Karnataka | Financial contribution (50% in the first year of the scheme and consolidated amount now) as premium for the beneficiaries; publicity, enrolment, collection of premiums, and issue of membership card to the beneficiaries through govt. machinery including post offices; verification and enrolment of the network hospital; coordination; supervision and monitoring of the scheme; the district collector and registrars' office play critical role. | Narayana Hrudayalaya conceptualized, designed and provided technical expertise and administrative support during the initial period; continues as the main coordinator; it is also one of the network hospitals; staff at NH work for the Trust. FHPL as the TPA, verifies and reimburses the claims of network hospitals for their services, manages grant funds, accounts, and maintains records; submit weekly reports on beneficiaries, claims, accounts of reimbursements. |
| Rogi Kalyan Samiti (RKS), JP Hospital, Bhopal | RKS is responsible for fixing user charges, improve infrastructure, patient amenities, purchase minor equipments and instruments, emergency medicines, supplies like X-ray films, chemicals, and improve the overall quality of care in the hospital. Maintain and manage separate accounts of funds. Ensuring that BPL patients get free services. | No private partner except eminent citizens being members of the society. |
| Revised National Tuberculosis Control Program (RNTCP), Hyderabad | Regular supply of free drugs and medicines to the DOTS centers and supply of X-ray films or lab requirements to the hospital; training of medical staff. | Initial screening, diagnosis (lab test), counseling, prescription of treatment and referral to designated DOTS centers by a referral card; follow-up; enrolment and coordination with the private practitioners and the government. Training and dissemination of the TB control efforts; private medical practitioners to refer suspected TB cases. |
| Emergency Ambulance Services, Theni District, Tamil Nadu | Two vans as ambulances with basic emergency equipments handed over to the NGO. One time purchase of communication | Free services to BPL patients. Ambulance to be equipped with life-saving first-aid facilities and drugs; deploy trained staff; provide round the clock services; |

|  | | |
|---|---|---|
| Urban Slum Health Care project, Adilabad district, Andhra Pradesh | equipment. Monitoring the overall effectiveness of the project. Rent free space; provision of equipment, drugs and financial support. Grant-in aid released by the district collector, to cover expenses towards staff salary, building equipment maintenance, tariffs for electricity, water, etc. District committee as recommendatory body. | give publicity; maintenance of ambulance in running condition; maintain accounts and log book. Appoint staff, manage and maintain the health centre, deliver MCH/RCH services, document and monitor the operational efficiency, conduct outreach programs, community mobilization, maintain medical records, accounts and submit monthly report. |
| Arogya Raksha Scheme, Andhra Pradesh | Annual premium for five years (paid in advance) on behalf of all the beneficiaries to the insurance company (Rs.15 million for 200,000 estimated beneficiaries). Issue eligibility certificate to beneficiaries (by ANM or PHC/CHC in-charge). Insurance company to empanel private hospitals; verify claims and reimbursement, manage funds, maintain accounts; compensate in case of accidents/deaths to beneficiary's child. Record keeping; inspect the quality of care. | Provide medical care services including hospitalization for ailments (maximum Rs. 4,000) up to five years. Verify bona-fide of beneficiaries; claim reimbursement from insurance company. Excess amount to be charged to the patient directly. Maintain records of the patients for claims verification. Submit periodic reports to the insurance company. Maintenance of registers. |
| Mobile Health Services in Sunderbans, North 24 Parganas district, West Bengal | Financial support; coordinate and liaison between the NGO and other concerned govt. departments, at both local and at state level. Provide all the approvals, documentary and information support; inspections of records and auditing of accounts; provide exemptions wherever needed, regular release of payments; supervision and monitoring. | Deploy one mobile launch and two mechanized boats with medical and diagnostic equipments, staff, and medicines; organize camps in the villages allocated; health education; arrange ambulances/other mode of transport for the patients; communication support; train health workers; maintain all clinical records and documents; manage accounts of the expenditure as per the assigned grant; conduct base-line survey with the help of health department; organize village health committees; make family visits. |

| Partnership project | Responsibilities of public sector partner | Responsibilities of the private sector partner |
| --- | --- | --- |
| Contracting in dietary, laundry and cleaning services, Baghajatin hospital, Kolkata | Rent free space for the contractors; infrastructure support, like water, electricity, common amenities, etc.; monthly payment. Supervision and monitoring of the performance on daily basis. Formal review by the hospital committee; ensuring of quality of food (dietary services by dietician); cleanliness of the premises (by hospital administrator) and disinfection of the linen and other laundry. Maintenance of record on fee collected from diet services, and volume of linen laundered. | The diet contractor is responsible for preparing the meal and providing free of charge meal to the BPL patients; appoint and manage staff (salary, with other perks); maintain records. Contractor for scavenging and cleaning appoints staff (their salary, and perks), purchase cleaning materials and chemicals and carryout cleaning of the hospital premises. Laundry contractor buys and installs equipments; responsible for collecting soiled linen on a daily basis, wash, disinfect, iron and return the linen to respective hospitals within 48 hours. Submit claims for reimbursement. |
| Shamlaji hospital, (Community Health Centre), Sabarkantha District, Gujarat | Government to release grant (equivalent to the budget released for a CHC) toward salary, for equipment maintenance, cleanliness, uniforms, medicines and supplies, diagnostic equipment, etc. Training of the staff, TA/DA during emergency duties. Supervision and monitoring through governing council and advisory committees; periodic (monthly) inspection and auditing of accounts. | Round the clock medical services in the hospital; outpatient and inpatient services; diagnostics, lab investigations; provide free services to the poor patients. Staffing and their management, creation of amenities to the staff, pay tariffs for water, electricity, property tax, etc. Maintenance of the building and premises; provide services under national programs; attend medico-legal cases; maintain records of patients, drugs, equipments; submit periodic reports including accounts. Maintain sufficient stock of medicines, supplies; provide food to inpatients; proper disposal of hospital waste; organize advisory committee meets. |

| Chiranjeevi Yojana, Sabarkantha district, Gujarat | District health officials to empanel the private gynecologists after verification. Reimbursement (or payment of advance) of the bills from the private doctors for treatment of emergency obstetric care; coordinate between district and local 'panchayat' and health functionaries; provide publicity; periodic visits to hospital premises for supervision and monitoring. Maintenance of records, accounts and reimbursement claims; check on quality of services; liaison with FOGSI and IMA. | Conducting deliveries, providing emergency obstetric care, provide drugs, maintain needed stock of surgical items and other supplies; use own OT/labor room and maternity ward. Patients not to be given any prescriptions or purchase of any medical supplies; maintain full patient record including condition of the mother and child when discharged, signature of the patient and health worker; submit monthly report. Submit certificates for BPL patients with bills for reimbursement. Return unused funds; maintain confidentiality of data. |

# 4   Stakeholders in public-private partnerships

Stakeholders are individuals, groups or institutions with significant direct or indirect influence over the way an organization functions and who shape an organization's policies, decisions and actions (Venkat Raman 2004: 102). The scope and range of stakeholders vary depending on whether the issue and interests are local, regional, national or international. Definitions of stakeholders include:

- 'any group or individual who can affect or is affected by the achievement of the organization's objectives' (Freeman 1984: 46).
- 'persons or groups that have or claim ownership rights or interests in a corporation and its activities, past, present or future. Such claimed rights or interests are the result of transactions with or actions taken by the corporation and may be legal or moral, individual or collective' (Clarkson 1995: 106).
- 'persons, neighbourhoods, organizations, institutions, societies and even the natural environment [whose] stake in an organization may take the form of a contractual claim, an exchange relationship, an investment or risk, or some other economic, moral, or legal right or interest' (Mitchell *et al.* 1997: 855).
- 'individuals or groups or organizations that have a stake in the decisions and actions of an organization and who attempt to influence those decisions and actions' (Blair and Bussler 1998: 9).
- 'actors who have an interest in the issues under consideration who are affected by the issues or who because of their position have or could have an active or passive influence on the decision making and implementation processes' (Varvasovszky and Brugha 2000: 341).

Stakeholders are thus individuals or groups or organizations who have a legitimate, compelling or sometimes even marginal interest in the decisions, actions and benefits from a project, programme or activity and who endeavour to influence such decisions and actions to the benefit of their own objectives or goals. Identifying the stakeholders and analyzing their expectations, needs and interests help project managers to comprehend the project environment. Managers would also be able to identify potential areas of convergence of interests and conflicts between stakeholders. For example, quality and cost control could interest the beneficiaries but may create disharmony between management and professional staff.

Stakeholder analysis also indicates the level of risks in dealing with certain stakeholders, for example, members of a political party or the media could support or create hurdles for a project or organization. Depending on the degree of cooperation or conflict with the stakeholders, stakeholder analysis helps in creating 'best' and 'worst case' scenarios and in developing strategies for effective stakeholder management. This chapter explores stakeholders under various types of public-private partnership, their respective stakes and their relative influence over partnership projects.

## Stakeholders in the health sector

The number and range of stakeholders vary depending on organizational characteristics such as ownership, organizations' products/services, degree of interface with the external agents, the stakeholders' interests and concerns with the organization. The roles stakeholders play are not static. Different actors take on different roles at different points of time depending on the issues and circumstances. For example, while examining the feasibility of different policy options on alcohol in Hungary, Varvasovsky (1998) identified 30 different stakeholder groups that had an interest in, or would be affected by, such a policy.

### Stakeholder types

There are many ways to categorize stakeholders. *Primary stakeholders* are those who are essential to the survival and well-being of an organization and who ultimately affect or are affected by it (either positively or negatively). They include owners, managers, staff, suppliers, customers and investors who may also be categorized according to gender, social or income class, occupational or service-user groups. *Secondary stakeholders* are intermediaries who influence the delivery of services to primary stakeholders but are not critical for the survival of an organization. They could be divided into funding, implementing, monitoring and advocacy organizations, including regulatory agencies, political interest groups, lobbyists, etc.

Stakeholders are also categorized by their organizational location (Fottler *et al.* 1989; Brugha and Varvasovszky 2000). *Internal stakeholders* are groups of people who operate entirely within the boundaries of an organization. In health care organizations internal stakeholders include administrators, clinicians, nurses, kitchen staff, housekeeping staff, etc. *External stakeholders* fall into three categories in their relationship to the organization: those who provide inputs to the organization such as suppliers, patients, donors and the financial community; those who compete with the organization for patients, staff and resources; and those with a special interest in how the organization functions such as regulatory agencies of the government and civil society organizations

(IIED 2005). Relationships between the organization and its external stakeholders are symbiotic and interdependent. Competitors, the second category of external stakeholders, seek to attract or directly compete for the patients or for skilled personnel. The third category of external stakeholders – special interest groups – are concerned with the impact of an organization's operations relative to their specific interest. They include professional associations, labour unions, the media, the local community and various political action groups. Conflicts often define their relationship. Ginter *et al.* (2002) classify external stakeholders into overlapping categories: political and regulatory, technological, social, economic, demographic and health care markets.

Some key stakeholders are neither clearly internal nor external but reside on the *interface* between a health organization and its environment. These include boards of trustees, parent organizations, taxpayers or other contributors (Fottler 1987; Fottler *et al.* 1989; Blair and Whitehead 1988). They are among the most powerful stakeholders for health care organizations. Whereas internal and interface stakeholders are at least partly supportive of an organization, many external stakeholders are neutral, non-supportive or even hostile. Among the stakeholders some are involved while others are excluded from decision-making processes. In some organizations subgroups such as unions or women employees could be stakeholders too (DFID 1995).

According to El-Gohary *et al.* (2006) stakeholders are further modelled as responsible, impacted or interested. *Responsible* stakeholders refer to organizations or individuals with some degree of responsibility or liability towards the functions of an organization. These are officials, service providers and program managers. An *impacted* stakeholder is an organization or individual who is directly or indirectly affected by the project and classified among three main sub-domains: staff, users and owners. Impacted stakeholders are further grouped as negatively or positively impacted. Finally, an *interested* stakeholder is an organization or individual not directly impacted by the project who would like to participate and provide opinions. The latter includes social institutions and media representatives.

The health care industry has at least four groups of key stakeholders by virtue of their control over critical resources and the substantial influence they exert on health care providers: physicians, patients, owners of health care delivery organizations and government officials (Dansky and Gamm 2004). Physicians are the most powerful stakeholder although patients and government are the most important. Governments are important because of their regulatory powers and authority. Patients can choose to use or not use a given provider. Physicians as individual caregivers choose the place of practice. For-profit organizations may be compelled to optimize resources for the benefit of shareholders. Public organizations may be more accountable to the taxpayers and public authorities while non-profit organizations are accountable to their donors, contributors and communities.

Blair and Whitehead (1988) and Blair and Fottler (1998) categorize stakeholders for health care organizations on the basis of their potential to support (cooperate) and potential to threaten (oppose). Accordingly they classified the stakeholders into four categories as 'supportive' (low threat–high cooperation), 'non-supportive' (high threat–low cooperation), 'mixed blessing' (high threat–high cooperation), and 'marginal' (low threat–low cooperation). Based on this logic, stakeholders are divided into partners, neutral, unstable and hostile (Venkat Raman 2004).

In the context of reforms, the health sector typically involves five groups of stakeholders: producer, consumer, economic, ideological and health development (Roberts *et al.* 2004). Producer groups include doctors, nurses, their unions, pharmaceutical companies, etc. Consumer groups include patients, pensioners, etc. Economic groups span health insurance industries, workers who gain or lose jobs, etc. Ideological groups include political parties, activists, etc. But a more critical stakeholder is the health-development groups such as multilateral development agencies, international health organizations, and non-governmental development organizations.

Compared to for-profit organizations, public health organizations have different sets of stakeholders. Stakeholders in non-profit organizations resemble those in public sector health institutions since most non-profit organizations are created to serve the void left by public sector organizations. Figures 4.1 and 4.2 respectively illustrate a generic set of stakeholders for a public sector health system and a private sector health system. These figures do not distinguish stakeholders as external, internal, primary or secondary. Detailed analysis of these stakeholders is discussed later in the chapter.

### *Public health systems*

Figure 4.1 depicts the gamut of stakeholders in a public health institution. For public health intuitions, stakeholders depend on service delivery levels that are local (primary care), block or district (secondary care), provincial (tertiary care) and national. In developing countries, key stakeholders at primary care service level are local community members (general public and community leaders), staff (physicians and other paramedical staff), community outreach workers and volunteers, local civil servants (from health and other departments), health facility administrators, political representatives (elected leaders) and other local health providers, social groups, and traditional practitioners (Farnsworth and Holden 2006; Horev and Babad 2005; Oyaya and Rifkin 2003). Health service units are supported by government funds. Their services are generally free and primarily accessed by the poor and other marginalized sections of society. Members of the local community are primary external stakeholders and, in a decentralized context, they are more powerful.

Physicians and other medical staff are also powerful stakeholders, as community members look upon them as providing succour to the suffering ('physicians as life savers'). However, the staff that are accountable only to the district or state authorities may be less concerned about the influence of the community. But in many countries, primary health institutions are administered by local government like village councils and municipal bodies. In the public health system, staff are powerful due to their ability to provide or disrupt the provision of services. They are well organized, have better bargaining power and possess ability to cause wider impact if they decide to disrupt the delivery of services.

At secondary and tertiary levels, stakeholders are qualitatively different and exercise considerable influence. Because secondary and tertiary health services are expensive and technologically sophisticated, the stakeholders have greater leverage in exerting their influence. Patients are more likely to be from middle-income groups or affluent and influential members of the community. Since they are located in urban areas other stakeholders such as media, health activists, suppliers and contractors, private sector providers, and staff unions have greater interest in the affairs of these health facilities. Because these institutions are under scrutiny, the district and provincial bureaucracy also takes greater cog-

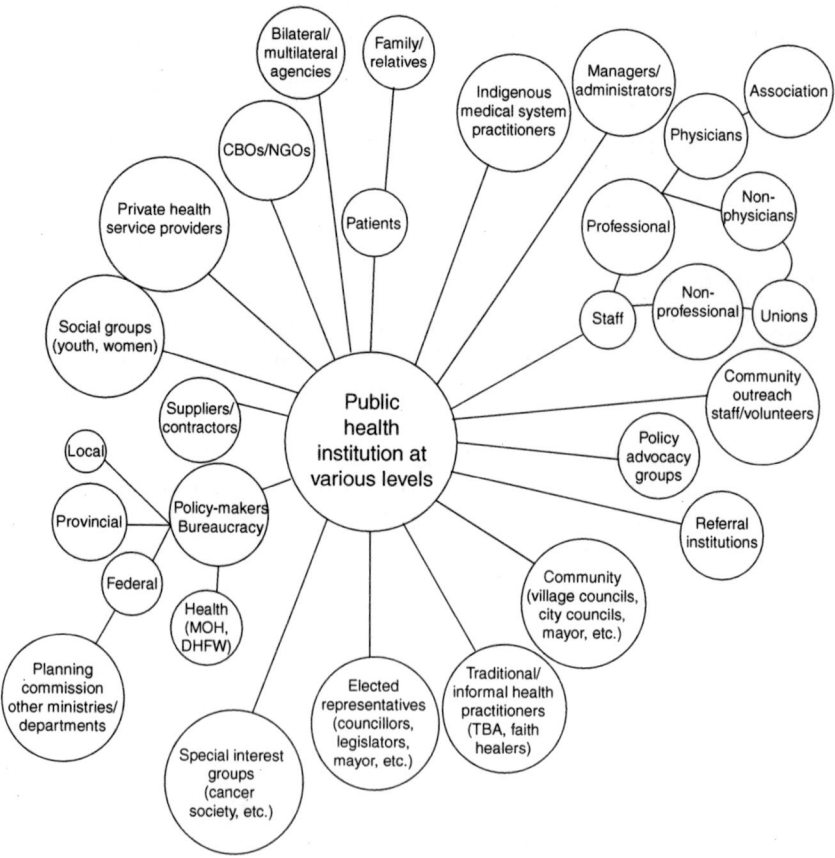

*Figure 4.1* Stakeholders in public sector health institutions.

nizance of their functioning. These institutions are constantly compared with the more efficient and resourceful private sector health institutions. Internal stakeholders such as hospital managers, physicians and other staff are under pressure to stretch resources to meet the burgeoning public demand. These institutions are often beyond their capacity in handling the volume of patients, partly due to failures at the primary care service level, but they continue to receive resources according to certain archaic norms rather than actual service volume.

India has several provinces where the health status of the population is equivalent to industrialized countries, whereas in other provinces it is worse than many sub-Saharan countries. In several such provinces, bilateral and multilateral donor agencies have been assisting the concerned government through pilot projects and programs. In these states such international agencies are critical stakeholders in terms of health policy and health systems.

Provincial governments also play critical roles in licensing, regulating and accrediting private sector health providers. At national level, the ministry of health and its departments provide policy guidelines, determine health priorities, provide technical capacity, facilitate international expertise and resources, combat diseases, and commit substantial resources. Other ministries or departments such as finance, economic affairs, women and child welfare, urban development, etc. are other critical stakeholders both at provincial and central level.

### Private health systems

The private health sector is more complex than the public health system and so the stakeholders are more diverse.

The private health sector is diverse in terms of ownership (individuals, groups, institutions), motives (for-profit, not-for-profit), systems of medicine (allopathic, indigenous), level of services delivered (from outpatient consultation to super-specialty services), size of operations, capital and technology deployed and geographical location.

Combinations of the above generate their own key stakeholders. For example, an individual physician with outpatient consultation in a rural area would be similar to a primary health center. Much of the private sector in health services delivery is comprised of individual owner-operated physician units. It is generally presumed that only affluent and the elite seek services from the private sector. But evidence from many developing countries indicates that the private sector accounts for a large proportion of outpatient and inpatient services, even among the poor.

Stakeholders in the private health sector are legion. Five factors determine stakeholders in the private sector. These are owners and ownership structure, capital and technology deployed, geographical location, degree of competition and the regulatory framework. Ownership determines the profit (or not-for-profit) motive as well as the governance structure (trustees). For-profit health institutions have boards of directors (trustees), shareholders, banks and other investors as their critical stakeholders. Likewise major stakeholders in the

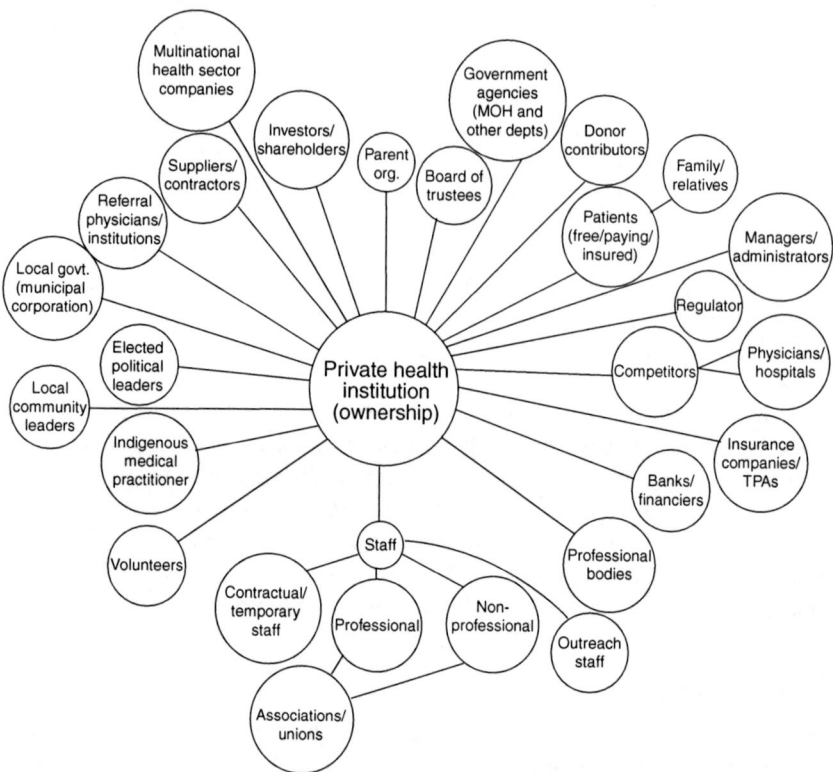

*Figure 4.2* Stakeholders in private sector health institutions.*

Note
* For-profit and not-for-profit not distinguished.

not-for-profit sector include donors, contributors and trustees. Capital, technology and geographical location determine the service level and thus the beneficiary (customer) profile, cost of care, quality and accessibility. Specialty services rendered by a private hospital in a densely populated urban area may perceive competitors as a threat whereas local political leaders in underserved, impoverished region could be powerful stakeholders. In the for-profit system, own-cost or insured patients are powerful stakeholders. Regulatory agencies are non-supportive stakeholders. Local health care providers ally with larger private hospitals to form referral links and gain mutual benefits in cooperation. Other stakeholders include health activists, special interest groups, local community leaders, suppliers and contractors and waste disposal providers.

Physicians and other professional staff are critical in determining the overall cost of inputs in clinical care. Medical staff poses the threat of changing their affiliation to another competitor and thus taking away patients. Therefore the private health system accords varied levels of importance to staff as stakeholders. Contractors who supply support staff, employers of beneficiaries are important critical stakeholders. Third Party Administrators (of health insurance companies) are emerging as powerful stakeholders due to their role in quality control, rational clinical practices, cost control, auditing, billing and reimbursement.

Professional associations such as medical societies, trade federations and commercial collectives advocate on behalf of the private health sector for policy changes to promote private investment, give tax incentives, reduce customs duty to import advanced medical equipment, protect local pharmaceutical and other commercial interests. These associations are powerful lobbyists.

The non-profit voluntary sectors also lobby through community mobilization, advocacy and policy dialogue. They demonstrate innovative interventions through pilot projects and micro models, some of which are up-scaled and integrated into health policy and planning at the national level. In India several community-level pilot projects such as Rogi Kalyan Samiti (patient welfare committees) have been up-scaled in several provinces. They lobby for more government patronage, grants, subsidies and more localized projects.

In summary, the key stakeholders for a health care organization are:

- government at different levels (local, district, provincial, federal);
- ministries of health, finance and planning as well as bureaucrats and functionaries;
- government policy research and advisory bodies;
- community-based organizations/non-governmental organizations;
- health service providers (individuals and institutions) at different levels and ownership (public, for-profit private, not-for-profit private);
- suppliers and contractors;
- national and international aid agencies;
- bilateral and multilateral donor and lending agencies;
- health personnel (professional and non-professional) (institutional and community outreach staff);
- managers and administrators;
- special program and project staff (disease control, immunization);
- elected political representatives;
- local community leaders;
- unions and staff associations;
- patients;
- special interest groups (cancer society, disabled, welfare, women, the elderly);
- professional associations;
- accrediting, licensing and regulatory agencies;
- health insurance organizations and Third Party Administrators;
- health activists;
- medical training and educational institutions;
- commercial interest groups, manufacturers of pharmaceutical products and medical equipment;

- shareholders and investors (corporate health institutions);
- board of trustees;
- charitable trusts and philanthropic foundations;
- policy researchers and academia; and
- indigenous traditional medical practitioners.

Most stakeholders are external to the health organization, yet are critical to its effective functioning. There are also other indirect stakeholders such as religious groups, chambers of commerce, the media, the judiciary, consumer advocacy groups, etc. who wield their influence in subtle manner.

Stakeholders, particularly key stakeholders, have different degrees of power to influence decisions that affect the policies and actions of an organization. Influence refers to how powerful a stakeholder is in persuading or coercing others into making favorable decisions. Importance refers to those stakeholders whose problems, needs and interests receive priority. Power may derive from the degree of dependence between the stakeholder and the organization.

There will often be stakeholders – especially unorganized primary stakeholders such as women, infants, poor patients and slum dwellers upon whom a health care project places great priority – but these stakeholders have weak capacity to participate in projects and limited power to influence key decisions (DFID 1995). They lack information appropriate for effective decision-making and some of them view the cost of participation as too high compared with the benefits. Certain secondary stakeholders like local NGOs seek to represent the interests of such powerless stakeholders. Other forms of power may be more informal such as charisma, expertise and personal contacts with the ruling class. Stakeholders' power is contextual and issue-based (IIED 2005).

### Stakeholder objectives and interests

Stakeholders do not have uniform objectives or interests. While 'overt' objectives are easier to identify, 'hidden' interests may contradict openly stated objectives of the stakeholders involved. Objectives and interests of stakeholders have a certain degree of volatility. In public-private partnership projects, some objectives (or interests of different stakeholders) such as equity, cost, quality and accessibility are particularly sensitive (El-Gohary *et al.* 2006). The stakeholders' objectives, interests, power and importance in the context of public-private partnership is discussed below.

### Government: Ministry/Department of Health and other agencies

In most developing countries, public sector health systems provide free health services that are the primary source of care for the poor. Delivery of curative health services is often the responsibility of either local or provincial governments. The funding for services is primarily through government budgets. At national level, the government and its agencies are involved in planning, financing, coordinating and regulating health services. They play a critical role in the production of human resources, resource mobilization and donor coordination. At provincial level, the government and its agencies are entrusted with program design, implementation, supervision, monitoring and control as well as enforcement of standards through licensing and regulation. They monitor the health systems in terms of outputs and outcomes, efficiency, capacity building and research. At the district and local levels, government agencies coordinate local stakeholders, manage expenditures, and are responsible for effectiveness and efficiency in health institutions, programs and projects. Beyond the Ministry of Health, other units of government at various levels play significant roles in policy approval, financing and monitoring the health system. Some of these non-health agencies exert significant influence on the public health system.

### Professional health staff

Health professionals, particularly physicians, are important stakeholders in any health care organization. They are concerned with professional autonomy, clinical quality and the working conditions which fit their professional ethics. They constantly endeavor to exert professional dominance. They are usually more influential because they are wealthy, well-organized and often subtle. Most health professionals in public health organizations, including physicians, are unionized and their unions play a dominant role in the health care system. These stakeholders are interested in continued employment, better wages and incentives, better working conditions and opportunities to enhance their career avenues or skills. They tend to oppose changes in the status quo such as legislative initiatives that threaten to limit their employment. Due to their technical skills, they are also the most influential stakeholders in determining the cost, quality and efficacy of patient care. They have an important say in whether to allow private medical service in public hospitals. Sometimes their influence ensures that professional rather than public interests prevail, and their professional prestige and status dominate the decision-making process. If their needs are not met, they tend to affiliate with competing organizations or shift patients from one place to another. However, the physician–hospital relationship is also mutually dependent. While patients are more likely to associate with physicians than hospitals, the physicians require a place to practice (Horev and Babad 2005).

### Non-professional staff

Though non-professional staffs are less powerful than professional staff in clinical aspects, they are among the powerful stakeholders. In the public health system, they derive their power and influence from their unions that are organized at regional and national levels. They provide the kinds of service that influence patients' perceptions of the health care organization. In primary care units, these non-professionals are influential due to their proximity to the community and local leaders. During the absence of professional staff, they act as 'physicians'. Their interests are related to adequate salaries and job security.

### Unions

In the context of developing countries, unions are often regarded as antagonistic due to their propensity to strike and disrupt services. In recent years, given the demand for performance and efficiency, public scrutiny, outsourcing of support services, recruitment freeze and resource crises, unions have been under severe pressure. Some unions are organized at the national level and exercise greater bargaining power. Professional associations, on the other hand, tend to exercise their power more subtly by advocacy and as members of policy groups. They are strongly united on issues that affect their turf. Professional associations, for example, steadfastly resist any steps to mainstream traditional practitioners of medicine.

### Members of the public (as beneficiaries)

The general public, an external stakeholder, regards health care as a right. The public is broadly categorized on demographic attributes such as gender, income, occupation, geographic location, health service needs, etc. People expect greater accessibility, better quality of both clinical care and service amenities, and reduced cost through efficiency. In principle the public would like to be treated equitably and with priority. However, in developing countries, people from poor social and economic backgrounds tend to be indifferent to inequities in health services. Historically, they have been the weak stakeholder in health care. They lack information about their rights to benefits and do not demand more information about health systems. Improving the quality of care is rarely a priority although access and equity are. The sources of power for patients include their ability to choose providers and their ability to influence other potential patients regarding these choices. Due to poor quality care or negligence, violence against health care providers has been on the rise in several parts of India so state governments have begun to enact laws to protect public health staff.

### Private sector

Private for-profit health organizations have resources that other stakeholders lack and use them to promote their interests vis-à-vis government and other providers of health care. Private corporate stakeholders play crucial roles in the provision of health services at six different levels (Farnsworth and Holden 2006):

- They deliver services to end-users directly as an alternative to direct provision of such services by the state.
- They produce welfare-related goods that are vital to the operation of state-

provided services. For example, health services cannot operate without medical equipment or pharmaceuticals. The state then regulates such firms in order to ensure that the cost of drugs remains low or subsidized by the public sector, and that the substances produced are safe and efficacious.

- They supply services to the state and other service providers but have no contact with the end-users. For example, ancillary services such as cleaning and catering are important primarily for cost control so such services have been increasingly contracted out to the private sector.
- They provide insurance and pensions. As insurance against sickness or disability, insurers pay for health or long-term care services.
- They invest in physical assets. Physical infrastructure such as hospital buildings are almost invariably designed and constructed by the private sector.
- They provide for their own employees and dependents, partly financed by employees themselves through statutory provisions such as sickness benefits, insurance and partly by non-statutory provision such as medical allowances.

In recent years private commercial stakeholders have become more influential. However, competition among them plus their need to operate within a framework determined by other stakeholders place them in an inferior position relative to other stakeholders (Horev and Babad 2005).

## Non-governmental and community-based organizations

Non-government organizations are perceived as able to 'get things done' faster, better and cheaper than government agencies. NGO staff have the reputation of being highly motivated and committed. Non-profits are thought to be more trustworthy by beneficiaries as well as better able to supply complex hard-to-evaluate services. The ideological charter of the non-profits allows them to attract mission-driven workers who often accept lower wages and who are able to comprehend the complexity of managing a variety of constituencies.

However, there are tasks that non-profits do not perform well. Non-profits typically have problems in raising financial resources. As they consider it unacceptable to raise equity, their assets are generally project specific. Even when non-profits can overcome capital barriers, there are problems of managerial capacity to handle large-scale activities. Many non-profit agencies are staffed by professional workers highly attached to their own professions and fiercely autonomous so problems of control and motivation increase with size. Even as funding pressures on non-profits grow, cost-cutting become more critical subcontracting by NGOs will be on the rise (Morse and McNamara 2006). The non-profit sector in developing countries is heterogeneous and highly dispersed.

*Hospital management*

Hospital managers are important internal stakeholders who determine the success or failure of service operations. They influence the cost, expenditure, quality, physical amenities, patient relationships, degree of motivation, productivity and performance among the staff, and hospital image. Sometimes health facility managers hold strong opinions about certain stakeholders that may conflict with generalized perception about such stakeholders. Such prejudices create conflicts and tensions between the stakeholder and the organization. Personality, leadership, business acumen, managerial style and skills are critical factors for the success of an organization as well as the reputation of successful managers.

*Trustees and boards of directors*

Boards of trustees possess formal authority and control. They may veto administrative proposals or decisions by management. The board usually represents a broad spectrum of influential citizens in the community and is concerned with community needs identified by them. The board is interested in improving or maintaining the image, profitability and overall effectiveness of its organization. If tasks are undertaken by the organization is incompatible with the envisioned goals of the board that controls the parent organization and its resources, the board has the power veto any such moves (Fottler *et al.* 1989).

*Elected officials*

Elected public representatives such as legislators and councillors exert influence in areas that affect their constituents. Since all public hospitals and some private non-profit hospitals receive grants from the public budget, these officials become critical in terms of their power to affect such resources. Elected public officials are concerned with services for their own constituents in terms of accessibility, regularity of services, availability of staff and drugs, working condition of equipment, cost containment and positive community image. They are also concerned with preferential treatment to those they refer to clinics or hospitals. In a developing country with decentralized governance, these officials acquire great powers in appointments, transfers, postings, contracts for buildings and support services, location of health facilities, and even the use of public resources such as vehicles for their own benefit.

*Donor agencies*

Bilateral and multilateral donor agencies are key stakeholders at the policy, planning and program design stages of the health sector. Donor agencies include the World Bank, DFID, GTZ, USAID, DANIDA, the Gates Foundation, United Nations agencies such as UNFPA, UNICEF, WHO, UNDP, UNAIDS and global alliances such as the Global Fund to Fight AIDS, Tuberculosis and

Malaria. The overt objectives of these agencies are to enhance economic and social development for the well-being of recipient states, but these also generate divergent responses.

The role of the donor agencies in health sector reforms is well documented but there are diverse perceptions of their results. Some are praised for unconditional aid; others are criticized for lack of conditional loans. Bilateral and multilateral agencies lend financial support on the condition that recipients will reform, improve or undertake large-scale changes. Apart from much needed financial resources and technical capacity, donors bring a wide range of experience from around the world. They aim to strengthen local ownership, help local institutional partners to develop capacity, and develop skills and confidence. However, significant proportions of the terms, conditions and project designs in external aid are prepared by foreign consultants with varying degrees of endorsement by recipient governments. Due perhaps to inadequate technical and managerial resources of recipient countries to prepare operational details that meet the criteria of donor agencies within an acceptable timeframe, some externally funded programs have limited local ownership. Local stakeholders often seem less concerned about success or failure than their foreign sponsors (DFID 1995).

*Special interest groups*

The health sector has many special interest groups ranging from clinical health activists to youth clubs that promote awareness of community health. Some special interest groups are local; others have national and international presence. There are direct stakeholders like a cancer society and indirect stakeholders like the media or the judiciary. Direct stakeholders such as cancer societies, anti-tobacco groups, heart foundations, tuberculosis associations and various disability-related associations campaign for special concessions from government or to bring about changes in policy to suit their members. For example, a cancer society may appeal to the government to reduce the taxes on cancer drugs; anti-tobacco campaigners may seek to ban smoking or the sale of tobacco. Similarly groups interested in HIV/AIDS may campaign for more testing and counselling centres, more anti-retroviral therapy units, etc. Indirect stakeholders such as the media and the judiciary may not play an active role until they consider an issue important for intervention.

*Health insurance organizations and third party administrators*

Most developing countries lack extensive voluntary health insurance. Medical insurance has traditionally been subsidized or provided by the public sector. Due to rapid growth of the private health sector as well as liberal economic policies, however, private health insurance companies have emerged as significant stakeholders in the health system. Compared to industrialized countries, health insurance is at a nascent stage but health insurance companies through their third party administrators have become an active stakeholder by scrutinizing clinical and accounting practices. But they are yet to become powerful stakeholders. In recent years social health insurance projects at community level have demonstrated the viability of local mobilization of resources. Experiments with several community-level health insurance programs are paving the way for rapid growth in the health insurance market.

### Stakeholders' power and influence

Stakeholders hold considerable potential for cooperation or conflict with the decisions and actions of an organization. The potential for conflict depends on three factors: the relative power of the stakeholder compared to the organization; the nature of the issue; and the degree of dependency on the stakeholder. The more an organization depends on the support of a stakeholder, the more powerful the stakeholder becomes and the more conflict and potential for threat exist. The more dependent stakeholders are on the organization, the more support and cooperation they will exhibit. Stakeholder power is manifest in the form of control of resources like funds and patients, the ability to impose costs, and regulatory restrictions (Venkat Raman 2004; Fottler *et al.* 1989). Effective program managers do not try to satisfy the needs of all stakeholders. They minimally satisfy the needs of marginal stakeholders while maximally satisfying the needs of key stakeholders. In doing so, managers make two critical assessments about stakeholders: their potential to threaten the organization, and their potential to cooperate with it (Freeman 1984).

Potential for threat or cooperation also depends on the specific context and history of an organization's relations with that stakeholder (Blair and Whitehead 1988; Blair and Fottler 1998). For example, the potential for cooperation or threat by medical staff depends on how competing hospitals manage their personnel and how they have treated them in the past.

Based on the potential to cooperate and potential to threaten, the stakeholders could be categorized as supportive, non-supportive, marginal and mixed blessing stakeholders. Supportive stakeholders include trustees, managers, employees, patients, parent organizations and the local community. Marginal stakeholders are professional associations and community-based groups. Issues such as cost containment could make some marginal stakeholders change their levels of threat or cooperation. Non-supportive stakeholders include competing organizations, employee unions and terminated contractors. 'Mixed blessing' stakeholders are medical staff, insurance companies and special interest groups.

Stakeholders tend to exhibit their power only when dealing with an issue of significance. In a significant policy issue like public private partnership, the stakeholders of respective public and the private organizations exhibit expectations relative to their influence. Stakeholders do not necessarily react as one would expect. For example, if management of a local primary health center is transferred to an NGO, the local community initially may react negatively but, over time, it may prefer such an arrangement. It depends on what the NGO does or fails to do.

## Stakeholders in public-private partnerships in health

Partnerships can be a significant problem in a multi-stakeholder context. If stakeholders are mainly external, these difficulties have two problematic dimensions (Bovaird 2006). First, each member of a partnership tends to push for its own priorities in the strategy adopted. Second, discontented stakeholders can exit from the partnership and strike new deals with other partners, often at relatively low cost. Private and public sector managers have conflicting priorities. In public-private partnerships, the dominant role played by the public sector creates difficulties in relationships and trust. One of the partners is likely to perceive itself as being manipulated, which leads to a strategic behavior by the other to use its expertise to evade control. This partner is likely to use its influence to persuade supportive stakeholders in its favor and perhaps against the actions of the other partner.

Despite such possible opportunistic behaviors, partnerships in multi-stakeholder environments generally intend to benefit all key stakeholders. For the public sector, partnership with the private sector may lead to capacity-building. For NGOs, partnerships may involve the provision of additional and much needed resources, and increased recognition and status (Jorgensen 2006). However, government as a stakeholder using public-private partnerships may experience a loss of control, threats to its authority or greater difficulty in holding private organizations accountable to public standards (Gazley and Brudney 2007). While governments offer non-profit partners financial resources, non-profit organizations in turn offer specialized expertise beyond the scope of government. However, non-profit organizations may lose independence or even private donations and volunteers. They also fear losing their ability to be critical of the policies and practices of the government, which is one of the reasons for the creation of NGOs.

Organizational stakeholders in the for-profit private sector are likely to view partnership with the public sector more suspiciously. While the private for-profit sector is driven by profit maximization, public sector stakeholders have altruism or public service as their overt motive. These differences in values and perceptions hamper collaboration between the two. Public sector trade unions always resist private sector partnership because they fear loss of jobs or reduction in opportunities and service conditions of employment. Service-users have sometimes expressed concerns about having service providers who are driven by the profit motive because they fear becoming objects of a profit calculation. However, as long at the quality of services is satisfactory, service-users are uninterested in the precise legal standing of the organization that provides the services (Bovaird 2006). Partnerships pose different stakes and risks to different stakeholders. Politicians and bureaucrats fear losing control over policy-making and service management. Donors believe that involvement of the private sector is essential for the success of a project whereas the government and bureaucracy may not want to see donor funds transferred to NGOs.

Lasker and Weiss (2003: 126–127) describe how community level stakeholders view partnerships:

> There are two types of partnerships, the 'Lead Agency' model and the 'Community Engagement' model. In the 'lead agency' model, partnerships are developed to involve a private organization to carry out a predetermined program. Most of the thinking, planning and design is done by the lead agency (ministry or government department or donor agency). Community residents or other stakeholders may or may not have been consulted. Their primary role may be restricted to help the lead agency obtain access to the community or provide local resources or legitimacy needed for the project. In the 'community engagement' model a broad array of community stakeholders work together in all phases of partnership. This model has potential to create greater synergy in the delivery of services, because diverse stakeholders have an opportunity to influence the partnership design. By involving a broad array of stakeholders, in all phases of its work, partnerships are in a better position to be not only more effective but also sustain their programs. Another irony is that partnerships that are run by professionals in health and human services tend to treat community stakeholders as objects of concern or sources of data rather than as peers in setting goals, objectives and in solving operational bottlenecks. The professionals usually determine the language that partnership shall use (for example 'taking care' of the community rather than 'working with the community').

In the health sector partnerships between public and private sectors (both for-profit and not-for-profit) involve a wide range of stakeholders. Figure 4.3 provides a generic sketch of the type of stakeholders involved. Partnerships may lead to the creation of a service delivery unit within the premises of the public sector health facility or in a private sector health facility.

Figure 4.3 illustrates the key stakeholders when public and private sectors collaborate in the delivery of health services. Service delivery units under such partnerships could be located in the public sector agency, in the private sector agency or as an independent agency. Four organizational adaptations are possible under such partnership:

- A private agency may be contracted to deliver support services within the premises of a public sector organization. Such services include security, cleaning, waste disposal, drug stores, laundry, kitchen and diagnostics (lab tests, X-rays, MRI, CT scan).
- If a partnership between the public and the private sector sets up a service delivery unit in the private facility, it could be a separate ward or a unit earmarked for the beneficiaries under the partnership. Such arrangements are made to cover patients through vouchers or service redemption coupons with a quota of patient volume in exchange for tax concessions and subsidies. The services covered are generally specialty care. In such arrange-

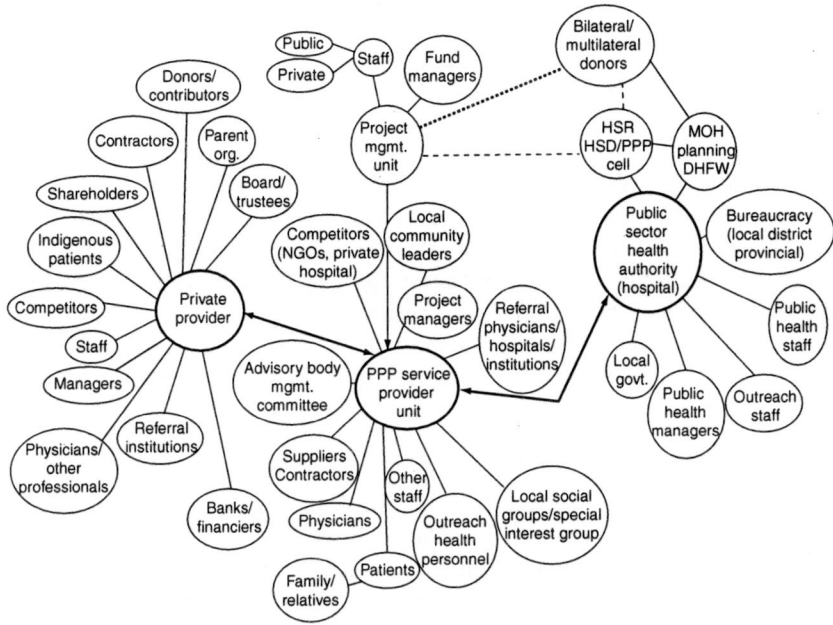

*Figure 4.3* Stakeholders in public-private partnerships in the health sector.*

Note
* Bold circles indicate key stakeholders.

ments, the critical stakeholders are the management board of the private hospital, hospital managers, target beneficiaries (patients), professional staff and the monitoring agency. Experience in India suggests that political leaders and high level bureaucrats are the decisive stakeholders.

- A third variant is 'contracting in' when an entire public health facility is transferred to a private agency that manages the unit and delivers services to the local community. Government health personnel are moved to other public facilities while the premises are occupied by the private agency.
- Joint ventures are under long-term contracts. If the partnership sets up a separate agency, key stakeholders would be the ruling political party, the bureaucracy, the funding authority and other civic agencies. Such arrangements have been common under the Private Finance Initiatives in Britain. In such arrangements health activists, consumer groups, opposition parties and professional associations become active stakeholders.

These organizational innovations with the private sector are due to the reform agenda championed by bilateral and multilateral agencies (but with the concurrence of policy-makers in ministries of health, planning, finance and economic affairs). In India, the Planning Commission played a critical role in envisioning a broad role for the private sector, in successive five-year plans. Such experimentation was piloted under the overall rubric of health sector reforms but more specifically under public private partnerships. Therefore bilateral and multilateral agencies are key stakeholders in public-private partnerships in health care in developing countries. Coordination between donor agencies and state governments has been facilitated by the establishment of health sector reform cells or donor coordination cells in the ministry.

Project management units were created to supervise day-to-day operations under a partnership arrangement. Supported by an advisory committee, the project management unit consists of staff from the public sector, private consultants and experts. To maintain broad support for such initiatives, advisory committees consist of community leaders, hospital managers, senior professional staff, elected representatives and district officials. The success or failure of these initiatives depends on a spectrum of stakeholders. In the following paragraphs we examine the key stakeholders under different forms of public-private partnership.

### Stakeholders in 'contracting-in'

Under a 'contracting-in' partnership, a private agency is 'hired' to provide clinical or non-clinical support services with an objective of efficient delivery. Non-clinical support services in a typical hospital include cleaning, laundry, kitchen, waste disposal, security and landscaping. In such an arrangement, stakeholders are limited to contractors, facility administrators and affected public health staff. Employee unions of public health workers play a crucial role. A hostile union could effectively sabotage the services of a contractor and his staff. Although the contractor is important for the success of a 'contracting in' partnership, the hospital management and staff unions are the dominant stakeholders.

Local political groups and bureaucracy are other critical stakeholders who influence the selection of a contractor. Hospital managers monitor the day-to-day performance of contractors, issue performance approvals and release payments. Patients are key stakeholders in diagnostic services, dietary support services, drug stores and lab-test services because such 'contracted in' services are meant to be free for poor patients. Key stakeholders in any 'contract' include the ministry of health with staff at district or hospital level, the donor agency through its reform cell, the hospital advisory committee and the private contractor. Other stakeholders include competitors for similar services (radiological diagnostics, pharmacy and lab tests). Public health personnel who have been replaced by contract staff are likely to be hostile stakeholders. The parent organization of the contractor, its board of directors, shareholders and professional staff are other stakeholders.

### Stakeholders in 'contracting-out'

Under 'contracting-out', a private agency or an NGO is contracted to manage an entire health facility to deliver health services to the local community. The government in return provides the budgetary support normally earmarked for the public health facility. The public health staffs are redeployed by government to other public facilities.

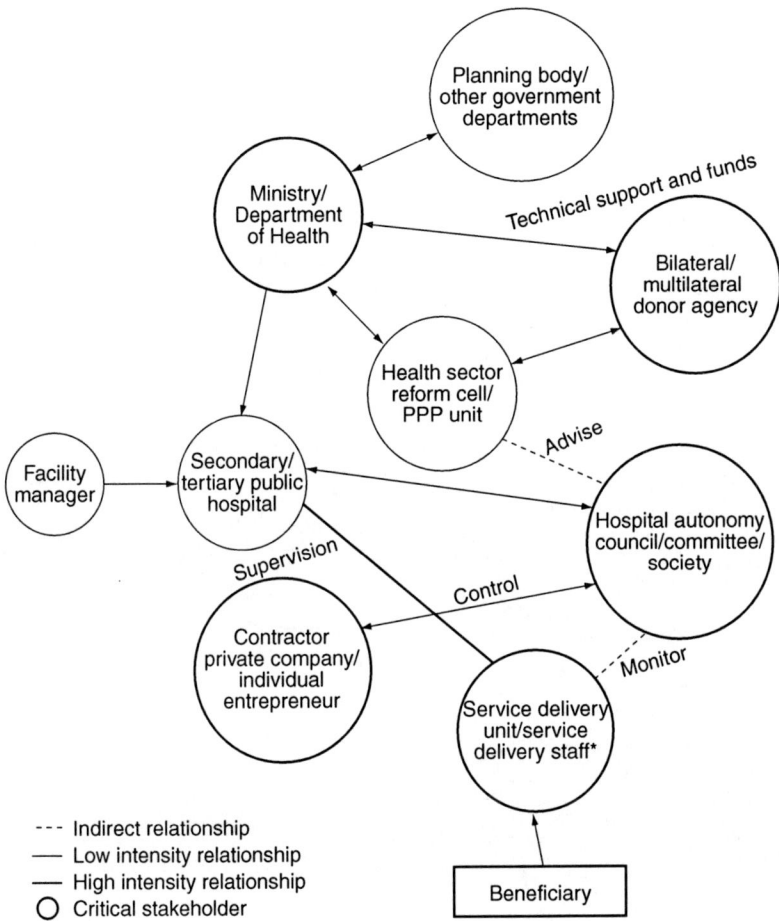

*Figure 4.4* Key stakeholders in traditional 'contracting in' partnerships.

Note
The service delivery unit is located in the public health facility.

Key stakeholders in 'contracting-out' arrangements are the ministry of health, district-level health authorities and the health sector reform cell (if involved in such an initiative). The success or failure of this model is often determined by the local community, public health staff, the private agency and the facility level advisory committee. The community is an important stakeholder because its members might perceive such a partnership as an attempt at privatization and could mobilize the community against such an arrangement – as experienced by Karuna Trust in Karnataka. With entrenched interests in the local community, public sector staff might connive with either the unions or local interests to sabotage such a partnership. As outreach staff, community health workers may not like to report to a more demanding new management. In this dynamic, patients

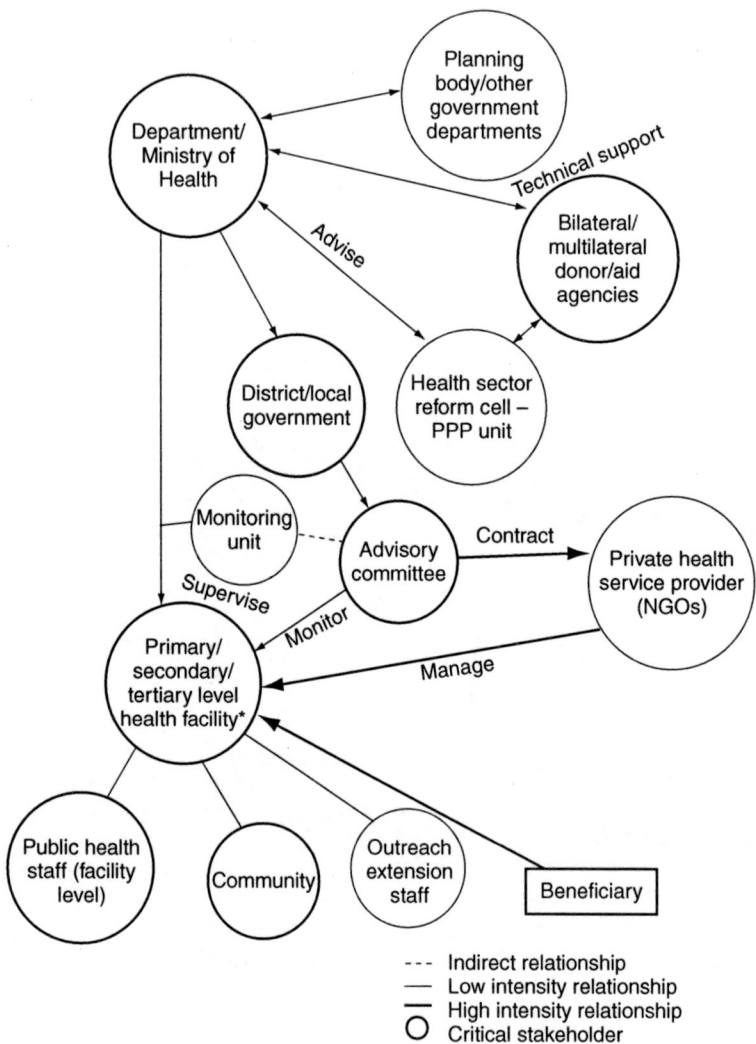

*Figure 4.5* Key stakeholders in 'contracting out' partnerships.

Note
Except for government personnel, the entire facility is transferred to the private provider.

are important beneficiaries since an affordable primary care service is available at accessible distance run by more 'courteous' and 'considerate' staff.

Sometimes a tertiary hospital is allocated to a private for-profit agency. In Karnataka a decision to give Raichur's Rajiv Gandhi super-specialty hospital to a corporate hospital chain was taken because public health personnel were reluctant to be posted in a remote, economically backward region. In this arrangement, the private agency is more powerful than government because it was able to negotiate a better business deal with a guaranteed profit. While the partnership intended to provide super-specialty services, there have been considerable difficulties in verifying and filtering eligible beneficiaries. Local elites seem to have garnered benefits with false credentials while the poor for whom the services are meant have no influence in making a case for their stakes. Hospital managers are afraid of antagonizing more powerful stakeholders or have no incentive to targeting benefits to the poor. Consisting of local and state officials, the advisory committee has been unable to identify a solution to this problem. This case illustrates how powerful stakeholders divert benefits meant for other less powerful but more deserving stakeholders, and how a more powerful private stakeholder is able to negotiate better deals with a managerially weak public stakeholder – in this case the state ministry of health.

### Stakeholders in a voucher scheme

Schemes for vouchers or 'service redemption coupons' have four sets of primary and key stakeholders: the beneficiaries, the government, the private provider and the NGO/CBO. With or without the advice of a donor agency, the government creates a special fund to provide health care services to a target population. With pilot projects in the Indian provinces of Uttarakand, Uttar Pradesh and Gujarat, the case concerns safe births by pregnant women in a private facility. The target population is to be identified through a network of NGOs or CBOs, each in a designated area in the region.

Beneficiaries are enrolled and given service redemption coupons (vouchers) to visit the nearest empanelled and accredited private nursing home or clinic. Service coupons are redeemed for antenatal check-ups as well as for delivery (whether normal or caesarean). When submitting redeemed coupons, private providers are paid from the special funds at pre-negotiated rates while NGOs are paid for their operational support. The project management unit coordinates between the government's district-level health authority, the NGOs and the private sector. In this partnership, apart from the four categories of stakeholders identified above, outreach workers play a critical role in the enrolment of beneficiaries. The community outreach worker is a critical link between the beneficiary and the private hospital. In all schemes the district-level health authority ensures the continued interest of the private partners through speedy release of payment.

### Stakeholders in a mobile health scheme

Under mobile health schemes, the principal stakeholders are the donor agency, the ministry of health, an NGO or private agency, and health functionaries in the mobile unit. In one mobile health scheme in Uttarakand a mobile van equipped with radiological diagnostic equipment along with basic test kits moves around a fixed circuit to conduct health camps. The van and its equipment were donated by a federal agency as a technology demonstration project. A local private research institute was entrusted with the operational management of the mobile

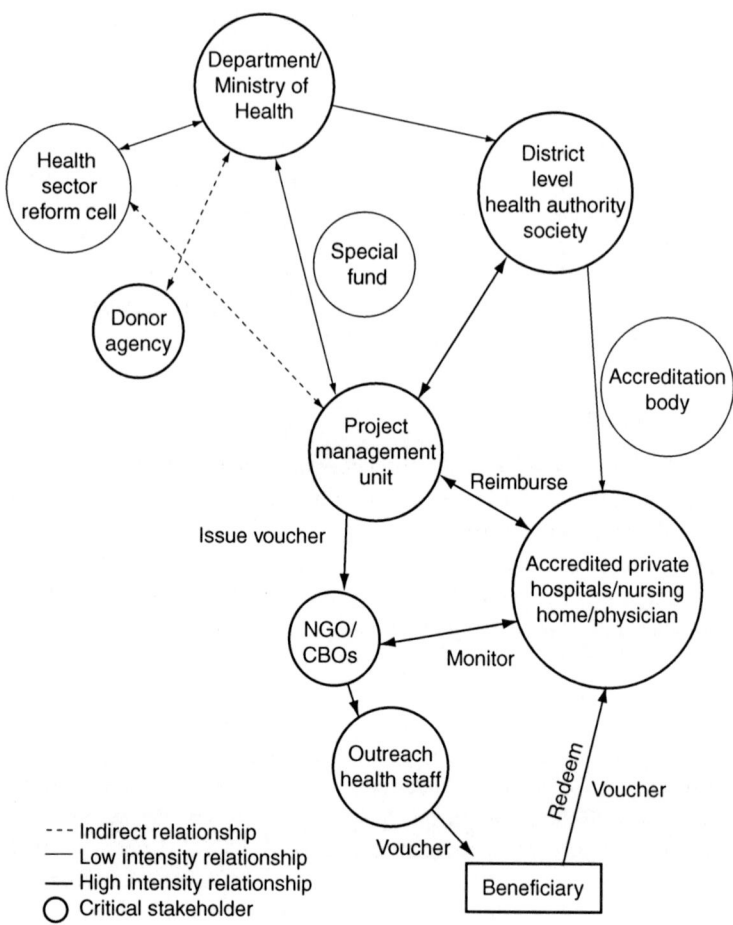

*Figure 4.6* Key stakeholders in a 'voucher' or 'service coupon' scheme.

van, its staff and equipment. The provincial government supplements the project with staff, funds, drugs and other supplies.

In another project, a multilateral lending agency prompted a provincial government to experiment with the launch of emergency ambulances that would be operationally maintained by a local NGO in Tamil Nadu's Theni district. The NGO in turn contracted the vans to locals for operating, maintaining and earning their livelihood through user-charges. In yet another project, an aid agency donated two launches to a local NGO to provide health services through outreach health camps in a riverine delta. The boats are maintained and health camps are conducted by the NGO with financial support from the provincial government.

In each of these projects, apart from the NGO, donor agencies, government and the mobile health units are the most important stakeholders. Other critical

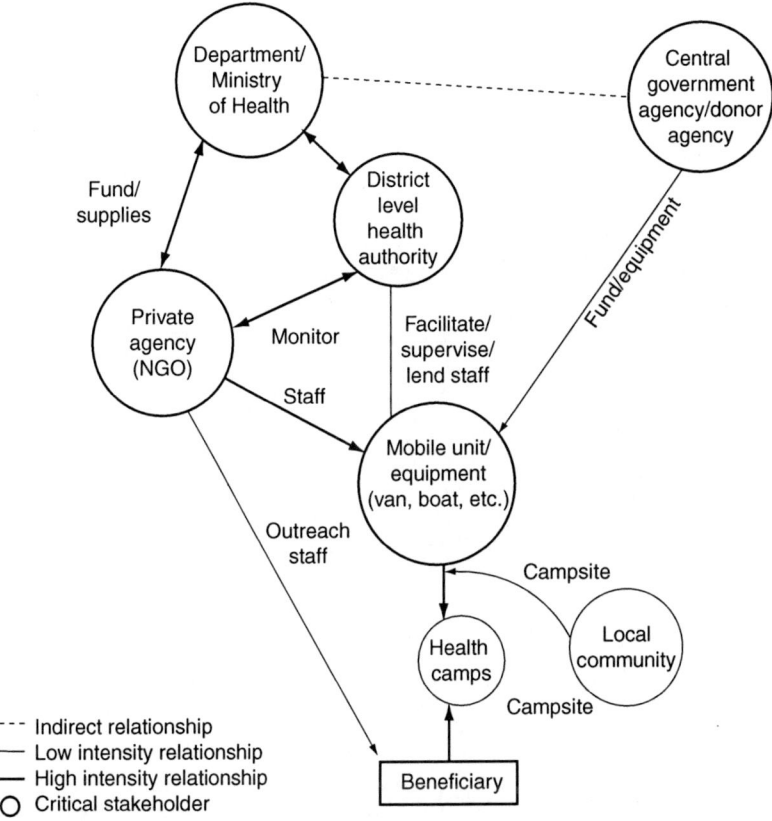

*Figure 4.7* Stakeholders in mobile health service projects.

stakeholders are outreach workers, community and the district-level health authorities. Outreach workers are able to sensitize a community about the mobile health schemes and are influential in utilization by the beneficiaries. The community is important in allowing health camps to be organized on local sites. District-level health authorities are responsible for supervision, monitoring, allowing public health physicians to participate in the mobile team, and providing performance feedback to government for the release of payments.

### Stakeholders in a tele-health/telemedicine project

In technologically sophisticated partnership projects such as telemedicine and tele-health, the most important stakeholder is the technology support provider. In Karnataka it is a federal agency, the Indian Space Research Organization. Equally important is the district hospital that benefits from the services and the private tertiary care unit that provides tele-consultation services.

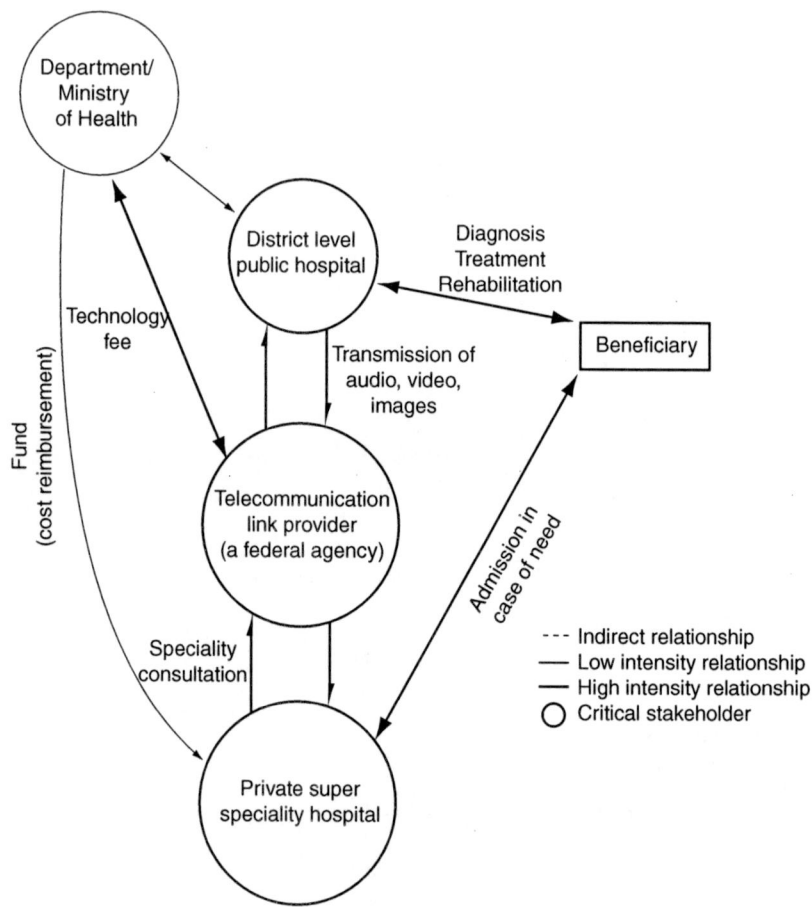

*Figure 4.8* Key stakeholders in a tele-health/telemedicine project.

The state government negotiated with a private specialty hospital to allow the latter's specialists to provide clinical advice based on radiological diagnostics reports generated in a remote government hospital and transmitted via video conference without physically transferring the patient. Physicians at the government hospital are able to get specialist opinions before commencing treatment or follow-up. In such a tightly organized partnership, each stakeholder is essential for the success of the project. Stakeholders are also tested on their commitment to the project. For example the state government may eventually have to pay fees to the technology provider for its equipment and satellite link because the federal space research agency will not be able to provide free services forever. Likewise the private hospital may be unable to allow its specialists to spend hours without an adequate fee. The government may be pressurized into seeking a more sustainable solution rather than an experimental project. Other stakeholders such as the government health staff and special interest groups might be question the cost-effectiveness of such projects. Figure 4.8 identifies the critical stakeholders in tele-health.

### Stakeholders in community-based health insurance projects

In Karnataka's Yeshasvini health insurance scheme, the stakeholders are many and all are equally influential. Interestingly the project has no involvement by the state ministry of health or departments affiliated to it. Figure 4.9 displays stakeholders in this partnership.

The primary stakeholder is the state department of cooperatives in collaboration with a network of private hospitals. The founder of a large private hospital envisioned this project in league with the state government. For a nominal

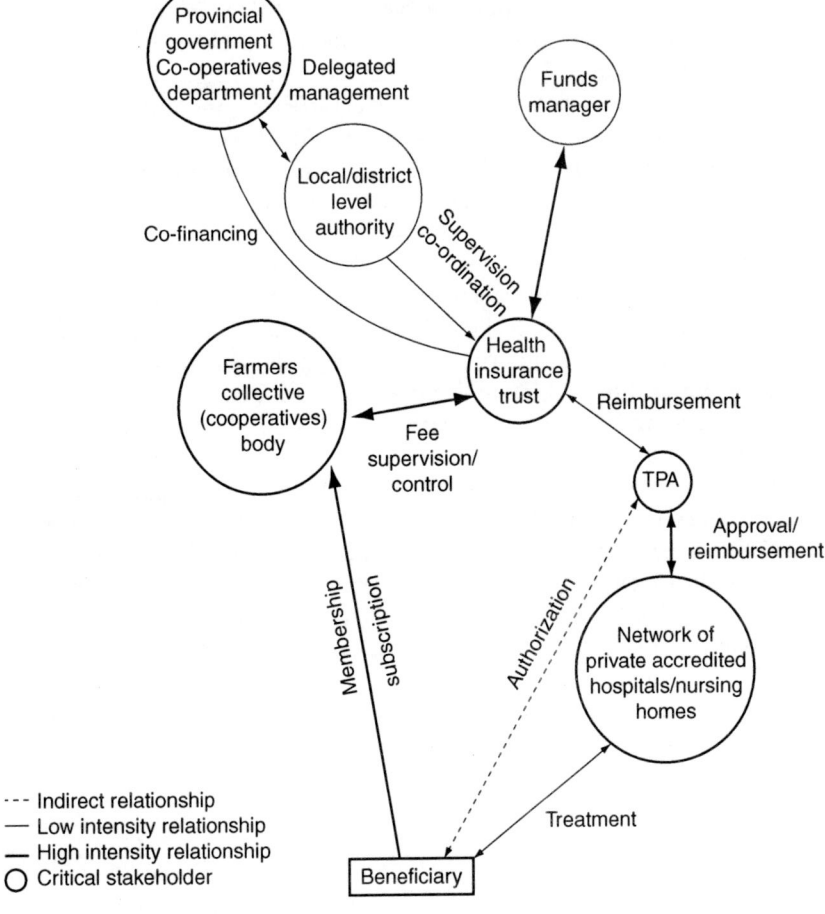

*Figure 4.9* Stakeholders in a community-based health insurance partnership.

premium, the project provides surgical care and covers hospitalization costs for members of agricultural cooperatives and their dependents. The state government co-pays the annual premium. Members and their dependents receive clinical services at any one of a network of private hospitals throughout the state. Membership funds are managed by a trust that in turn hired a professional fund manager for this service. The fund manager in turn appointed a third party administrator to verify claims and the treatment received. District-level officials (particularly district collectors) are entrusted with monitoring the project. Each stakeholder is critical for the success of the project. The other significant stakeholder is the registrar of cooperatives. Of all stakeholders, the farmers' cooperative society, the funds manager and the private hospitals are the most important.

### Stakeholders in a public-private mix

Unlike the previous models, public-private mix (PPM) is not conventionally regarded as a public-private partnership but as an added dimension in collaboration with the private sector for treatment of diseases. PPM is used to denote involvement of private individuals and institutions in a range of services from testing to follow up. India's Revised National Tuberculosis Control Program (RNTCP) has been largely funded by the World Bank with private sector involvement as one of its critical components. Funds from the federal government are routed to district-level societies formed to overcome bureaucratic redtape. In collaboration with the district-level disease control societies, state governments engage private hospitals or private physicians in the detection, referral, treatment, drug administration and tracking of drug defaulters.

Under PPM, private individual physicians are the most important stakeholder. Patients attend a private clinic without recognizing the symptoms of TB. If the physicians are well-trained, they diagnose and treat the disease appropriately; otherwise, they indulge in wrong prescriptions that lead to drug resistance and complications. Other important stakeholders are private health facilities that patients easily approach without stigma. Private facilities need appropriate diagnostic facilities to test and treat patients. For continued treatment, a range of trained health personnel is needed to administer DOTS – Directly Observed Treatment, Short-course. Community outreach workers and volunteers are other stakeholders without whom the program could not successfully operate.

Sometimes professional medical associations and philanthropic foundations provide support in mobilizing the private sector as part of disease control. Public TB clinics are also important due to their role as facilitator and in providing capacity-building initiatives to the private sector. Figure 4.10 depicts the stakeholders in a public-private mix.

### Summary

The health sector has a tradition of involving stakeholders in planning and implementing community health programs. The Alma Ata declaration advocated

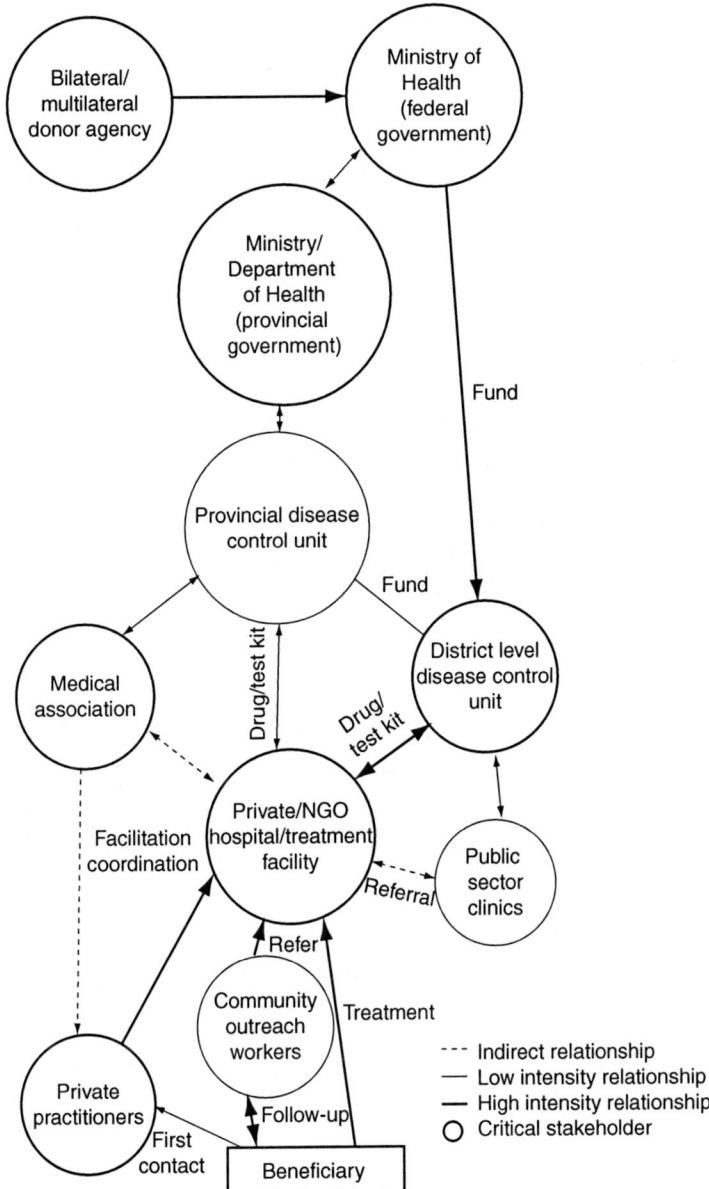

*Figure 4.10* Stakeholders in a public-private mix.

wider community involvement. Community Needs Assessment has been a strategy followed by developing countries in successfully implementing primary health care services. Under public-private partnerships the stakeholders have a range of objectives. Their influence is more than conventional community participation programs. Key stakeholders under public-private partnerships in the health sector include the government at local, state and national level, the ministry of health and its agencies, health staff unions and associations, private health providers, community-based civil society organizations, patients, local leaders, bilateral and multilateral donors and planning authorities. The importance of other stakeholders depends on the degree of their involvement in a partnership. Figure 4.11 illustrates the phases involved in stakeholder management.

It is prudent for both public and private sector managers to identify critical stakeholders in projects under public-private partnership. For a project to be successful, it is important to map the range of stakeholders, their motives, their influence and their resources in order to identify the scope for negotiation, coordination and facilitation of their stakes. For example, in projects like voucher schemes, community health insurance schemes or PPM, prior consultation with stakeholders provides a clearer picture about the needs of each stakeholder and therefore more precise program design and implementation plans.

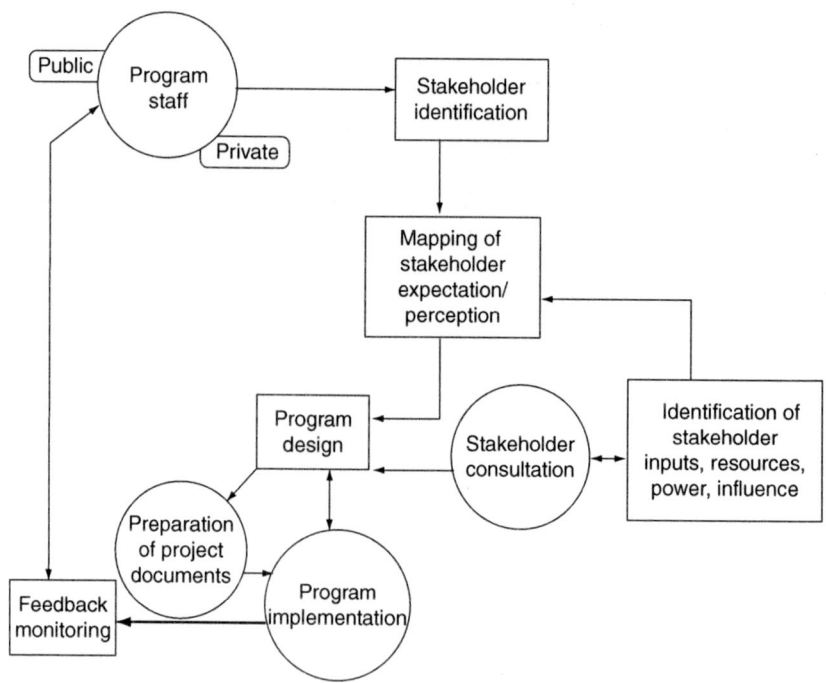

*Figure 4.11* Process of stakeholder management.

# 5 Comparative public-private partnerships

Public-private partnerships are contextual. As public policy, they vary in scope, coverage, objectives and form, all of which depend on the pervasiveness of the private sector in a given country, the level of a region's economic development, political ideologies, social contexts, regulatory capacity of a regime and the quality of governance. Experience with public-private partnerships across the world has generated policy issues about enabling conditions, legal contexts, organizational and managerial structures, financing mechanisms, scope and coverage of services, constraints and bottlenecks, and the appropriateness of one form over another. This chapter reviews partnerships in across the world with specific attention to the delivery of health services.

As noted in Chapter 1, primary reasons for the introduction of public-private partnerships are resource constraints in the public sector, rapid growth of the private sector, high proportion of private out-of-pocket expenses by the poor, and the concerns about equity, efficiency and quality in the health system. Evidence indicates that a substantial private sector is thriving in low-income and middle-income countries in Latin America and Asia, although less so in sub-Saharan Africa. It is estimated that private out-of pocket health expenditures in at least 50 countries account for half or more of total health expenditures[1] (England 2004: 8; WHO 2000). Given the assumption that collaboration with the private sector would deliver better quality health services more efficiently with improved access, many governments have been exploring ways to tap the private sector and to reduce the pressure on public budgets (Hodge and Greve 2007). While evidence on such assumptions is limited, public-private partnerships tend to appear in countries whose governments suffer from heavy debt burdens, where aggregate demand is sizable, and where markets are large enough to allow cost-recovery (Hammami *et al.* 2006). Partnerships are also more likely in countries with low inflation, less corruption, an effective rule of law and prior experience with successful partnerships.

Although contracting had its origins outside the health sector, contracting out in the health sector has become common in all OECD countries (England 2004). Contracting private physicians for the provision of primary care services has had a long history in Europe (Mills and Broomberg 1998). During its initial stages, contracting covered non-clinical services such as catering, laundry and housekeeping but contracting later was extended to clinical services, ancillary services and clinical preventive services (England 2004). Experiences in OECD countries suggest potential benefits from contracting such as cost-savings, improved productivity, improved quality, transferring risk of service delivery, increased service availability, greater innovation and responsiveness, and allowing governments to focus on their core responsibilities (Liu *et al.* 2004).

As a general rule, collaboration with private partners in the social sector begins with infrastructural projects. The World Bank database on private sector participation in infrastructure (PPI) reveals that industrialized countries like Australia, Canada, Ireland and the Netherlands adopted public-private arrangements to provide services in water and waste management, education, health and other social sectors (Hammami *et al.* 2006). Wherever substantial investment is needed beyond the financial capacity of government, partnerships have taken the form of Private Finance Initiatives (PFI). The most common forms of PFI in infrastructure projects are build-own-operate (BOO), build-own-transfer (BOT) and build-rehabilitate-operate-transfer (BROT), which account for almost three-quarters of all projects (Domberger and Fernandez 1999). Although OECD countries have the most experience with public-private partnerships in infrastructure projects, low-income and middle-income countries are beginning to catch up. According to the World Bank database, most infrastructural partnerships are in Latin America and the Caribbean, followed by East Asia and the Pacific, Central Asia and Eastern Europe. South Asia, sub-Saharan Africa, the Middle East and North Africa lag well behind.

A survey of 7,500 public-private partnerships in Australia described their typical attributes when delivering public services in an industrialized economy (Domberger and Fernandez 1999). Contrary to popular belief, saving money is not the main motive for public sector attraction to partnerships; rather, access to market skills and technical expertise are the primary reasons. The pace of innovation and technological change is such that in-house capability of the public sector to keep pace is difficult. Improving quality of services, cost-savings and better accountability were ranked in respective order as the other motives for PPP. Most partnerships were small and of short duration – perhaps due to the risk-averse nature of the public sector. One way to reduce risk is to enter into short-term contracts so that, in the event of a partnership failure, the damages are limited. Private partners are generally chosen on the basis of open tender preceded by a preliminary 'expression of interest'. Management costs and the size of the projects are inversely related as smaller contracts are relatively more expensive to manage.

In terms of savings, contractual cleaning services save half of previous expenditures. Contracting medical and health services saved up to 22 percent of pre-partnership costs. In the case of IT services, the saving was actually negative due to the rapidly changing nature of the service specifications and the generally high-priced contracts. The degree of competition and efficiency levels prior to contracting are the main determinants of the savings. There is lack of expertise in the public sector to monitor performance rigorously and effectively. Where performance monitoring is adopted, contracts perform 38 percent better in comparison to where they do not exist. When performance monitoring is absent, savings turn negative.

Public-private partnership arrangements in industrialized countries generally follow modified versions of the UK's Private Finance Initiatives (PFI) or the 'contracting' model of the US but there is a wide array of types (Hodge and Greve 2007). Broadly these include institutional cooperation for joint production and risk-sharing (as in the Netherlands); long-term infrastructure contracts with specified outputs in legal contracts (as in the United Kingdom); public policy networks with loose stakeholder relationships (see Chapter 3); civil society and community development symbolizing cultural change (as in Hungary); and urban renewal with downtown economic development (as in the US).

## Europe

Europe has two variants of organizational arrangements for health care systems: the National Health Service model and the Social Insurance model (Grimmeisen and Rothgang 2004). Under the NHS model the state plays a major role in financing, providing and regulating health services. In the social insurance model, the state has a less intrusive role because health services are largely financed by contributions through so-called sickness funds that, over time, have become parastatal organizations. Services are delivered through a mix of public and private (for-profit and not-for-profit) providers while the state restricts its role to regulation.

Scandinavia has a long tradition of preferring cooperative arrangements and cultivating consensus to forge partnerships between organizations. The urge for partnerships in Scandinavian countries rests on cultural values that stress cooperation, consensus and participation. The flexibility inherent in public-private partnerships provides a viable alternative to competitive bargaining. While central governments in Scandinavia focus on infrastructure-related private partnerships, regional and local governments forge partnerships for the delivery of public services. However, Scandinavian countries do not have identical approaches to public-private partnerships. In Denmark contracting public services has occurred since the 1980s. In the 1990s, a few local governments entered into sale-and-leaseback (up to 30 years) arrangements with the private sector for schools. In Denmark and Sweden, approximately 12 percent of local government service provision is contracted out to private service providers. Such services include cleaning, waste disposal, administration, elderly care, nursery homes, child care and ambulances. Prosperous Norway, which can easily afford public funding for services, has been debating the incentives for government to embark on partnership with the private sector (Greve 2003).

Over the years Sweden has reformed its public health system. Health care delivery is decentralized to county councils that implement their own user-fee schedules within a nationally set cap per individual. The philosophy of user-fees is to encourage users to ration their consumption of services rather than to generate revenue for the health care system. Another reform, although not widely implemented, is transferring hospital and other clinical services to for-profit operators. In 1999 Stockholm City Council transferred the operation of St Görans Hospital to Capio AB, a publicly traded company with business in the UK and other European countries. Capio bought the hospital's equipment and also hired its staff. The contract between the county council and Capio specified prices, volume and types of services as well as outlined terms of the lease of the hospital buildings. The stated objectives of this move were to remove the public monopoly on health care as well as its associated barriers to improving efficiency and to transfer the risk of cost-escalation to the private sector. However, the experiment caused concerns, such as high-need patients waiting longer than less ill patients (Fooks and Maslove 2003).

Most European health systems rely on a mix of public and private funding, with a large portion of funding from taxation and social health insurance. European countries have traditionally funded health care through compulsory social health insurance for every citizen, regardless of ability to pay. The main source of private funding is from voluntary private health insurance and out-of-pocket payments. In all European countries other than France and the Netherlands, out-of-pocket payments form a larger proportion of private health expenditure than private health insurance (Mossialos *et al.* 2002). In most of continental Europe, social health insurance funds contract with independent providers. In Scandinavia, private providers deliver a substantial amount of primary care. In Norway in 2001, two-thirds of primary care services were provided by privately contracted doctors whereas 19 percent were delivered by salaried doctors (Loevinsohn and Harding 2005).

In Switzerland all permanent residents have been legally obliged since 1996 to purchase health insurance from a limited number of insurers, whether public or private. Insurers must register with the Federal Office for Social Insurance, which monitors their activities and scrutinizes their accounts. Insurance companies are not allowed to make profits from their compulsory insurance activities and contributions are community-rated. Out-of-pocket payments are made for services not covered by the public system or to which access is limited such as dentists, pharmacists (for over-the-counter or de-listed drugs), laboratories and hospitals for private treatment (WHO 2002b). Switzerland has used an incremental approach to establish public-private partnerships (Lienhard 2006). Despite a public sector no longer able to ensure cost-effective quality services, the Swiss have not pursued large-scale privatization (Teicher *et al.* 2006).

Countries such as Germany, France and the Netherlands use insurance-based health systems supported by employer/employee payments where both parties contribute a percentage of the wage bill to health insurance funds. The German government permits high earners to opt out of the social health insurance scheme on condition that they are covered by a private scheme. The Dutch government excludes approximately one-third of the population from compulsory membership of social insurance schemes and Spain does so for civil servants (Glennerster 2003).

Europe has four models of private sector involvement in the health sector: private loans direct to a hospital; private loans to a regional health body; public-private partnerships where the private sector's role is to build, design and operate non-clinical functions of a hospital; and public-private partnerships where the private sector's involvement includes management of a hospital's clinical functions (Thompson and McKee 2004). The models generate four types of interaction between the public and private sectors: parallel public and private systems, co-payment systems, group-based systems and sectoral systems (Tuohy *et al.* 2004). Under the parallel system health care services are provided both publicly and privately. A co-payment system entails partial subsidies from the public purse with proportional contributions through private payments or from private insurance. The group-based system allows some sections of the population to use free health care while others pay for the same services. In a sectoral system some categories of service are provided free for all while other categories involve private payments. The US health care system exemplifies the group-based model in which free health services are available only for certain social groups. The current health care system in the UK combines elements from all four types but most closely resembles the parallel system.

In terms of capital financing for public hospitals, mechanisms include grants from central and regional governments, accumulated savings, surcharges on hospital fees, private loans and public-private partnerships. Private investment and finance are also available through loans from commercial banks and development banks as well as raised through bond markets. There is a basic distinction between the use of private loans as capital for hospital projects and the creation of longer-term public-private partnerships in the management of the finished hospital. Hospitals in the Netherlands, Germany, France, Sweden and Finland take loans directly from the private sector to finance hospital construction projects without establishing a formal public-private partnership – although in Germany all loans are subject to approval by the Lander (state governments) where decisions are based on health care need and whether the cost of funding in this way would be less expensive than using public funds. The Netherlands, with its entire hospital sector in private ownership, relies almost entirely on the private sector for its capital financing; around 85 percent of funds for a typical Dutch project come in the form of money loaned directly to a hospital. The balance is made up by the hospital's accumulated savings or other private sources such as philanthropists, institutional investors and commercial health care agencies. Hospitals in Sweden and Finland are able to borrow but applications must be made to the regional administrative level. Sweden's county councils have excellent credit ratings and are able to raise capital through bank loans with no restrictions on how the money is used. The situation in Denmark is in flux. Hospitals in Copenhagen are owned by a public corporation but the Frederiksberg county council is currently exploring outright privatization of facilities, with the goal of increasing utilization by privately insured patients (Thompson and McKee 2004).

England and Italy have developed a form of public-private partnership that involves the private sector in the subsequent management of non-clinical functions. In England the PFI allows private consortia to bid to finance, build and operate a hospital for a minimum 25-year period during which time it is effectively leased back to the NHS. The first wave of Italian hospital construction under public-private partnerships is just beginning, mainly in the Lombardy region, following the adoption in 1998 of a law that introduced private finance techniques and structures. This law created two options for private financing: for the private sector solely to finance and build the hospital, and for the creation of a longer partnership whereby the private entity stays to operate the hospital for a period of time (De Angelis 2002). Private consortia compete through public tender as in the UK.

Elsewhere in Europe, Greece has introduced partnerships to finance public sector infrastructure. Ireland's National Health Strategy, published in November 2001, indicated openness to some form of public-private partnership to finance expansion of the hospital sector. Spain has developed a form of partnership called the 'Alzira model' after the first hospital that was built under the new legislation and opened in 1999. In this model, a private group of insurance and construction companies builds the hospital and manages its services for ten years. During this period, the regional health authority prospectively pays a capitation fee for each member of the catchment population. This approach differs from the British and Italian models in that the private sector manages both clinical and non-clinical elements in the hospital and is given responsibility for health care of a defined local population. At the end of the ten years, if the private group does not have its contract renewed, ownership of the hospital will be transferred to the regional health authority (Trescoli 2002).

Many countries in continental Europe have established single-purpose organizational entities that promote public-private partnerships but the Nordic countries have organized themselves in a more decentralized way. Countries with special organizational units for public-private policy suggest a clear top-down push for partnerships across government. Countries that have not established centralized units indicate a bottom-up approach with room for greater local experimentation. Germany, Sweden and Denmark are examples of the latter trend (Hodge and Greve 2007).

In NHS-based systems in northern Europe (Scandinavia and the United Kingdom), hospitals are almost entirely public with fewer than 10 percent of private beds. The percentage of private hospital beds is higher in southern European countries with NHS systems; in Italy, Portugal and Spain the share of private beds is between 20 and 30 percent, about half being private for-profit. An emerging trend in private sector involvement in the hospital sector is the contracting out of support services such as hotel and diagnostic services. In many instances, these have proved to have lower direct costs than when they were publicly provided. In western European countries with social health insurance systems, hospitals are also mainly public but the share of private beds (mostly not-for-profit) is larger than in countries with NHS systems. Only in the Netherlands are most hospitals legally constituted as private not-for-profit entities. Due to a natural purchaser–provider split in these countries, all public hospitals have a degree of managerial independence and take autonomous, often corporatized, institutional forms (McKee and Healy 2002; Busse *et al.* 2002; Jakab *et al.* 2002).

In France public-private partnerships have attracted great interest among politicians and managers. The World Health Organization regards the French health system as one of the best in the world with expenditures lower than elsewhere in Europe and the US. The system is a public and universal mode, flexible and based on social equity. Opening the health sector for partnership is under discussion for it is proposed to entrust the private sector with minor surgeries and ambulatory day-care while prices will remain unchanged for patients. Partnership with the private pharmaceutical companies has also been successful in France. For example, projects of education for patients organized by a major company in collaboration with doctors and nurses to create awareness about chronic asthma, diabetes and obstructive pulmonary diseases showed not only a better use of drugs but also a reduction of hospitalizations and emergency admissions (Keramidas and Bout-Colonna 2007).

## The United Kingdom

The United Kingdom has a long history of providing public services through the private sector with different models of private provision. The UK model has evolved a complex balance of public and private delivery with public and private financing. The forms of legal contract range from a highly complex national contract for the services of all self-employed general medical practitioners to a relatively simple local contract for the provision of on-site catering. Although the direction of health services has been towards an increased use of private sector, the aim underpinning the National Health Service at its creation in 1948 was that the state would *finance* and *deliver* free health care for all. At the same time, an element of private provision was retained as the medical profession retained significant rights to provide services on a self-employed contractual basis. During the decades that followed, the original structure, objectives and values of the NHS were adapted to reflect the political preferences of ruling governments. Consequently the current health care system relies on increasingly complex interaction between public and private sector providers. For example, the UK hospital sector is predominantly financed through public payments but accommodates a small private market. Meanwhile, services such as dental care or prescription drugs require co-payments and additional charges for certain groups of people. The UK system is further complicated by the fact that health is now a devolved issue so the governments of England and Wales, Northern Ireland and Scotland have the freedom to modify existing structures (Asenova *et al.* 2007).

The NHS uses three types of contracts: block, cost and volume, and cost per case (Allen 1995, 2002). Block contracts provide unlimited services for a fixed annual sum. The risk lies entirely with the provider. Providers may opt for opportunistic practices to reduce their costs by lowering the quality of care. In such situations the purchaser has to incur a large *ex post* transaction cost for frequent monitoring. Cost and volume contracts are a kind of compromise where, if certain volumes of services are exceeded, further sums must be paid. Cost-per-case contracts stipulate that the provider is remunerated at an agreed rate in respect of each case treated. The risk is borne by the purchaser. Due to lack of adequate information on cost of care or about the process of acquiring cost information, the *ex ante* transaction costs could be higher and time-consuming.

In contrast, Allen (2002) pointed out that in any conventional contract in the NHS where the providers set their prices, there are severe financial constraints on the providers. Based on average costs, prices are fixed; there are no cross-subsidies or carryovers from one procedure or specialty to another. Decisions on investment or service expansion cannot be taken independently. Trusts are required to make a return of 6 percent per annum on their net assets. The NHS management sets a cash-limit for each trust on net external borrowings for each financial year, and prior approval is required for such borrowings. Maynard (1993 cited in Allen 1995) argued that such constraints on mobilization or deployment of resources will lead to less than desired efficiency. The NHS contracts are thrust on the districts by law; therefore there is no 'voluntarism'.

Under the Conservative government during the 1980s and 1990s, there was a concerted effort to 'roll back the state'. The role of ministries and bureaucracy was kept to the minimum through privatization, contracting-out and delegation of management authority for the provision of public services. Complex organizational systems evolved (autonomous public bodies, independent regulators, charities, private firms, internal contractors) to play critical roles in designing and delivering public services. While concern was expressed about the increased degree of institutional 'hybridity' and fragmentation within the state administrative machinery, the Labour Party – which had been critical of the 'privatization' strategies of the Tory government – continued after assuming power in 1997 to promote collaboration with the private sector while maintaining public sector values (Flinders 2002).

In the early 1980s, contracting in the public sector in the UK was sporadic (Boviard 2006). By the late 1980s and early 1990s, however, relational contracting began to appear as a major force in 'block contracts' within an NHS internal market (LeGrand and Bartlett 1993) and 'generalized service agreements' in social services (Kirkpatrick *et al.* 2001). Since then, relational contracting has become conventional wisdom in public service contracting, including the health sector. In the UK, partnership-oriented procurement from the private sector has had several manifestations that are divided into PPPs as strategic service delivery partnerships between organizations; PFIs aimed at accessing capital finance from private sector partners; and purchasing consortia that seek economies of bulk purchasing and lower transaction costs rather than any synergies in the service delivery process.

In the health sector, the Labour government found new ways of integrating private sector into health services delivery. Health Action Zones were established in 1997 to involve voluntary and private sectors; in 2004 Foundation Hospitals were established to operate as semi-independent public companies in competition with other trusts (Farnsworth and Holden 2006). The government also deliberately set out to recruit senior private sector managers for key positions within NHS boards (Carvel 2003). It is now the norm for long-term care to be provided in the private sector while hospital provision is predominantly undertaken directly by the state. As a harbinger, a private consultancy firm 'Secta' was awarded a £1.3 million contract in 2003 to take over the 'failing' Good Hope Hospital Trust in Birmingham. Secta is also involved in several PFI projects in the NHS. The private sector was invited to bid for contracts to run fast-track surgeries that are being set up by the government to tackle waiting lists (Dean 2003). In 2004 the construction firm Jarvis was awarded a joint contract with Interhealth Care Services, a Canadian health company, to build and run orthopedic units for patients waiting for hip or knee replacements (Carvel 2004a). The government also commissioned Netcare, a South African private health company, to conduct cataract operations from 2003, putting pressure on Primary Care Trusts to sign up even against local wishes (Carvel 2004b).

The main thrust of NHS reforms under the Labour government has been the nature of decentralized purchasing (Hudson and Hardy 2001). Rather than concentrating on practice-level purchasing, the focus has been on activity at the local level. In 1997 an NHS White Paper proposed that the chief responsibility for purchasing health care should move from the existing 100 health authorities and 3,600 GP fund-holders to around 500 Primary Care Groups (PCGs), each covering a community of around 100,000 people. While accountable to health authorities, PCGs are free to make decisions about how they deploy resources within the framework of a Health Improvement Program drawn up by the Health Authority. Normally each PCG has a majority of GPs on its governing board plus representatives from community nursing, social services and the local community.

Among the models to engage the private sector, two initiatives are considered significantly prominent: Public Interest Companies (PIC) and the Private Finance Initiative (PFI). While PFI originated in the late 1980s under a Conservative government, PIC as a distinct type of PPP emerged in 2001 under a Labour government. PICs have a wide variety of organizational forms such as not-for-profits, not-for-profit distribution organizations, mutuals and social enterprises. Foundation Hospitals have been created under PICs. Without shareholders PICs deliver public services and are legally independent of government (Maltby 2003; Birchall 2002). PICs have been found appropriate when there is no clear purchaser–provider difference. The notion of shareholder is replaced by stakeholder membership in order to increase the sense of accountability towards the local community or users. Although largely funded by the state, PICs are allowed to raise money through the private market but under government supervision. Elected boards drawn from the local community manage the foundation hospitals (Flinders 2005).

While PICs are of recent origin, PFI has a much longer history. PFI was introduced in 1992 with the aim of increasing the role of the private sector in the provision of public services that had previously been 'off limits' to it. PFI was vigorously promoted by the Conservative government. Under PFI schemes, the private sector raises finance from the capital market and builds a project. For instance, to build a health facility, a PFI will involve the collaboration of a construction firm and a bank and be administered by a consultant firm. Costs are recouped through user-charges to individuals (Teicher *et al.* 2006). However, PFI differs from privatization because the public sector remains a key actor in the project as both facilitator and main purchaser of services. It also differs from contracting-out as the private sector provides the resources as well as the services.

The PFI process is relatively simple. After receiving approval from the treasury, the local authority or public body issues a tender to the private sector for the specific project. Using a public sector comparator (as a benchmark to obtain value-for-money), a risk assessment is conducted on each bid. This evaluation leads to the award of a contract that forms a partnership in which the private partner finances, builds and manages a facility (school, hospital) in return for a long-term contract (25 years or more) under which the government commits itself to pay an annual fee during the entire duration of the contract for the use of the facility. PFI contracts vary significantly in terms of size and scope (from £100,000 to £4 billion – such as the Channel Tunnel rail link). Although the Labour Party had long been suspicious of PFI, the party came to find value in this model because it theoretically provided the possibility of funding major public sector projects without raising income tax or public borrowing. PFI offered a trade-off to the Labour Party's traditional misgivings about the role of the private sector by meeting the government's desire to invest in and improve public services without increasing taxes or borrowing. PFI has been important part in public sector capital investment in the health sector in the UK. Between 1995 and 2003, 563 PFI projects were undertaken and over 600 new public facilities were established. The Department of Health issued 126 contracts for 34 hospitals and 119 other health schemes with a total capital value of £2.9 billion (Flinders 2005).

Comparison of PFI and PIC public-private partnerships in the UK reveals a mixed experience. On the dimension of efficiency, PFI delivers increased efficiency in the building and managing of prisons and constructing roads but not in skill-intensive sectors like hospitals (Dunnigan and Pollock 2003; Gaffney and Pollock 1999). Instead of transferring risk to the private sector, PFI tends to transfer risk to the government, users and taxpayers – particularly in designing, building and managing hospitals (Pollock *et al.* 2002). Also PICs and PFI increase the number of quasi-autonomous public bodies or 'hybrid bodies', thus increasing the complexity within the administrative landscape.

The complexity is exacerbated by frequently creating other quasi-autonomous organizations to oversee and regulate the activity of these partnerships. Each such organization has an autonomous relationship with different ministries (Flinders 2005). Such 'dense' inter-organizational networks make coordination difficult. Since most PFI contracts are between 15 and 30 years, the private partner becomes more powerful when the contract needs to be renegotiated because, by then, the government would have lost its own ability to provide the services (Pollock *et al.* 2001: 11). Arguably PFI-based partnerships for public services disrupt traditional accountability structures, especially under different political regimes that may not agree with such models. However, if community engagement is built into the partnership, accountability may be strengthened.

Perspectives on PFI-type partnerships vary according to different researchers. Hodge and Greve (2007) observe that PFI is based on two premises: to reduce pressure on government budgets, thus allowing a greater capacity to spend on other policy priorities, and better value for money in the provision of public infrastructure. However, the claim that more money may be available for other policy initiatives has been largely discredited. Bowman (2001) reports that PFI partnerships are seen by some in the UK 'yet again screwing the taxpayer' with private project sponsors are caricatured as 'evil bandits running away with all the loot' (cited in Hodge and Greve 2007). Shaoul (2005) contends that the merits of PFI have been exaggerated through 'convenient' evaluation criteria by those favoring expansion of the PFI model. She concludes that, at best, PFI has turned out to be very expensive without accountability.

Although PFI had enjoyed considerable popularity in policy circles, there has always been some doubt about its success. The reasons for skepticism include the lack of independent evaluators, poor evaluation rigor, inadequate definition of benchmarks against which partnerships are to be judged, evaluations by auditors-general who may not question government policy, the use of inaccurate discount-rates of net benefits, inaccurate estimates of risk transfers from the public to the private sector, and predicted benefits being estimated at a premature stage of a long-term contract (Hodge and Greve 2007). Nonetheless, PFI partnerships have been popular elsewhere in Europe, the US, Canada and Australia in the construction of buildings, tunnels, ports, sports stadiums, wastewater management systems, construction and operation of prisons, education, transportation and such social policy arenas as human services, welfare provision and emergency services.

## The United States of America

Public-private partnerships in the American context appear paradoxical as they would be expected to proliferate. Contracting in the health sector became popular in 1990s as government-run Medicaid programs began to contract with privately managed care companies to provide health care for beneficiaries. By 2000, two-thirds of local health departments were supposedly contracting out public health services including maternal health, pediatric care, communicable disease, family planning and environmental health (Liu *et al.* 2004). However, since the mid-1990s there has been a steady reversal of private sector involvement, which is to say a return to public services and traditional invitations to tender. American municipalities have become increasingly averse to sub-contracting and are taking on several services themselves (Keramidas and Bout-Colonna 2007).

Since 1965 Medicare and Medicaid have provided intersecting systems of short- and long-term care for the elderly and for the poor, respectively. A large measure of private sector involvement has existed since the inception of this dual approach, not only for provision of services but also insurance schemes. Medicare coverage in particular is regulated by forms of cost-sharing such as premiums, co-payments, deductibles and co-insurance (Friedland 2005). This reliance on private agencies has lead to questioning the desirability of such trends, particularly for vulnerable social groups (Asenova *et al.* 2007). In the state of New Jersey, an effort to outsource public health responsibilities for tuberculosis and sexually transmitted diseases failed due to 'critical infrastructure weaknesses [which] resulted in a complete deterioration of services'. Pennsylvania, which outsourced much of its laboratory services, is re-establishing state capacity due to vendor instability (Avery 2000).

Hospitals in the US display ownership types that are categorized as public (veterans' hospitals; municipal hospitals), not-for-profit (religious or charitable organizations) and for-profit (publicly-traded chains of hospitals with a commitment toward shareholders profit). American hospitals are usually not-for-profit general hospitals. Although reviews of these hospitals in the literature are inconclusive, for-profit hospitals arguably perform better than other hospitals on indicators of quality, performance and efficiency. Managed care organizations such as health maintenance organizations (HMOs) combine insurance and delivery functions and use their client-based buying power to negotiate better rates from providers. HMOs include both for-profit and not-for-profit organizations. Managed care institutions reveal how competition leads not-for-profits to behave in ways similar to their for-profit rivals (Essig and Batran 2005).

The US has a long tradition of contracting with the private non-profit sector. Such contracting has led to long-term relationships characterized by a decline in competitive bidding and a decreasing importance of price after the initial contract. But the cost of managing contracts has been high – up 20 percent of a contact's value. Primary health care services in states like Texas and California have been contracted to serve low-income people without health insurance. Models of service delivery include private for-profit health maintenance organizations and private providers contracted by local agencies. Reviews of the tender and bidding processes in American health care indicate very complex relationships among market players, characteristic of products or services, incentives and the political influence of provider associations. These reviews imply that competitive bidding does not always lead to cost savings. The managed care system puts primary care physicians under financial risk (Mills and Broomberg 1998).

Public-private partnerships have been a basic characteristic of the political and social welfare system in the United States. Cultural and ideological perspectives in American society do not allow government an exclusive role in the area of public services, particularly health care at the federal level. Federal and state governments rarely deliver services themselves but rather involve private organizations in managing and delivering public services. Typically these partner organizations are non-profit entities that account for half of the country's hospitals, colleges and universities (Smith and Lipsky 1993). Government financing accounts for more than half of the income of non-profit social service agencies and, at any given point in time, there are hundreds of contractual arrangements between public and private non-profit entities. Government support is extended in the form of direct payments, tax exemptions, preferential regulatory treatment and deductibility of donations. Public-private partnerships usually take the form of short-term purchase-of-services contracts. As purchaser, the government exerts varying control over beneficiaries, service delivery and discharge decisions for clients. Under this arrangement, public and private agencies are involved in a mutually dependent but unequal relationship because the government is more of a sponsor than a partner.

Since the Reagan Administration the US has undertaken a major restructuring of how health and welfare are funded. There has been a reduction in the level of government funding for non-profit activities across the board. Fifty-seven federal grant categories were consolidated into nine block grants, and the funding for social service agencies was shifted from reimbursement plans of conventional contracting to performance contracts that emphasize efficiency and capacity. Given the emphasis on efficiency and performance, the for-profit private sector organizations began to garner contracts to manage and deliver welfare services. The non-profit sector has been forced to compete for government contracts, too. As government spending on the health sector shrinks and as competition amongst for-profit providers increases, non-profit organizations must rely on alternative funding sources, including commercial income. Experts fear the consequences of this trend on the beneficiaries. They also fear that non-profit organizations may lose their service ethos, become overly professionalized, and resort to 'vendorism'. Some non-profits are already commercialized to the extent of selling theme license plates, opening health clubs and off-site museum stores, leasing mailing lists, sponsoring conferences, publishing journals, loaning their logos, licensing and patenting discoveries, among many other strategies to generate income through fees.

The health field has witnessed mergers and conversions to for-profit status among non-profit hospitals and other health care organizations. How these conversions affect hospital pricing is a major concern. For example, the YWCA of Greater Milwaukee recently faced a 40 percent reduction in revenue as the Wisconsin legislature consolidated existing social service programs. On its own, the YWCA did not have the resources to bid competitively for the new $40 million welfare-to-work contract. Its response was to seek a partnership with two for-profit firms to build the scale and managerial capacity to win the contract. In several other cases, non-profit partners have formed coalitions either among themselves or with for-profit firms.

Another trend has been a new kind of mutual dependency among for-profit firms and non-profit organizations. For example, the government contracts with for-profit firms for the management of social programs, then contracts with non-profit organizations for service provision. For-profit firms may have the technical expertise and organizational capacity to manage large-scale delivery systems, but they often lack local access and the specialized expertise necessary for the provision of services. For-profit firms come to rely on non-profit organizations to help them fulfill their contracts at the provision end of the delivery system. For-profits become the middleman between government purchasers and non-profit providers (Moulton and Anheier 2001).

## Canada

Almost all hospitals in Canada are in the not-for-profit sector with approximately 70 percent of health expenditures paid through public sources. Other than health care for the defense forces, the aboriginal communities and provincial psychiatric hospitals, however, very few Canadian health services are directly delivered by the public sector. The private not-for-profit sector is the dominant force in Canada. With their independent community-based boards of directors, Canadian hospitals have a long tradition of providing services to local communities but they are inaccurately classified as part of the public sector. The reason for such confusion is because these not-for-profit organizations receive about nine-tenths of their budget from public sources. Fueling the confusion is the definition of 'public sector' by different provinces. The province of Ontario, for example, classifies municipal hospitals as 'public'. It also replaced some of the formerly independent hospital boards with regional health authorities, thus further blurring the public-private distinction (Deber 2002).

Canadians have traditionally used phrases such as 'alternative service delivery' or 'partnering with the private sector' rather than 'privatization'. During the 1990s, opinion surveys indicated strong support for the use of public-private partnership to build and deliver services, including health services (Carr 1998). In 2002 Ontario decided to construct two hospitals under public-private partnerships that resemble the PFI in the UK. Requests for proposals invited private partners to design, finance, build, own and maintain the hospitals although the funding of hospital clinical services remained the responsibility of the ministry of health and the hospital boards. The provincial government's decision to build hospitals through public-private partnerships had several problems – particularly lack of consultation with relevant stakeholders, lack of public debate, lack of clarity about accountability and insufficient transparency (Auerbach 2002). The wisdom of using private capital was likewise questioned because, unless the public sector provides risk-free lending or guarantees a subsidy, the private sector must borrow money for the same project at a higher interest rate. Auditors-general in Ontario and New Brunswick each raised concerns about similar projects in the health and education sectors and argued that public sector ownership would generally have been more economical. Canada's auditor-general was also concerned about accountability due to diminished availability of financial, audit and performance information from the non-government entities formed by these arrangements. In the case of the Royal Ottawa Hospital, for example, bundled into the financial justification for public-private partnership was a significant reduction in inpatient beds as well as greater reliance on outpatient group home-care.

Nonetheless Ontario and British Columbia have keenly explored cooperative options for the private sector. The provincial government in British Columbia decided to finance long-term care through public-private partnerships and to build hospitals through a public finance initiative. The province of Ontario has used bonds to augment funding for hospital services and allows the use of public finances to purchase clinical services from for-profit providers. The university health network in Toronto financed its renovation through a bond issue. In 1984, as perhaps the first case of public-private partnership in Ontario, management of a not-for-profit hospital in Hawkesbury was contracted to a for-profit private health care organization without much success. The province requires that hospitals and their communities provide a portion of capital expenditures but the hospital was unable to raise its share. Through a request for proposal the provincial government then sponsored a competition to find an operator who would pay for the community's share of capital in exchange for a ten-year management contract for all non-clinical services. A US company – American Medical International (AMI), a chain of then 130 hospitals operating in 13 countries – was the only qualified bidder. Although AMI did achieve some economies of scale in operating costs, the management contract was not renewed and the hospital was returned to not-for-profit management (Bennett 2001).

In 2001, the provincial not-for-profit Cancer Care Ontario (CCO) contracted with Canadian Radiation Oncology Services (CROS), a for-profit business organization, to treat breast cancer patients who would otherwise have been referred at far higher cost to the United States. At the time, there was spare capacity in terms of the necessary equipment for radiation treatment and diagnosis but a shortage of personnel willing to work for the wages offered by Cancer Care Ontario. The private clinic accordingly used the facilities of a large not-for-profit teaching hospital – Toronto Sunnybrook Regional Cancer Centre – by operating a second shift weekdays after normal working hours. The private clinic was far cheaper than sending overflow patients to the US ($3,500 versus $18,000) but no comparison is available to indicate whether it is cheaper than care in the existing not-for-profit clinics (Deber 2002).

In laboratory services, several provinces in Canada involve the private sector. In 1995 Alberta negotiated a tariff with a private sector laboratory at 30 percent below the hospital laboratory. The use of for-profit operators to provide ancillary services is increasing in Canada, which Canadians seem to find acceptable (Romanow 2002). Home care is another service in which the for-profit sector is effectively involved. However, one of the for-profit firms responsible for quality testing of the drinking water supply in Ontario did not perform up to the required standard, which led to the death of seven people and affected thousands. This case highlights the importance of effective regulation in such contracts (O'Connor 2002).

While there is rarely controversy in Canada about the role of the not-for-profit private sector in the delivery of services, there is considerable debate whether the private for-profit sector should engage in the direct provision of services through public financing. Canadians believe that no one should be able to purchase service ahead of someone else who cannot afford the fee (Fooks and Maslove 2003). During 1997–2001, auditors-general in several provinces expressed concern about whether partnerships might have implications for international trade obligations. And in 2001 Alberta's auditor-general called for more stringent controls on the contracting of clinical services.

As in the UK, several provinces in Canada have a history of mixed (public and private) provision of health services. A case in point is British Columbia where in 2004 all housekeeping services in 32 hospitals and extended-care facilities in the province were contracted out to three large multinational corporations. The health authorities also contracted out hospital food services and security services. In addition, support services (housekeeping and food) in many for-profit long-term care facilities were contracted out on long-term contracts. Commenting on the rapid pace of contracting, Cohen (2006) observed that the impact on the staff of the privatized housekeepers had been severe. Their wages were cut almost in half, benefits were eliminated or drastically reduced, and union protections abolished. Overnight these workers went from being the highest-paid to the lowest-paid housekeepers working in health care in Canada; the new rates were between 14 and 39 percent lower than anywhere else in Canada and 26 percent below the national average. The harsh working conditions, lower levels of compensation, poor training and heavier workloads endured by the privatized workers militate against the provision of a quality service (Stinson *et al.* 2005).

The size and scope of this privatization place British Columbia at the international forefront in the privatization of health support housekeeping services, outpacing even the United States and Britain – two countries with several decades of experience in privatizing such sectors. In the US in 2003, for example, only 6.8 percent of hospitals reported that they contracted housekeeping services (Towne and Hoppszallern 2003), down from 27.4 percent in 1999 (Sunseri 1999). Such complexity arose due to poor conceptualization of the need for contracting. The need for contracting had been based on a study conducted by a politically affiliated research organization that compared the costs of ancillary support services in hospitals – cleaning, laundry, food services, trades and clerical – to 'hospitality' services in hotels. Based on this comparison, it concluded that hospital support workers in British Columbia were overpaid (Ramsey 1995).

## Australia and New Zealand

Public-private partnerships emerged in Australia after years of contracting and privatization based on federal competition policy (Teicher *et al.* 2006). Although the federal government introduced the policy, the states were the principal stakeholder because most contracts were under their jurisdiction (O'Faircheallaigh *et al*. 1999: 107). Since 1995 a shift to marketization of public services has led to increasing use of contracting out and the introduction of user-fees (Makin 2003). The operational definition of a public-private partnership in Australia is 'that government has a business relationship, it is long term, with risks and returns being shared, and that private business becomes involved in financing, designing, constructing, owning or operating public facilities or services' (Hodge 2004: 37).

In the health sector, the Australian federal and state governments introduced private participation in more than 50 public hospitals through several different mechanisms. They include 15 BOO transactions (a private firm builds, owns and operates a public hospital), four conversions (a hospital is sold to a private operator who runs the hospital), four transactions (private management of a public hospital that the government continues to own), three build-own-leaseback arrangements (a private firm constructs a new public hospital, then leases it back to the government), and 30 co-locations (a private wing is located within or beside a public hospital). These initiatives were driven by a need for new capital, a perceived need to transfer operational risk and a desire to increase efficiency (Taylor and Blair 2002).

Australia's first large public-private partnership – La Trobe hospital – was a failed experiment. The private sector company operating the facility lost money and eventually returned it to the government (Bennett 2001). A more successful example is the Mildura hospital contract, awarded in 1999. The government selected a private operator to design, build, own and operate a new 153-bed hospital under a 15-year contract. The existing public hospital was closed and its employees transferred to the new hospital. The operator is required to provide appropriate clinical services to all patients who attend the hospital without charging them. In turn, the provider receives from the government annual payments based on the forecast mix of clinical patients (with funding capped at a specified number of patients) plus a small block grant to cover such costs as teaching. For quality control purposes, the provider is required to maintain the hospital's accreditation by an independent agency, provide monthly reports on clinical indicators and have high-volume treatments reviewed by external peers. The contract includes penalties for non-compliance, including the ultimate sanction – 'step-in rights' for the government – and it requires the operator to provide a performance bond of about 5 percent of its annual revenues. Mildura's results have been impressive. Capital costs for the new hospital came in 20 percent below those for public sector comparators, and the hospital provides clinical services at lower cost than government-operated hospitals. Moreover, all performance targets have been met, patient volumes increased by 30 percent in the first year, and the operator made a profit.

New Zealand provides insights into how contracting for health services has evolved (Ashton *et al*. 2004). Historically the country had a tax-based publicly funded health system that provided free services through a network of state-owned hospitals plus fee-based services by private general practitioners. During the past decade, however, New Zealand's health sector underwent a series of reforms. Prior to 1993, 14 locally elected area health boards received population-based budgets to provide secondary and tertiary care as well as public health in geographical areas. In 1993 the responsibilities for the 'purchase' and 'provision' of services were separated. Four Regional Health Authorities (RHAs) were set up to purchase all primary, secondary and tertiary health services as well as social care, and 23 Crown Health Enterprises (CHEs) were under contract with RHAs to provide services alongside private providers. In 1997, while the purchaser provider split was retained, the four RHAs were replaced by a single national purchasing organization – the Health Funding Authority (HFA) – in order to reduce the costs of contracting. CHEs were restructured into government-owned not-for-profit institutions called Hospital and Health Services (HHSs) that provided the same services under contract with HFA. Again in 2000–2001 a restructuring occurred in which 21 locally elected district health boards were created to purchase some services and provide others. During these successive reforms, the process of contracting was shaped by factors such as financial constraints necessitating considerations of efficiency, organizational systems attuned to competitiveness, a more mature legal framework, and a desire for uniformity across the country.

During the initial stages of reform, no national guidelines existed for contracts. RHAs were given considerable autonomy, which lead to lengthy and detailed contracts, prolonged administrative procedures, adversarial relationships and a lack of uniformity in contracts. These problems were overcome at later stages of reform. Most contracts were placed with the current providers (most of them public sector providers) through selective contracting. Due to either higher prices or lack of support services, private providers were limited in number. Contracting became competitive when there were many providers with surplus capacity, when purchasers wished to buy additional services on a spot-contract basis, when more funds were available for new services and when the current provider supplied poor quality service. Providers were more often changed due to poor quality than to price. Over the years, the RHAs learned to specify volume and price of services in a contract. Additional volume provided over and above a contract was generally not reimbursed.

Many general practitioners in New Zealand joined umbrella organizations called Independent Practitioner Associations (IPAs) that negotiated on their behalf and helped to counter the weight of the RHA as a single purchaser. Some IPAs negotiated 'budget-holding' contracts that provided them with a pool of funds to cover the costs of some services. Primary care is also provided by not-for-profit organizations to targeted populations – often disadvantaged ethnic minority groups. Volume and price were not pre-determined under the contracts with these providers who were generally paid through capitation. Most contracts did not follow a uniform pricing strategy but did specify some measures of quality, including guidelines related to patient dignity and privacy, culturally appropriate services, information sharing, employment of qualified staff, hours of access, clinical quality, written policy guidelines and physical ambience.

Given annual funding arrangements, the duration of most contracts was one year but contracts ranged from three-four months to two/three years. Based on information supplied by the providers, performance was monitored by measuring the volume of services provided and components of quality of care. While monitoring of quality includes audits of services provided against set standards, purchasers often lacked technical skills to interpret the information gathered. Sanctions for poor performance include termination of a contract or retrieving the resources.

In the later reforms, the health funding authorities relied on relational contracting by working closely with the providers in planning the services. National level consistency in contract terms included specification of services, pricing schedules and duration. These changes reduced transaction costs, shortened the negotiation period, and reduced the legal and administrative costs of providers.

Despite subsequent restructuring, contracting remains at the core of New Zealand's health care system. Both providers and purchasers benefit from contracting. Written contracts help providers to comprehend the importance and linkage between volume, cost and quality as well as innovative styles of service provision. Selective contracts open an opportunity for ethnic minorities like the Maori to bid for providing health services to their own community. Despite managerial limitations such as shortage of skills in contract management during the initial stages of reform, experience has confirmed the benefits of contracting in the public health system of New Zealand (Ashton *et al.* 2004).

## West Asia and the Mediterranean region

A recent study documents the experiences of contracting out publicly financed health services to the private sector in ten countries of West Asia and the Mediterranean area (Siddiqi *et al.* 2006). Contracting was analyzed on the basis of factors that influenced institutional capacity of health ministries in the region. Table 5.1 summarizes the comparative information.

Most countries undertook contracting to improve access, efficiency and quality of health services. Bahrain and Lebanon have national policies to engage the private sector. In the Islamic Republic of Iran and Morocco policies of decentralization provided the underlying reason for contracting out. Urged strongly by multilateral and bilateral donor agencies, Afghanistan contracted out health services to expand basic health services that had been disrupted by years of conflict. In Tunisia contracting to private providers decreased the cost of treatment incurred on patients who would otherwise be sent to foreign countries. Pakistan contracted through non-governmental organizations to access populations at risk of HIV infection. Jordan sought to improve the use of private hospitals and to save capital investment on public facilities. Egypt contracted out to improve coverage and quality of services and increase access to advanced medical technology available in private hospitals. Other reasons for contracting out in these countries included disillusionment of the general public with directly provided services, the concern of the public sector to improve access,

Table 5.1 Contracting health service delivery: the Mediterranean and West Asia

| Country | Rationale to contract | Private sector/ NGO motive | Political, bureaucratic, legal support | Public sector characteristics | Private sector characteristics | Risk | Monitoring mechanism |
|---|---|---|---|---|---|---|---|
| Afghanistan | Years of war-disrupted public sector | 80% services provided by NGOs; $4.5 per capita for basic package | Weak; donor influenced push for contracting | Ministry lacks experience; contracting unit established | NGOs have vast experience of providing services under donor funding | Long-term sustainability, if donor funding stops | Balanced scorecard system |
| Bahrain | Improve efficiency and cost control; active government policy | Assured regular revenue; increase scale of operation | Strong political, bureaucratic and legal framework | Dedicated unit in finance ministry; clear rules/procedures | Limited capacity for local providers | Failure of contractor; need for alternatives | User feedback; previous track record |
| Egypt | Increase coverage; improve quality; utilize technology of private sector | Assured regular revenue; guaranteed clientele | Part of reform process; legal framework exists | Four technical units in the ministry to support contracting | Private sector predominant in ambulatory care; mostly non-accredited | Fee for service and capitation system are only piloted | Performance indicators (30) on quality, coverage and utilization |
| Iran | Decentralization; provision of services to rural and poor | Access to government resources | Political and legal support exist | Enhanced access, quality and efficiency in primary care for rural poor | Mainly in urban hospitals; lack experience in primary care | Managers in both sector lack skills | Performance-based contracts. Negative incentives |
| Jordan | Improve efficiency and accessibility; | Use of spare capacity; assurance of | Political and legal framework | Long experienced in contracting, | Lack skilled managers; experience in | Delayed payments; concern over | Weak monitoring system; new |

| | optimize public sector investment; reduce waiting list in government hospitals | revenue; increased credibility by public sector affiliation | exist; bureaucratic framework is not flexible | including costing and pricing | negotiating contracts | quality of care from private sector | system being piloted |
|---|---|---|---|---|---|---|---|
| Lebanon | Utilize private infrastructure; avoid service duplications | Access to major insurers; utilize excess capacity | Adequate legal framework; lack political support to improve contracting | Experienced in contracting, but it is fragmented; does not limit cost of care | Major provider; over-supply of specialist services | Providers exceed demand; contracts not performance-based | Poor capacity to monitor; political factors affect monitoring |
| Morocco | Decentralization; improve access; overcome budget constraints for investment | Recognition of private sector; chance to partner public sector | Decentralization gave impetus to contracting; no clear policy on clinical services | Experienced in contracting | Limited experience in clinical contracting; technologically advanced | Ensuring quality of services | Monitoring indicators not well defined; information system not in place |
| Pakistan | Improve access; expand provision of sensitive services (HIV/AIDS) | Expand programs; recognition from community | Political support but bureaucracy unsure; legal framework adapted | No dedicated unit in ministry; limited experience in contracting | Wide range of private providers; varied capacity | Delayed payments; block payments | Limited information system; weak quality monitoring |
| Syria | Clinical services not contracted | Access to government funds | No political or bureaucratic support; only non-clinical services | Major service provider; expanding the infrastructure | Technologically advanced | Ensuring quality of services | Limited capacity of monitoring information system |
| Tunisia | Curtail cost of seeking treatment abroad | Only super-specialty services were contracted | Supportive political/legal framework | Extensive experience; contracts not given directly to private facilities | Technologically advanced | Reimbursement on flat rate; no co-payments | Medical inspection in place |

Source: abridged from Siddiqi et al. 2006.

efficiency and quality of services, optimization of hospital bed occupancy and better targeting of vulnerable populations. The non-state health sector was interested in contractual arrangements to assure of a regular source of revenue, to enhance recognition and credibility, to increase the volume of work and to utilize spare capacity.

All countries had some experience with contracting clinical services with the exception of Bahrain and the Syrian Arab Republic where only non-clinical services were contracted out. Except for the Syrian Arab Republic, all countries have policies that promoted contracting but Afghanistan's policy was the most explicit. Bureaucratic support depended on prior contracting experience. Jordan, Lebanon and Tunisia had extensive experience while experiences in Afghanistan, Egypt and Pakistan were more recent. Most ministries had limited capacity for cost and price analysis; transaction cost estimates were rarely done. Most countries had some type of competitive bidding process to award contracts although Pakistan did not have an independent contracting unit and lacked the institutional capacity to award contracts. Although bidding procedures were in place in Iran, local reputation and recommendations by experts were often the criteria for provider selection. In Egypt, Jordan, Lebanon, Morocco and Tunisia private providers had access to advanced medical technologies that made them attractive as contractees for secondary and tertiary care services.

With the exceptions of Egypt and Afghanistan, no performance indicators were included in the design of contracts. Because management information systems were inadequate to monitor the performance of private providers, performance was measured through third-party evaluations. Payment methods for most contractual arrangements were either fee-for-service or block grants. Delayed payments were a particular problem in Jordan and Pakistan. Some of the risks entailed by contracting out were differing interpretations of loosely worded contracts, limited numbers of providers in rural areas and parties with vested interests gaining control over the contracting process. There is also a lack of commitment among governments to contract once donor funds dried up.

In Egypt, the Family Health Fund (FHF) is the main contracting agency, which splits financing from service provision. FHF ensures competition among providers and is considered as a forerunner of the National Health Insurance Fund. The FHF is also piloting the purchase of a package of primary care services for registered families through contracts with accredited private providers and NGOs as well as internal contracts with the reformed public sector facilities. It has identified a set of 30 coverage, utilization and quality indicators for monitoring performance.

In Pakistan, contracting out 163 primary health care facilities in Rahim Yar Khan district showed that utilization, physical condition of facilities and patient satisfaction had improved and out-of-pocket expenditure had decreased. However, the quality of care, drug availability and accessibility to remote communities did not improve and there was little effect on the coverage of preventive health services. In Iran, contracting seemed to have improved access and quality and decreased the cost of services. In Afghanistan, in regions where peace has been restored, four-fifths of health facilities are operated by NGOs. As the core of national health policy, the ministry contracted out a basic package of health services at an average cost of US$4.50 per capita.

Jordan, Lebanon and Tunisia have had extended experience with contracting out hospital services in secondary and tertiary health care. In all three countries, payments are based on fee-for-service with no co-payment system. Limitations are fragmentation of the contracting process between different agencies, the limited leverage of public over private sector, the inability to contain escalating health care costs and lack of public sector capacity to monitor performance. Jordan's ministry of health has partnered with private sector hospitals to secure obstetric and renal dialysis services for government-sponsored patients including civil service employees. A survey of 30 acute care private hospitals in Amman found that 96 percent had treated ministry-sponsored patients during the past year (Banks and Shahrouri 2003). Most hospitals, however, expressed dissatisfaction with the government as a client, including problems of delayed reimbursement, disputes over diagnosis, and overall distrust between the private sector and the ministry of health. While private hospitals are willing to undertake public-private partnerships, they do not agree to contract provisions such as clinical practice guidelines and a computerized link with the ministry to monitor contract performance.

In Bahrain, Morocco and the Syrian Arab Republic, the health ministries con-tract out services for the maintenance of medical equipment and hospital build-ing as well as support services such as cleaning, catering, gardening and security. Contracts are awarded through competitive bidding. Payments are made on a quarterly or annual basis with monitoring mechanisms varying among countries. A third party in Bahrain – a Tender Board in the Ministry of Finance – ensures transparency in the selection process.

The authors conclude that contracting is complex and cannot be a solution for all problems of the health care system. Not everything can or should be con-tracted out. The legal and administrative framework for contracting health ser-vices needs updating in most countries in the region. Many health ministries lack a dedicated unit for contracting and there is limited capacity in the public sector to design, negotiate and award contracts, undertake cost, price and volume analysis, optimize payment methods and effectively monitor contract performance. The purchaser–provider relationship is an important determinant of the success of the contracting process. Whether providers find purchasers intimidating because they have greater negotiating power or authority or whether there are other reasons remains to be explored. It is equally important to compare the transaction costs of contracting out with the explicit and hidden costs of directly managed public systems that incur large costs in monitoring staff and output quality.

## Africa

It is a myth that the private sector in health is not well developed in African countries. Data from 26 sub-Saharan countries indicate that the poor use the private sector extensively; on average more than two-fifths of health expenditures are paid out-of-pocket (Osewe 2006). The main source of health financing is private payment (Guinea 91 percent; Mauritania 74 percent; Burkina Faso 54 percent). The private sector delivers 49 percent of health services in Kenya, 55 percent in Cameroon, 65 percent in Ghana, 69 percent in Mali, 59 percent in Niger and 68 percent in Uganda. For economic reasons the rural poor are unlikely to seek care outside the home but, when they do, they use the informal private sector in the form of traditional healers and shops. In Ghana and Niger, the poor primarily go to private pharmacies; in Burkina, Guinea and Mozambique they mainly use traditional healers. Between 1992 and 2000 the use of the public sector in Malawi declined by half whereas the private sector grew considerably. Three-quarters of Malawians now seek health care from the private sector. In sum, the private sector in sub-Saharan Africa plays a significant role in health care delivery for both the rich and the poor.

As in other developing regions, the private sector in Africa is diverse and consists of a wide range of institutions, organizations and individuals. The formal not-for-profit sector is predominantly comprised of religious trust hospitals. It is estimated that NGOs provide most of the rural health care and depend on grants and subsidies from the government. The informal for-profit private sector in Africa is dominated by traditional healers on whom it is estimated up to four-fifths of Africans rely partly or solely (WHO 2002a). These providers are often more accessible because they live in the community, have credibility and use centuries old traditional remedies. Traditional birth attendants also play a major role in health care delivery, especially in areas where women do not have access to antenatal care services or, if they do, still prefer delivery at home. Community workers are informal not-for-profit providers who are successful as health educators and promoters.

The quality of care is better in the private sector in some places and in the public sector at other places. In South Africa, for example, sexually transmitted infections were more often properly diagnosed in the private sector compared to the public sector. In Senegal, under a national anti-malaria program, drugs from the private sector failed more often than those from the public sector (Marek *et al.* 2005). Overall, there is no conclusive and significant variation between the public sector and the private sector in terms of cost of care in Africa, but there are incidences of overcharging and 'under the table' payments in both sectors.

The private sector has been absorbing a large proportion of the public sector's human resources. In Ghana migration of medical and paramedical staff from the public to the private sector has been high. Senegal attempted to solve the problem by contracting private medical institutions to train additional staff for improving the supply of human resources. Also nurses are contracted for two years to augment the supply of public sector staff. Such contractual staff are posted in remote areas but receive better pay than their civil service counterparts (twice as much for medical doctors and thrice as much for nurses). Similar attempts have been made in Kenya, Tanzania and Mali. Beyond the formal sector, training of traditional healers has also been tried. Health providers in

Africa face a range of challenges: poor infrastructure, limited access to supplies and equipment, and loans at high interest rates, all of which escalate the cost of care.

The growth of the formal private sector in many Africans nations has been stimulated by the structural reform programs of the World Bank and the IMF. Their terms restricted the flow of resources in the public sector, which led to rapid expansion of the private for-profit sector. Significant proportions of public health staff have either joined the private sector or established their own facilities. Rapid growth in the private sector is occurring throughout Africa so policy-makers are beginning to explore different options of working with private providers. Policy-makers confronted two possible strategies: harness the capacity and potential of the private sector, or shift publicly provided services into private control to improve delivery of services. The latter has been extensively used in rural South Africa to expand health coverage and improve the efficiency and quality of health services (Osewe 2006).

Policy-makers in sub-Saharan Africa are considering a number of strategies such as regulation, contracting, social franchising, training of private providers, provision of information to patients, and vouchers. With the exception of South Africa, regulation is poor in African countries due to weak institutional capacity and lack of self-regulation. Contracting has sometimes been used, as in Zimbabwe where over half of rural health care is provided through church-related hospitals under contract with the Ministry of Health. The government procures medicines and provides staff salaries and equipment. Social franchising has been used in disease-control programs like STI in Cameroon, HIV testing and counseling in Zambia, and family planning in Ethiopia. In some African countries, training was provided to private providers for improving the quality of services; in Kenya shopkeepers were trained in dispensing proper drugs to treat childhood fevers while in Tanzania doctors, nurses and pharmacists were trained to provide anti-retroviral therapy. The provision of information to patients has been used in Ghana to educate the community about services for orphans and vulnerable children. And Tanzania has used vouchers for subsidized insecticide-treated bednets to protect pregnant women and children under five against malaria (Osewe 2006).

Collaboration with the private sector in Africa occurs in public financing of the private sector through health insurance and vouchers and in partnership for service delivery through leasing, contracting, concessions and franchising. Experiences of these dimensions are described below.

Health insurance is rare in the region except in South Africa and, since 2003, Ghana. Community based financing arrangements devoted to health services – called 'mutuelles' in West Africa – originated from simple drug-revolving funds that had been set up by civil servants who were not satisfied with coverage provided by the state. In Senegal, Guinea and Burkina Faso their number multiplied seven-fold in six years from 76 in 1997 to 547 in 2003.

Vouchers are mechanisms for subsidizing the provision of particular services to targeted groups through the use of a token that can be redeemed to purchase all or part of a good or service. The objective is to select specific health interventions that are cost-effective, directly target vulnerable groups, simplify administration (reducing the possibility of irregularities and false claims) and reduce provider-induced demand. Voucher programs can be competitive or non-competitive. In a competitive program, the providers of health services seek to obtain the business of the voucher-holder and thus create a market in which the voucher-holder can choose the provider. In a non-competitive scheme, a designated service provider is charged with delivering services.

A typical competitive voucher follows a sequence of events. Funds are transferred to a voucher agency that then produces and distributes vouchers to a target population (either by itself or through a third-party organization). The recipient of a voucher presents it at the service provider of his or her choice in exchange for specified goods or services. The service provider returns the voucher to the voucher agency along with any required information, which then pays the provider an agreed-upon sum for each voucher redeemed. The voucher agency reports program outputs and outcomes to the government or donor providing the subsidies (World Bank 2005).

Several lessons are evident about voucher schemes in Africa (Mushi *et al.* 2003; Erulkar 2003; Skibiak *et al.* 2001). A substantial amount of time – often years – is needed for people to understand and use a voucher program so multiple communication channels are essential. Careful monitoring is required, especially at the beginning of the program. Targeted beneficiary groups that are easy to identify and reach – such as pregnant women – contribute to the success of the program. Rather than subsidizing the provision of a good or service through public facilities, a voucher program strengthens commercial providers while serving public health goals. In the initial stages, the poorest are unable to take advantage of vouchers and participate only later in the life of a program. Minimizing the misuse of vouchers is more difficult in larger, nationwide programs than in carefully controlled programs limited to a few districts. The use of third parties to distribute vouchers – particularly social organizations – may strengthen outreach. For services of a sensitive nature such as sexual and reproductive health services, the point of contact – both in distributing the voucher and obtaining services – may be critical for ensuring comfort and confidentiality and thus acceptance of a voucher program. Better results can be obtained if the distributor of the voucher and the provider of services are the same. And training of providers ensures quality of services.

Competitive voucher programs in Africa are evident in three examples: purchasing insecticide-treated nets in Tanzania, delivering emergency contraception in Zambia, and providing reproductive health services to young people in Kenya. Each project is briefly described.

Tanzania employed a competitive voucher scheme to subsidize insecticide-treated bed-nets in two southern districts. Targeted at pregnant women and women with children below five years of age, vouchers were distributed through public and private maternal health clinics when the women and children came for treatment. Each voucher worth 500 Tanzanian shillings could be used as part-payment for the purchase of a treated net (total cost of 3,000 shillings). The nets were also available through a network of public and private providers, shopkeepers, health workers and village leaders. These agents were given a credit of 500 shillings plus a 50-shilling handling-charge for each voucher when they purchased the nets. The project was effective and voucher return-rates were very high although there was indirect evidence of misuse. Evaluation of the project revealed that a substantial amount of time – several years – was required for people to understand and participate in the program. The voucher program did, however, increase coverage of treated nets and served as a promotional tool to increase awareness of their health benefit (Mushi *et al.* 2003).

The voucher program in Zambia was undertaken as part of a study in Lusaka and its suburbs to experiment with the most effective channel for delivering 'youth-friendly' contraceptive services. Four different types of health workers – peer counselors at public health clinics, clinic-based outpatient health care providers, private pharmacists and community-based sales agents – were trained to provide information on emergency contraception pills (ECPs) and distribute vouchers for them. Potential users were given information and a voucher that could be redeemed for a pack of ECPs, either by the same health worker or by any of the project's participating providers. Once a card was redeemed for a pack of pills, the supplier noted the age of the beneficiary on the back of the card. The number of vouchers given to each category of health workers was recorded to keep track of the number of contacts made. Providers were supplied with stocks of ECPs. At the public clinics vouchers could be redeemed for ECPs free of charge while private pharmacies were permitted to charge 13 US-cents (the normal price was US$3.75). Pharmacists emerged as the most frequently used provider of ECPs but peer counselors were popular among younger clients (Skibiak *et al.* 2001).

In Kenya a three-year community-based project was targeted on young people living in Nyeri, capital of the Central Province that is the homeland of the Kikuyu, Kenya's largest ethnic group. The project's objectives were to delay the onset of sexual activities among unmarried youth not yet sexually active and to create a reproductive health information and service environment that would be responsive to the needs of young people. The project had two components: information and referral, and service provision. Adult educators were used in the information component. Young parents from the community served as 'Friends of Youth' (FOY) and were paid an honorarium for their services. They were trained and assigned an area of operation. By the end of a pilot period (1998–2000), about one-third of young people in the project area had had direct contact with a FOY.

In the service component, a network of private and public service providers were used to reach young people. Twelve service outlets participated in the project (seven private clinics, two public facilities, a lab, one chemist and one counselor). FOYs issued vouchers and a list of service providers to young people. In turn, service providers used the voucher to refer young people to labs for tests, if needed. The voucher entitled the young person to services at a subsidized cost. The young person paid 50 Kenyan shillings (US$0.60), the providers waived their consultation fee, and the Family Planning Association of Kenya paid for additional costs including lab tests and drugs for treating sexually transmitted infections. If a young person could not pay the fee, it was waived. The cost of subsidizing the services was approximately $7 per contact. During the three-year project, 2,800 young people were referred and received services through this system – about half of whom received treatment for sexually transmitted infections (Erulkar 2003).

Contracting is widely used in Africa to deliver primary care services, training, ancillary services and nutrition interventions. In most countries, governments contract with both for-profit and not-for-profit providers – the latter including community-based organizations and religious organizations. In nutritional support programs in Senegal and Madagascar, community-based NGOs and local contractors were more effective (Marek *et al.* 2005). In almost all cases, the reasons for governments to contract are based on the need to reach underserved areas or to provide services for which the government had limited capacity rather than an explicit policy to encourage private sector provision.

Contracts are predominantly either fee-for-service or lump-sum payment mechanisms. Quality, performance and sanctions against non-performance are often poorly defined. Competitive bidding has been used more often among non-governmental organizations than among for-profit providers. The contracts with the latter tend to be negotiated non-competitive agreements. Given the lack of competition within the private sector in most sub-Saharan countries, the policy goals of efficiency and cost-reduction are jeopardized. Governments lack the capacity to negotiate and enforce contracts. Consequently the government has an unfavorable risk-sharing position with respect to the contractor; there is little monitoring of contractors or enforcement of sanctions. Because incentives to contractors are weak, there are very few efficiency gains from contracting. In Zimbabwe, for example, a long-term contract between a private hospital and the government leads to enormous cost burden due to the government's lack of capacity to screen patients or monitor the contract. In some cases, like a community nutrition project in Senegal, NGOs are undertaking part (or all) of the job of administering contracts, thus relieving the government of a role for which it is often not well equipped. Congo and Burkina Faso also use delegated contract management, which encourages small local institutions to participate in health initiatives.

Governments often lack sufficient information about the private sector or the cost of services, thus weakening their bargaining position and reducing any efficiency gains from contracting. In a contract between the South African government and a for-profit hospital company, for example, the efficiency gains were more beneficial for the private agency in the form of higher profits (Loevinsohn and Harding 2004). Burkina Faso, Senegal, Uganda and South Africa have created partnership units in their ministries of health to serve as an interface with the private sector and to become specialized in dealing with the private sector. A major challenge for public-private partnerships is related to ensuring the legal rights and responsibilities of every stakeholder. Ghana and Senegal have created legal and regulatory framework policies for contracts, yet payment for the services to the private providers is often long delayed by government bureaucracy.

Contracting in Africa has had a mixed record as indicated by the following cases. The Ministry of Health of the Government of Zimbabwe had a long-term contract with Wankie Colliery, a 400-bed hospital, to provide services to patients who otherwise would have gone to a public hospital as free patients. The hospital contract was based on fee-for-service. A government official stationed in the hospital certified the eligibility of the patient and the hospital sent the bill for treatment to the ministry. Signed in the 1950s without any competitive tendering, the original contract was prompted by the absence of government hospitals in the region. The contract does not specify rates or any formal monitoring of quality of services or operations. Due to the lack of competition as well as the government's inability to offer services, the monopoly position of Colliery in the district was entrenched. Failure of the government to screen patients for their ability to pay or to ascertain their need for hospital services led to excessive provision. The contract led to high costs, a result of overuse by those who should have paid for the services. The contract was eventually terminated due to disagreements over revisions (McPake and Hongoro 1995; Mills 1997).

Provincial governments in South Africa's Eastern and Western Cape have had long-standing contracts with private general practitioners (as part-time district surgeons) to provide medical services in defined rural areas. Private physicians are paid a basic fee to provide a list of specific medical services but the contracts do not specify standards for quality or other terms of engagement. While sanctions for negligence, breach of conditions, or misconduct are included in the contract, no examples of such behavior are specified. There is very little monitoring or supervision. Inter-personal relations govern the interactions between purchaser and provider. Governments depend on the practitioners for service, and providers depend on the contract for their income. Only factors like the desire to maintain one's reputation, personal obligations and commitment to the community determine the quality of service. Because contracts are more relational than classical, the practitioners decide for themselves about how to deliver services with professional and ethical standards being the key motivation (Palmer and Mills 2003; Palmer 2003).

Leasing is a potential form of partnership but it is relatively rare in the health sector in Africa. Equipment leasing, which transfers usage rights to an operator in the delivery of services, is not often used although in Guinea in 2004 a CD4 counter bought by the government had been leased to a private laboratory that ensured its maintenance and tested HIV-positive patients. In South Africa several public hospitals have leased surplus bed space to the private sector.

Concessions are another form of partnership with the private sector that require management of public assets for a defined period or new construction. Concessions are common in South Africa where an advanced hospital concessions system has been developed. The Inkosi Albert Luthuli Hospital in Kwazulu-Natal, for example, was designed to provide the region with state-of-the-art tertiary care. A consortium, which included Siemens medical systems, provides advanced tertiary care services during a 15-year concession period. The government closed five old hospitals in Durban in order to concentrate its resources on this hospital. It is estimated that this concession would save government 370 million Rand during the partnership.

A similar model was used to refurbish Pelonomi hospital in Blomfontein. In 2004 the Free State Government and South Africa's leading private health care provider, Netcare, entered an agreement to update the entire hospital facility. In addition Netcare would take over one wing of the hospital to provide services through its own staff and equipment for privately paying patients. Netcare shares access, under strict contractual agreement, to some of its other facilities with the public medical staff – an arrangement that benefits all parties. The public facility employees have access to sophisticated equipment while patients have access to updated facilities. As co-location of a private wing within an existing public facility, the Pelonomi concession is recommended for other countries of the continent.

Franchising has been used in the African health sector during the past decade. A typical structure involves the franchiser setting performance criteria, training the franchisees, monitoring their performance, and marketing the brand name to target populations. Franchisees are accountable to the franchiser and pay dues or royalties. Examples of franchising include essential drug provision, family planning and HIV/AIDS treatment. Population Services International (PSI) operates a majority of franchises in Africa.

In 2000, with a grant from the Bill and Melinda Gates Foundation, Population Services International launched 'TOP Reseau', a franchise for reproductive health care in Madagascar. After extensive training to improve both technical and management capacity, the 17 clinics in the network – all in Tamatave city and surrounding rural areas – were invited to join the franchise. The clinics, which display a TOP Reseau logo, benefit from marketing and media promotion on television and radio, and from referrals from other components of the project coordinated by PSI. TOP Reseau builds its client base through the work of peer educators in schools, community events and other areas. In addition to reproductive and sexual health related services, the clinics offer family planning counseling, pregnancy testing and counseling, immunizations, breast exams and pap smears. The project faces high costs, especially the payments to peer educators (LaVake 2003)

In Kenya in 1996, an NGO 'KMET' began a reproductive health franchise in Kisumu province, a geographically hard-to-reach area. As franchiser, KMET trained private doctors, consultants, midwives and nurses in safe abortion practices and post-abortion care. The providers were given a free initial kit and regular delivery of contraceptive products for their clinics. Franchisees pay an annual membership fee which makes them eligible to participate in a revolving loan program. The services include family planning, STI management and home-based care for HIV/AIDS. Community-based workers were trained for outreach activities. KMET received financial support from Family Planning

International Assistance (FPIA) and family planning commodities from the government, which are passed on at no cost and placed in condom distribution boxes in bars and other locations frequented by at-risk populations. KMET has 125 franchisees, apart from its own clinic, and 200 members registered with the agency.

In 2000 Kenya's Sustainable Healthcare Enterprise Foundation (SHEF) launched a franchise of drug shops, all under the Child and Family Welfare (CFW) brand. Owned and run by community health workers who have undergone training, the shops sell 18 essential drugs and are permitted to charge user-fees. Non-CFW drugs are not allowed to be sold by a franchisee. In 2003 the network expanded to include clinics operated by nurses and new services such as HIV/AIDS counseling, home-based care and de-worming of children. By 2003, SHEF/CFW operated 40 franchised drug shops and 20 franchised clinics, over four-fifths of which operate in a self-sustaining manner (Montagu 2003).

Given the informal as well as formal private sector in Africa, governments have experimented with ways to taps its resources and to collaborate with it in the delivery of health services. Despite the array of models, however, public policies for partnership with the private sector face many challenges. There is little agreement on possible strategies about how to engage the private sector as well as conflicting objectives among stakeholders. Given the historical pattern of segmentation between the public and private sectors in almost all fields of endeavor as well as entrenched ideological positions, there is no foundation for collaboration with the private sector on an equal basis.

Likewise, with exceptions, there are few examples of successful partnerships on which to base decisions or to seek to replicate them. Matters are exacerbated by limited technical skills among government staff and the lack of ability to design, negotiate and monitor contracts. Indeed, public employees are often unwilling to support health sector reform for fear of losing their jobs; consequently more attention is paid to the content of reform or design than to implementation. As the private sector in Africa is poorly organized, governments find it difficult to deal with a plethora of players that lack a coherent entity. Forums for consultation are likewise limited so adequate information is not exchanged. The international penchant for vertical health programs also places a strain on health sector staff that are already overstretched. Consequently even existing national health programs are undermined. While these conclusions apply to other middle-income and low-income countries as well, they are particularly evident in sub-Saharan Africa.

## Asia

While various models of public-private partnerships are being implemented in Asian countries, one of the most prominent strategies to involve the private sector has been the control of tuberculosis through a public-private mix. During the past decade over 40 public-private mix projects have been undertaken in 15 countries to involve private practitioners in TB control in order to align their practices with national and international standards. Private sector practitioners involved in these projects range from private general practitioners and specialist chest physicians through not-for-profit non-governmental organizations and private hospitals to unqualified village doctors and informal private practitioners.

The genesis of the strategy of public-private mix in TB control programs is the fact that private practitioners are the first point of contact for any patient. However, these private practitioners are often non-qualified or semi-qualified practitioners – particularly in rural areas but in urban areas as well. In Bangladesh, which has a large private health sector, unregistered non-qualified 'gram dakteri' (village doctors) are by far the largest group of health care providers in the private sector. Comprised of semi-qualified or unqualified allopathic practitioners, practitioners of traditional or mixed systems of medicine and drug vendors, they provide most of the outpatient care in the country, especially for the rural poor.

A study of 15 initiatives across eight countries that involved both for-profit providers and not-for-profit NGOs as intermediaries found that 13 of them targeted individual self-employed for-profit private practitioners (Lönnroth *et al.* 2006). Table 5.2 provides a cross-country comparison of private provider involvement in TB control functions under collaborative agreements. In all cases except Vietnam, no cash incentives are made to the private provider, and the private partners operate under (free) drugs-for-performance contracts. In all initiatives, private providers were trained to follow standardized procedures for diagnosis, treatment and monitoring as per the respective national guidelines. The 'drugs-for-performance contracts' were largely informal or verbal in relation to for-profit providers although certificates and/or signposts stating that the provider had been 'accredited' by the government were used in some cases. None used formal competitive tenders. A contract could be ended either by the private provider exiting the agreement or by the government withholding further drug distribution. Eight of the initiatives involved intermediary not-for-profit organizations. All these not-for-profit organizations had a formal agreement with the government. In all but two initiatives, the treatment success rates were above 80 percent which is as good or better than the treatment success rate in public facilities and better than treatment success rates of around 50 percent reported in previous studies of TB treatment results in the private sector.

The relational contracts were not exhaustive and did not define penalties of breaches beyond the understanding that either party could withdraw from the collaboration if the performance of the counterpart was unsatisfactory. This arrangement implies that 'soft' relational contracts were indeed effective in most initiatives and sustained over several years, but the process of reaching an agreement on collaboration was extensive, sometimes stretching over a year or more. Mutual mistrust, lack of experience with public-private collaboration and lack of experience with public health work in the private sector are among the barriers to creating a viable working relationship between private and public stakeholders.

Table 5.2 Public-private mix for TB control in developing countries

| Location | Type of private provider | TB control services | | | | NGO intermediary |
| --- | --- | --- | --- | --- | --- | --- |
| | | Referral | Diagnosis | Treatment | Defaulter retrieval | |
| *India*: Hyderabad, Pune, Mumbai | Physicians and non-allopathic practitioners | Yes | No | Yes | Yes | Yes |
| *India*: Kannur and Delhi | Physicians and private labs | Yes | Yes | Yes | Yes | No (Kannur) Yes (Delhi) |
| *Bangladesh*: Damien Foundation | Non-allopathic practitioners | Yes | No | Yes | Yes | Yes |
| *Bangladesh*: Dhaka | Physicians and labs | Yes | Yes | Yes | Yes | No |
| *Myanmar*: Yangon (Shwepyitha), Yangon (SQH Franchise), Mandalay | Physicians | Yes | Yes | Yes | Yes | No |
| | Physicians and labs | Yes | Yes | Yes | Yes | Yes |
| *Nepal*: Kathmandu | Physicians and pharmacies | Yes | No | Yes | No | Yes |
| *Philippines*: Makati | Hospital | No | Yes | Yes | Yes | No |
| *Vietnam*: Ho Chi Minh City | Physicians and pharmacies | Yes | Yes | Yes | No | No |
| *Indonesia*: Yogyakarta | Hospitals | No | Yes | Yes | No | No |
| *Kenya*: Nairobi | Physicians | Yes | Yes | Yes | No | Yes |

Source: modified from Lönnroth *et al.* 2006.

'Relational' collaboration requires dialogue, openness to change and stepwise development of collaborative terms whereas preparing formal contractual terms on paper seems less important. Strong commitment for supervision and monitoring was an important success factor in several initiatives at it requires the contracting public agency to have sufficient management and supervision capacity to monitor private providers. Many initiatives were small-to-medium-sized and run by dedicated individuals. In such situations the need for formal contracts is limited, but contracts become much more important when applying models nationwide.

The Government of India has developed guidelines for private sector involvement in the control of tuberculosis, including a set of standard schemes for different roles in TB care with well defined criteria for participation as well as clearly defined financial conditions. However, despite a clearly articulated policy, private providers in India prefer informal agreements. The pros and cons of formalized schemes versus informal agreements are not known, but the upscalability of drug-for-performance contracts, without monetary incentives, is possible. Two NGOs in Bangladesh (Damien Foundation and Bangladesh Rural Advancement Committee) in collaboration with the National TB program of Bangladesh enlisted non-professional care providers in the implementation of a DOTS strategy and covered more than 100 million people (Salim *et al.* 2006). Public-private mix models could apply to other interventions such as antiretroviral therapy, diagnosis and treatment of sexually transmitted diseases and prevention of malaria.

In Pakistan's North West Frontier Province, the government-run district headquarters hospital in Mansehra and the private Frontier Medical College (FMC) in Abbottabad forged a partnership to create a teaching hospital. The private medical college, which charges its students relatively high tuition, offered a capitation fee to the district hospital. The hospital in turn invested the money to raise its facilities to the level needed by a teaching hospital. This arrangement also improved the quality of education for the students. Despite initial opposition to the idea from local residents who feared that privatization of the local hospital would increase fees they were won over when they saw the quality of health care rise without an accompanying increase in patient costs.

The factors critical in this partnership project were exceptionally detailed and thorough contracting arrangements such as clear statements of ownership of assets, agreements about services for poor patients, continued civil service status of employees plus a bonus for them under the partnership (an incentive to support the arrangement), a commitment that the government would not reduce its salary payments despite the capitation fees received by the hospital, and the development of a hospital fund to ensure that capitation fees were used for hospital development. In addition there was strong leadership by a widely respected and well-connected local doctor. The hospital also had autonomous status with a hospital board, characteristics not usual in public hospitals (ADBI 2000: 6).

The city government of Yogyakarta, Indonesia, sought bids on private health insurance to cover health services for the poor. Takaful Muhammadiyah – a religious non-profit organization with many years of experience in health care management and provision – was invited to manage the health budget of the city and transfer funds to city health centers on a capitation basis. Incentives were incorporated into the arrangement to encourage well-performing partners. Although concern has been expressed about the cost of care, this partnership produced measurably better outcomes such as improved health status of the poor, improved ability of city health centers to provide services, and greater patient satisfaction.

In Mongolia, under the health systems development program, the ministry of health planned and organized family group practices in Ulaanbaatar. The objectives were to provide primary care, contain costs and reduce hospital expenditures by addressing most primary care needs at the local level rather than at hospital level. The program also reduced the number of health personnel in public service because the family practitioners, who had previously been civil servants on salary, became independent providers in the private sector. Group practices are entities that work under contract with the local government and that are financed through capitation payments with performance allowances. The family group practitioner model is new in Mongolia but, like GPs in Europe, trained family doctors are physicians oriented toward preventive medicine and public health. The family doctors are supposedly drawn from the community and provide services more cheaply than specialists. All patients must first visit a family doctor who decides whether the patient needs specialist services or hospitalization. Specialists then refer the patient back to the family doctor for follow-up. Through this system, the family doctor plays an important role in keeping hospital inpatient days as well as more expensive specialist services as low as possible. Local governments in Mongolia have started to contract out non-core hospital services like laundry, cleaning and catering (Jeugmans 2000).

The Korean health care system is dominated by the private sector in the provision of services through a mix of public and private financing. Private hospitals and clinics comprise over 90 percent of all medical institutions, account for nearly 90 percent of the beds and over 90 percent of specialist doctors in the country. Since four-fifths of Koreans live in urban areas, development of health institutions has been skewed towards the private sector. The government's role is primarily in disease prevention, health promotion, regulation of fee structure and negotiating benefits under national health insurance. National health insurance is compulsory for all employers with five or more employees, with co-payments from the employers and subsidies from the government. The largest proportion of health finance comes from social security followed by out-of-pocket payments. Subsidized health insurance is also available to the self-employed rural people. The government-financed medical aid program allows the poor to access health services in private sector (Jeong 2005).

## Latin America and the Caribbean

Latin America and the Caribbean have extensive experience of engaging the private sector in forms of collaboration to harness its resources and improve the delivery of services to remote geographical areas. Although contracting is the most common form of engaging the private sector, the type of contracting is not uniform across the region. As summarized in Tables 5.3 and 5.4, an analysis of 27 cases of contracting in 14 countries in the region identified five hybridized versions of contracts that are neither completely time-based payment nor outcome-based payment (Slack and Savedoff 2001).

In a Type I 'Partnership' arrangement, the government supports private providers or NGOs by monetary payments, training, infrastructure provision or other contributions. The provider bears most of the financial risk with a focus generally on access rather than efficiency. In Uruguay, for example, church-based NGOs supported by donor funding provide services for mentally retarded children while the government contributes drugs and medicines. As a result, payments are often in kind. For example, the NGO might add ten children to its existing patient population in return for government provision of drugs for 100 children. In such a case, the provider's risk is limited and the incentive for increased efficiency is weak.

In Type II Population-based Historical Contracts, based on the size of the population to be served, the provider is allocated a fixed amount of funds that is not adjusted to cost-overruns. The provider bears the risk of any deficits but also keeps any surplus.

Type III Per Capita Contracts for Insurers involve a fixed payment for each person affiliated with the insurer. Depending on the competition, payments tend to be variable. However, in both types II and III the provider bears the financial risk with a focus on efficiency. Providers may introduce co-payments or

*Table 5.3* Types of partnership contracts in Latin America and the Caribbean

| Type | Payment mechanism | Contract characteristics | Risk-taker | Focus for provider payment |
|------|-------------------|--------------------------|------------|----------------------------|
| I | 'Partnership' contracts | Purchaser donates/ contributes training, infrastructure or part of funds (not at full cost) | Provider | Accessibility Efficiency |
| II | Population-base/ historical contracts | Population-based historical resource allocation to provider | Provider | Efficiency |
| III | Purchaser–insurer contracts (per capita) | Resource allocation on per capita basis | Insurer | Efficiency |
| IV | Service-based with volume restriction | Resource allocation with volume rationing | Provider | Efficiency Accessibility |
| V | Service-based (no volume restriction) | Resource allocation with no volume restriction | Mainly purchaser | Accessibility |

Table 5.4 Models of partnership contracts in Latin America and the Caribbean

| Type of contract | Country | Initiated | Service | Purchaser | Provider |
|---|---|---|---|---|---|
| I Partnership | Brazil | 1987 | HIV/AIDS prevention and care | Ministry of Health (MOH) | Civil Society Organizations |
| | Bolivia | 1985 | Outpatient care | Municipal Government/USAID | PROSALUD-NGO |
| | Dominican Republic | 1999 | Reproductive health | MOH/Provincial Health authority | PROFAMILIA-NGO |
| | Haiti | 1996 | Women's health | MOH | MARCH-NGO |
| | El Salvador | 1996 | Rural health program administration | MOH | FUSAL-NGO |
| II Population-based | Guatemala | 1997 | Primary care administration | MOH | Provincial health providers |
| | Haiti | 1990 | Tuberculosis control | MOH | NGOs |
| | Costa Rica | 1998 | Primary care/outpatient care | Government (social security fund) | COOPESALUD (NGO) |
| III Per capita-insurer | Peru | 1994 | Management of health centers | MOH | CLAS (Local community) |
| | Argentina | 1971 | Primary and secondary care | National health insurance program | Private insurers |
| IV Service/restricted | Nicaragua | 1994 | Primary and secondary care | Social security administration | EMP (Private providers) |
| | Uruguay | 1960 | Primary and secondary care | Social security administration | Private insurers |
| | Columbia | 1990 | Reproductive health | MOH | PROFAMILIA-NGO |
| | Brazil | 1970 | Reproductive health services | Municipalities | BEMFAM-NGOs |
| | Columbia | 1998 | Primary and secondary services | Social security institute | Private providers |
| | Brazil | 1983 | Inpatient services | State/municipalities | Not-for-profit hospitals |
| Type V Service/ no restriction | Uruguay | 1980 | High-tech services | National health fund | Private providers |
| | El Salvador | 1990 | Ambulatory specialty care | Social Security Institute | Private physicians |
| | Nicaragua | 1994 | Specialized hospital care | Social Security Institute | Private hospitals |
| | Peru | 1991/1992 | Minor surgery/primary care | Social Security Institute | Private hospitals/clinics/doctors |
| | Chile | 1979 | Ambulatory and hospital care | Social Security Institute | Private |
| | Uruguay | 1970 | High-tech services | MOH | Private hospitals |

Source: Slack and Savedoff 2001.

user-charges to pass on the financial risk to the user or they may renegotiate with the government for additional resources. Under fixed payment systems, the provider may avoid risks by rationing the range of services, reduce the quality of services or enroll healthier patients. In Guatemala, there is population-based payment to Proveedora de Servicios de Salud based only on rough cost estimates of the basic package of services to be provided to each individual. However, the service package is not well defined. In Argentina, per capita contracts between the national health insurance program and provider groups indicate a chronic problem of under-service, improper incentives under the payment mechanism and almost complete absence of consumer choice. In Peru, the CLAS (local health administration committees that are non-profit, community-administered institutions) are financed through block grants from the Ministry of Health, which holds each CLAS accountable for reaching targets agreed upon in the local health plan. Such an arrangement avoids under-provision of services. In some cases, in order to reduce the financial risk, insurers or providers must enroll a sufficiently large population, which could be a problem in smaller countries. In Nicaragua, public or private medical care insurers are paid a per capita amount by the Social Security Institute in Nicaragua but these are not chosen on a competitive basis.

Type IV providers (Service-based Contracts with Volume Restrictions) are paid a fee per service, but the number of services to be performed is restricted. Although the provider may not bear the risk of quantum of services, the rates per service – which are agreed in advance as prospective payment – may not cover the full cost. The provider therefore focuses on controlling costs below the preset fees, which limits the user's access to services. From the purchaser's point of view, this system is more advantageous than types II or V contracts. In Brazil, the municipalities and states pay private providers for hospital services based on agreed prices per diagnosis and on an authorized volume of services based on historical figures which are agreed between the individual providers and the municipality. Up to an agreed maximum, providers are reimbursed for each individual discharge form submitted. Such a mode of payment tends to reduce service levels. As a result, hospitals are reluctant to treat severely ill patients, discharge patients too early and reduce the use of necessary technologies. Administrative costs and problems have, in extreme cases, forced the government to abandon this payment mechanism. In 1998 in Colombia the then new government abolished the per capita payments for groups of doctors and introduced a system of prospective fee-for-service payments to individual doctors. Each doctor was given a limited account to provide services to a limited number of patients but the administrative burden was huge. The government quickly lost track of the number of services performed and rationing became difficult. Colombia witnessed another type of 'limited volume fee-for-service' where payment is partly service-based and partly population-based. Contracts with the Ministry of Health to provide reproductive health services based payment half on the expected volume of services and half on retrospective reimbursement. However, by artificially inducing demand, providers could increase their retrospective reimbursement.

Type V, 'Fee-for-service Contracts without Volume Restrictions', have two variants – one prospective, the other is retrospective (cost reimbursement). Both variants may increase access to services and promote flexible use of resources but they may lead to opportunistic behavior by the providers in terms of over-reporting the volume of services in order to increase revenue. Cost control then becomes a problem. Studies in Uruguay found that private high-tech providers, under contracts, reported 20 to 25 percent more costly services compared to public facilities. Chile's contract with private providers on a fee-for-service basis simply pays private hospitals well below cost – at the 1979 rate increased by little more than inflation. Consequently, hospitals charge patients high co-payments in order to make up the difference, which has led some patients to self-rationing. There are problems of equity and quality as well.

In Central and South American countries, the judicial system is said to be weak and unable to monitor the obligations under the contract or to enforce any penalty for deviance in a contract. Even on quality assurance, Latin American and Caribbean countries have weak systems of monitoring. In Chile, where a government agency contracts with private providers, accreditation occurs only once. There is no subsequent technical monitoring to assure that providers' quality standards are maintained, no tool for patient feedback, and providers are practically unregulated. In Nicaragua, contracts specifically list exclusions such as expensive and chronic services. But in Guatemala and Colombia, where the basic package of services has not been defined, the responsibilities for many preventive public health functions are not clear. Consequently, measures like vaccination and control of tuberculosis appear to have worsened. In Brazil service outputs are spelled out by focusing on volume, mix, quality and price whereas no easily measurable outputs are designated in contracts in Costa Rica (Slack and Savedoff 2001).

A review of contracting experiences in the New World found intricate contractual agreements (Abramson 1999; Abrantes 2003). In Latin America and the Caribbean, the public sector chooses to contract primary health services to NGOs in order to extend coverage, increase the availability of medicines and medical supplies, and improve the quality of care. A review of contracting in five countries found that the services contracted out were largely related to the delivery of reproductive health, outpatient primary care or health promotion (Abramson 1999, 2001). Selection of the NGOs ranged from direct invitation to public bids, and some were based on model projects that continued under contract. Only in Guatemala were the NGOs' credentials made explicit. Methods of budget allocation varied from global budgets calculated on the basis of geographical area and population to case-based reimbursement (half in advance on a monthly basis). One instance was a block grant. Three cases had explicit performance indicators but without a definitive geographical focus for the agencies providing services. The percentage of revenues contributed by the public sector ranged from 25 to 100 percent except in the Dominican Republic where revenue from the government was less than 1 percent.

In Colombia a legal framework of laws passed in 1993 supported public sector contracting to private agencies, despite resistance from opposition groups.

Resistance was predicated on the fear that contracting would threaten labor stability. This legal framework paved the way for radical reform in the Colombian public health system (Bitrán and Yip 1998). These laws provided for government restructuring (including decentralization) and redefined the role of the government as a purchaser of health care and its role in the oversight and regulation of care. As a result, a broad range of contracts between state agencies and providers – including NGOs – can be found in the Colombian health sector. Competition among providers, which include public agencies, private for-profit providers and NGOs, was expected to improve access to care as well as better management, more efficiency and higher quality of care. The government viewed contracting as a cost-efficient means to boost the coverage and quality of health services.

The Colombian NGOs and other private sector providers restructured and reorganized themselves, improved their physical and technological infrastructure, and implemented efficient financial and administrative systems to avail the new opportunities in health provision. The private agencies charged user-fees on a sliding scale based on patient income, the services provided, and the classification of patients under the social security system. Exemptions from user-fees have been made for many categories of patients. Decentralization of health service contracts in Colombia faced complexities in the form of maintaining uniform management information systems for contracts and in defining performance indicators for monitoring. With many agencies trying to implement the contracts at different levels of the government, discrepancies arose between facility records and central information systems. As a result, there were considerable delays in payments to providers.

Guatemala adopted contracting in order to expand access to and improve the quality of health services for rural and indigenous populations, many in remote areas. This arrangement was part of a peace agreement with indigenous rebels in order to end a decades-long civil war. Under the new agreement, government made commitments to reduce maternal and infant mortality by half, to eradicate polio and measles, and to allocate half of public health expenditures to disease prevention in these areas. Since the Guatemalan Ministry of Health does not have the physical infrastructure or human resources to provide care for uncovered populations, it turned to community-based NGOs in order to extend coverage to the poorest sectors of society and to provide a defined package of basic health services. Guatemala has a history of community-based NGOs providing social services to low-income indigenous communities. Interested in expanding access to their target populations, these NGOs reacted favorably to the government proposals to use NGOs to strengthen alliances between the health ministry and communities. The government pays an NGO via a global budget, a fixed amount paid prospectively and based on the population in the geographic area that the NGO serves. Payments are made quarterly. To handle the NGO contracts and monitor funds, a special cell was created within the Ministry of Health. The unfamiliarity of this new contracting method and the large number of contracts have made it difficult for the Ministry to make advance payments as stipulated by the contracts. Delay in payment has been a problem for many NGOs because they are small and lack strong financial bases. When there have been delays in payments, the organization has resorted to other funding sources such as bank credits to continue operations.

Health cooperatives play an important role in health care systems across Latin America and the Caribbean with varying degrees of success. Cuba, Brazil and Costa Rica have experimented with cooperatives to deliver health care services. In 1988 Costa Rica introduced the first health care cooperative. Founded by the employees of primary health care units, each health cooperative is an autonomous legal entity that assumes responsibility for management of a facility for a specified period under a lease from the Costa Rican Social Security Institute (CCSS). All equipment and infrastructure are transferred to the cooperative. Cooperatives purchase inputs such as drugs and medical supplies from CCSS or directly from the market. They receive a yearly capitation fee (no user-fee allowed) based on the estimated number of members in the geographical area. However, they are allowed to charge non-insured individuals who seek care. An administrative council awards and manages the contracts. All workers in the cooperatives are legal shareholders as well as partners who periodically receive earnings generated by the cooperative but part of their salary is regularly deducted to augment capital. The cooperatives operate under private law and enjoy income-tax exemptions but are obliged to present annual financial statements to the CCSS. They are also expected to evaluate their own performance (Gauri *et al.* 2004).

Latin American health sector reforms and new governance structures like decentralization have led to greater autonomy for health authorities to engage the private sector – especially the not-for-profit sector – in the delivery of health services. Community-level NGOs found new opportunities to influence the local government, which had not been possible (or attempted) at the national level. For example, after the passage of the 1994 Popular Participation Law in Bolivia, many municipalities obtained ownership of health facilities. A National Mother and Child Insurance scheme enrolled both public and private providers in the delivery of maternal and child health services. PROCOSI – a network of NGOs based in La Paz – worked closely with the government in designing the policy. PROCOSI also helped auxiliary nurses and other paraprofessionals to expand their role to deliver services previously carried out only by physicians. PROS-ALUD – the largest NGO in Bolivia – is another significant not-for-profit player in the health care market. It has helped the government to conserve resources as well as expand the access and coverage of priority health services to under-served populations.

In the Dominican Republic, INSALUD – an umbrella network of 62 NGOs – is not only involved in policy-making processes but also facilitates NGO access to government resources at local level. It develops and implements norms and standards to be followed by health sector NGOs as well as advocates transfer of public funds to NGOs. INSALUD has helped government officials to overcome their historical lack of understanding of NGOs participation in the health sector.

In Ecuador duplication of services in both public and private sectors is a serious problem, even though a large proportion of the population lacks health service coverage. Another umbrella organization for NGOs – APOLO – is entrusted with improving primary health care by developing models that deliver high quality services and that are equitable, sustainable and replicable at local and provincial levels (Putney 2000).

## Comparisons across countries

Public-private partnerships in general, and contracting in particular, have been primarily driven by health sector reform ideologies influenced by multilateral and bilateral agencies such as the World Bank and other donor agencies (Mills 1998). Although contracting in health services originated in OECD countries in the early 1990s, it spread to developing countries by the mid-1990s. In recent years contracting with the private sector has become commonplace around the world. Many publications provide lists and summaries of such experiences (Waters *et al.* 2002; Rosen 2000). The services provided under the contract system range from primary care through reproductive health to HIV/AIDS.

A review of contracting experiences in ten low-income countries concluded that contracting with NGOs to deliver primary health or nutrition services seems to be effective (Loevinsohn and Harding 2005). Contracting yielded positive results in achieving the health service delivery goals, and contractors were more effective than government agencies in terms of both quality of care and coverage of services. As Bangladesh's experience with rural community nutrition indicates, contracting can provide large-scale services, yet can also be more cost effective than directly provided government services. Non-governmental entities did better even when they had the same or fewer resources than public institutions. Furthermore contracting can increase coverage, even in poor remote areas. When contracts explicitly included targets for reaching the poor, contractors were able to improve health services for the most marginalized groups. While contract management is often difficult for governments, it does not seem to prevent improvements in service delivery.

Another review of contracting identified its effects based on empirical evidence (Liu *et al.* 2004). Most evaluation studies focus on access rather than measuring the impact of contracts on other critical issues such as equity, quality and efficiency. While studies suggest that contracts deliver services at a lower cost than public providers, it is not been possible to demonstrate whether contracting increases efficiency. Table 5.5 summarizes the data around the world.

Evidence indicates that contracting out primary health care services increases access, utilization level and coverage. Indicators of access include quantum of services, population covered and the availability of services. Contracting is more effective in improving access to health care services in comparison to government provision of services. Overall, the literature supports the premise that contracting improves accessibility to health care (Loevinsohn and Harding 2004).

*Table 5.5* International experience with contracting

| Country/reviewed by | Provider (contractee) | Objective/services contracted |
|---|---|---|
| *Bangladesh/* Mahmud *et al.* 2002 | NGO | • Improve access to primary care for the poor from urban slums |
| Loevinsohn 2002 | | • Primary care services – immunization, obstetric care, family planning, IEC, treatment for diseases |
| *Bangladesh/* Chowdhury 2002 | Private rural health workers | • Improve knowledge, skills on ORT/ reduce diarrhea deaths • Education of mothers; skills training on preparation of oral rehydration solution |
| *Bangladesh/* Karim *et al.* 2003 Loevinsohn 2002 | Female community workers | • Improve nutritional status of children and women. • Growth monitoring; nutritional support to pregnant and lactating mothers/ children |
| *Bolivia/* Lavadenz *et al.* 2001 | NGO | • Expand access to birth delivery/improve quality of care • Primary care with focus on maternal and child health |
| *Brazil/* Connor 2000 | NGO | • Improve access and quality of prevention and treatment of HIV/AIDS |
| Barnett *et al.* 2001 | | • Strengthen health institutions for AIDS control |
| *Cambodia/* Loevinsohn 2001 | NGO | • Improve access to and quality of basic health care • Basic health services (immunization, family planning, ante-natal care, provision of micronutrients, care for diarrhea, acute respiratory tract infection and tuberculosis) |
| *Costa Rica/* Abramson 2001 | NGO | • Increase access; improve quality; increase efficiency • Primary health care services |
| *Georgia/* England 2004 | NGO | • Provide cardiac surgery to children from poor families • Cardiac surgery for congenital abnormalities up to 13 years age |
| *Guatemala/* Nieves and La Forgia 2000 | NGO | • Improve access to basic health services by the poor • Basic health care services |

*Table 5.5* continued

| Country/reviewed by | Provider (contractee) | Objective/services contracted |
|---|---|---|
| *Guatemala/*<br>Barnett *et al.* 2001<br>Barnett and Putney 2000 | NGO | • Improve access and improve quality of prevention and treatment to HIV/AIDS<br>• HIV/AIDS prevention and treatment |
| *Haiti/*<br>Eichler *et al.* 2002 | NGO | • Strengthen the capacity of the NGO providers and improve performance of NGOs in providing maternal and child health<br>• Maternal and child health services; family planning services |
| *India/*<br>Murthy *et al.* 2001 | NGO/GPs/ hospitals | • Improve quality of DOTS strategy in detecting/treating TB<br>• Implementation of DOTS strategy |
| *India/*<br>Loevinsohn and Harding 2004 | NGO | • Improve quality of care for child health<br>• Treatment of childhood illness according to WHO guidelines |
| *Madagascar/*<br>Marek *et al.* 1999 | NGO | • Improve access to nutritional services<br>• Growth monitoring for children and education for women |
| *Romania/*<br>Vladescu and Radulescu 2002 | Individual GP health providers | • Improve efficiency on preventive services, access to primary care and patient satisfaction<br>• Provision of preventive and curative primary health care |
| *Senegal/*<br>Marek *et al.* 1999 | NGO | • Improve access to nutritional services; decrease malnutrition<br>• Growth monitoring for children and education for women<br>• Referral to health services for severely malnourished |
| *South Africa/*<br>Mills *et al.* 1997 | For-profit hospitals | • Improve quality and reduce cost<br>• Provision of hospital services |
| *Zimbabwe/*<br>Mills *et al.* 1997 | NGO/hospitals | • Improve quality and reduce cost<br>• Provision of hospital services |

Source: modified from Liu *et al.* 2004.

Studies that link contracting with equity are limited, but available studies show significant improvement in access by the targeted beneficiaries (i.e. poor), indicating an improvement in equity. In Georgia, the state social health insurance program that contracted an NGO hospital to provide cardiac surgeries for children aged 3–14 from poor families with no co-payment (costs were covered by social insurance) showed a significant increase in utilization of the services by the poor (Gotsadze and Levan 2003). In Cambodia a contracting-out project explicitly addressed the issue of equity by including 'reaching the poor' as its objective (England 2004; Loevinsohn 2001). This project demonstrated that contractors are better able than the government to reduce inequities in accessing the services (Loevinsohn and Harding 2004). Contracting out also reduced out-of-pocket payments by over 70 percent and effectively targeted the poor in Madagascar, Senegal and Bangladesh (Marek *et al.* 1999; Mahmud *et al.* 2002; Loevinsohn 2002).

In Brazil (Connor 2000; Barnett *et al.* 2001), Guatemala (Barnett and Putney 2000), Costa Rica (Abramson 2001) and Bolivia (Lavadenz *et al.* 2001), the projects had explicitly stated quality improvement objectives but lacked well-developed quality indicators, thus making it difficult to gauge whether substantive improvements in quality occurred. The same argument applies to Romania's primary health care project (Vladescu and Radulescu 2002), Bangladesh's urban primary health care services (Mahmud *et al.* 2002; Loevinsohn 2002), Haiti's maternal and child health and family planning (Eichler *et al.* 2002) and India's TB control through DOTS programs (Loevinsohn and Harding 2004), uni-dimensional process indicators such as patient satisfaction, patient waiting-time and percentage of disease treatment interventions (using standardized medical protocols) were used as proxy quality indicators. In Madagascar and Senegal's access to nutritional support project (Marek *et al.* 1999), Bangladesh's program for training mothers in oral rehydration therapy (Chowdhury 2002) and India's TB control project (Murthy *et al.* 2001), health outcomes were used as indicators of quality. Indicators for measuring health outcomes are also disease or condition specific. Cambodia's project for improving access to basic health services for the poor (Loevinsohn 2001) as well as South Africa and Zimbabwe's projects for hospital services (Mills *et al.* 1997) used multidimensional measures such as structure, process and outcomes to monitor and evaluate the quality of care.

A review of contracted projects in South Africa and Zimbabwe demonstrated that contracted providers deliver services more efficiently at lower unit costs than their public sector counterparts while still maintaining quality (Mills *et al.* 1997). In Pakistan, Bangladesh, India and Cambodia, non-governmental entities performed better than public institutions with similar amounts of financial input (Loevinsohn and Harding 2004). But research in Ghana and Tanzania found no systematic differences in cost between contracted private providers and public hospitals, yet considerable difference in quantum of services and the quality of care from contracted agencies such as church hospitals compared to public hospitals (Gilson *et al.* 1997). Literature suggests that contracted services can sometimes be more expensive than direct provision. For example, the positive health outcomes of the Rural Nutrition Services Project in Bangladesh were achieved at a relatively high cost (Loevinsohn and Harding 2004). One of the major constraints in the analysis of cost efficiency is the non-inclusion of transactional costs (procurement and administrative costs) of the purchaser.

A number of factors are essential for the success of contracting in developing countries. Successful public sector reforms introduce a distinct separation of functions between payer and provider and include the transfer of public sector staff from the state budget to be contracted by providers. A system of accreditation and licensing must be established for providers who treat public and private providers equally and thus regulate market entry. Policies for public financing of service provision for the poor must be explicit. A competent purchaser organization must exist that is able to contract with providers, and likewise a national system to identify the poor that is based on simple criteria and avoids complex means-testing.

Services being contracted must be relatively well defined, and tendering based on clear technical criteria must be transparent. The services being contracted should be specified clearly and contracts should be based on outputs rather than inputs or processes including quantum of services and the quality to be achieved. Contracts should allow the provider to manage operations and not be overly specified in detail on how the provider allocates resources or how those inputs are procured. And payment mechanisms should be well thought out and preferably tested in advance for their incentive value to the provider.

Likewise, contracts should specify how and when payments are to be made and precisely how and when non-performance by the provider could instigate delays or non-payments. Management of the contractual relationship should be planned in advance and, where appropriate, specified in the contract by detailing which party is to be responsible for what activities. Indicators should measure the extent to which the poor access services, perhaps through household surveys rather than through beneficiary records; and regular monitoring meetings should be arranged between the purchaser and provider to understand implementation problems. Finally, bidding procedures should be explicit, documented and transparent to all stakeholders; and external third-party assistance should be involved in the evaluation of bids and the awarding of contracts.

While reviewing the conclusions of case studies and research studies, an important observation appears. If a government has the capacity to contract for clinical services, it is likely that it also has the capacity to deliver these services directly by itself. But government contracts obviously pay little attention to contract performance measures. It is possible to hypothesize that one reason why the public sector is currently unable to provide services effectively or efficiently is because it lacks an understanding about performance indicators. Otherwise, if those in charge can use contracts to obtain performance from private contractors, they might as well use their influence to get the required performance from their own workforce.

The World Bank (1997: 87) has been skeptical about the capacity of governments in developing countries to contract-out complex services such as health care: 'It takes considerable capability and commitment to write and enforce contracts, especially for difficult-to-specify outputs in the social services.' Based on the experience of contracting in Latin America, Abramson (1999) found that the public sector had not consciously developed a capacity to manage the new forms of governance such as public-private partnership or outsourcing. Under the garb of health sector reforms, health ministries in many countries are reorienting their functions from one of direct health care provision to one of financing, purchasing and regulating (Björkman 2005; Bossert *et al.* 1998). The public sector needs to develop internal structures and strengthen the management skills to undertake such changes in its functions. The public sector needs the capacity to choose indicators for designing, negotiating and monitoring the implementation of such contracts. Contracting for services delivery is not a solution to weak public sector management; rather it places new demands on government managers.

With their relatively informal organizational structures, non-profit private sector agencies not only do not possess well-developed financial and administrative systems but, even if they have some competence, they need to modify their own systems according to the public sector contract requirements. NGOs that enter into health service contracts with a government purchaser generally face a number of challenges in responding to the demands of the new client. Contracting often requires an NGO to professionalize its institutional management systems. This often requires an NGO to upgrade its information systems. The current organizational structure, operational systems and internal culture of NGOs differ markedly from those of the government. They use different accounting, financial and technical systems. NGOs need to modify or strengthen their institutional capabilities. They have to adjust (or create from scratch) reliable management information and record-keeping systems. NGOs must calculate the internal costs of services that it will provide under government contracts by breaking out fixed and variable costs such as depreciation of vehicles and equipment, staff incentives, inflationary factors, or the need to prorate administrative and other costs under their program operations.

Many NGOs are not accustomed to a donor imposing conditions upon them. In the worst case, an NGO's social mission may be compromised by its shift to a market-oriented financial structure (Dees 1998). This situation is likely to occur when an organization that has long depended on philanthropic contributions, international grants or charitable institutions for its funding enters into a formal contract with a government agency. Once the NGO has committed itself to the terms and conditions of such a contract, its funding will be conditioned on compliance with these terms. As long as the ultimate beneficiaries under a government service contract are the same population towards whom the NGO's social mission is geared, then notwithstanding changes in work style, the organization can sustain its mission while receiving government funding. NGOs also fear, however, the implicit control that the public sector may impose on them.

Notwithstanding these difficulties, the scope of contracting has more than doubled over the past decade. Far from limiting government involvement in health care, contracting may ensure that publicly financed health care remains relevant.

## Note

1 Representative percentages are Georgia (90), Cambodia (90), Myanmar (87), India (82), Nigeria (79), Sudan (79), Kenya (78), Pakistan (77), Cambodia (76), China (75), Cameroon (75), Vietnam (74), Indonesia (76), Nepal (71), Morocco (70), Thailand (67), Bangladesh (64), Uganda (62), Paraguay (62), Ethiopia (61), Peru (60).

# 6  Observations and policy lessons

While collaboration with the private sector is an important policy to deliver health services throughout the world, the rationale, objectives, processes and implications of this policy are contextual and varied. Poorly performing public health systems and a rapidly burgeoning private sector raise concerns about equity and access to health services for marginal sections of society in most low-income countries. Therefore governments have been exploring alternatives beyond directly delivering health services on their own. The compulsions of market forces and a growing realization that public and private sectors can potentially gain from one another have facilitated this policy shift.

Collaboration with the private sector is particularly critical in low-income countries where populations lack access to formal health care institutions and remain vulnerable to the economic impact of seeking services from the private sector. In countries with middle and high income, efficient use of resources in the health sector appears to be the primary trigger for exploring greater public-private collaboration. While partnerships hold great potential, they entail complex challenges at policy and operational levels. These issues relate to the taxonomy of the private sector, the operational meaning of partnership, the scope and objectives of partnerships, the role of stakeholders and the political, legal and institutional challenges at policy level as well as organizational and managerial concerns at the operational level. Based on experiences in India and elsewhere in the world, this chapter summarizes these issues and their policy lessons.

## The private sector

One challenge in public-private partnerships is to define the private sector and understand its structure and characteristics. While the public sector is relatively easy to comprehend, deciphering the private sector is more complex. The latter varies in size (individual practitioners to large hospitals), ownership (religious groups, charitable trusts, corporate sector, community-based organizations), motives (for-profit, not-for-profit, philanthropic), systems of medicine (allopathic, indigenous, faith-based), sources of funding (donations, grants, commercial borrowing), service level (primary to tertiary care), market segments (medical education, medical technology, curative service, long-term care), geographical area (tribal, rural, slum, urban), resources and technology deployed (number and quality of staff, equipment, physical standards), cost and regulatory control (unlicensed quacks to certified international standards). Private providers include diagnostic centers, ambulance operators, pathology labs, pharmacy shops, blood banks, commercial contractors and professional associations. There are also many unqualified informal providers. Despite these variations, the private sector is often classified into 'for-profit' and 'not-for-profit' groups, thus stimulating serious objections by community-based organizations. The public sector finds it difficult to collaborate with such a heterogeneous and disorganized private health sector since the former is accustomed to engaging only organizations with formal administrative systems.

Growth of the private sector has been extensive in some countries; in others it has been modest. In Asia growth has been concentrated in the hospital sector whereas in Africa retail drug outlets have multiplied. Understanding such trends helps to develop viable policies. For example, it may be easier to introduce change when private sector growth has been relatively weak. Some countries actively encourage the growth of the private sector by providing subsidies and incentives as state policy. Governments also seek to use this leverage in the delivery of health services to the poor, although with less than satisfactory results. Regulation of the private sector continues to be a major challenge, which is compounded by variation in the quality of governance. In the absence of effective regulation, the behaviour of the private sector and its consequences shape the policy of public-private collaboration. In India, perverse behaviour by the private sector and a lack of demonstrable control over it by the government have led to great suspicion about policies that promote public-private partnership.

All the above indicate a need for understanding private sector characteristics, behaviour, experience and perceptions before initiating any policy on public-private partnerships. Regions within developing countries also display asymmetries in the private sector. In India some states have a more extensive private sector than others. Informed decision-making requires a clear picture of what the private sector is currently doing. Therefore information must be compiled about the size, composition and distribution of private providers in health sector. But there are major gaps in data about small-scale and informal private providers. There is likewise a need for comprehensive analysis of the use of private sector services by the poor. These requirements involve large investments to build up national health informatics through demographic and health surveys.

However, better data on private sector practices are not enough. Better understanding is needed of the causes of private sector behavior and performance, the impact of private sector behavior on the poor, and the nature of interactions between the public and private sectors. Questions include whether the public sector has access, leverage or regulatory control over the private sector. Information is needed about the geographical location of private providers, and whether the public sector is absent or whether the private sector is thriving in places where public sector facilities are already available. The economics of service delivery by the private sector must be ascertained in terms of capacity, cost of services and utilization level. Formal collaboration with the private sector requires clear understanding of these issues and concerns at the outset.

Another critical factor is whether a sufficient number of private firms exist that are capable of managing contracts. Availability of contractors with sufficient experience and capacity is a problem is many countries, especially in Africa and Central America. On the other hand, countries like India, South Africa and Thailand have sizeable numbers of private health providers and commercial contractors, thus making contracting of services a possibility. However, the availability of private firms alone may not be a sufficient condition for successful partnership because public contracts are generally less profitable. If the private sector grows rapidly it is likely that investment opportunities in the region exist in abundance so the private sector may not be keen to undertake partnerships with the public sector. When growth slows, as in South Africa, there may be more interest in government contracts.

## Partnership

While theoretical definitions abound, the term 'public-private partnership' is difficult to define at operational level. In common parlance, almost every interaction between the state and the private sector is labelled a 'partnership'. Even contractual transactions and grants-in-aid, the traditional form of supporting the non-profit sector, are termed partnerships. Such generalizations debase the core content of partnership which contains five essential principles: relative equality between the partners, mutual benefits to the stakeholders, autonomy, accountability and mutual commitment to agreed objectives. The public and private sectors vary in their interpretation of each principle of a partnership. Both government and the private sector harbour deep suspicions about each another in terms of motives, methods and objectives. Many non-profit organizations have been formed due to dissatisfaction with government policies and actions. Overcoming mutual suspicions is critical for a partnership to commence, much less to continue.

Sometimes government bureaucracies have very little patience for definitions or guiding principles. Instead they initiate conventional contracting under competitive tendering processes and assume such transactions to be public-private partnership. Because the label of public-private partnership has a contemporary appeal, overly zealous pro-reform officials enter into contracts with the private sector and call them partnerships. Ideally relationships are built on trust and on understanding of mutual objectives but these evolve over long periods of time. Prior informal consultations, clarity about one another's objectives and an expressed commitment to public health goals facilitate the process of building a strong relationship. Whatever the degree of trust, partnerships must be guided by clear terms and conditions, defined structures and performance indicators.

## Motives and objectives

Health systems seek common objectives such as accessibility, equity, efficiency and quality, but these are interpreted differently by the public and private sectors. Public sector priorities lie with equity, accessibility and quality while the for-profit private sector emphasizes efficiency, flexibility in resource deployment and profitability. In most countries, the public sector has the obligation to provide health services free or at minimum cost to its citizens. In Africa the private sector is dominated by the non-profit sector that tends to share common objectives with the public sector. Elsewhere the private commercial sector predominates with priorities that differ from the public sector. Rapid growth of the private sector in developing countries during the past decade has caused overcapacity of service facilities, which has led the latter to explore new avenues for business in order to avoid losses. The non-profit sector that previously received funds through unrestricted government grants, private donors and international aid agencies, has been facing cutbacks. Consequently not-for-profit organizations have become resource savvy by undertaking commercial operations to sustain themselves.

In many developing countries bilateral and multilateral donors mandate engagement with the private sector, even though the public sector lacks sufficient technical or managerial capacity to undertake partnerships. As governments often regard themselves as the only legitimate providers of public services and solely accountable for the delivery of public goods, whatever they do is said to be for the benefit of their citizens while contributions and roles played by other parties are discounted. Given divergent ideas about efficiency, collaboration with the private for-profit sector seems to be a daunting task for the public sector. Opposition to collaboration with the private sector emanates too from a fear that such moves are attempts at privatization and at abandoning state responsibility for health services. On the other hand, public views about the non-profit private sector are generally favourable.

Despite these entrenched views and perspectives, great potential exists for the public and private sectors to work together to provide services in the public interest. It is important for the public sector to recognize that the private sector has relatively easy access, greater innovativeness and a credible image, and that it is technologically better equipped, better managed and usually more efficient. The private sector can help to expand geographical coverage as well as newer frontiers in clinical services. In turn, the private sector needs to understand that its scope of clientele is the society at large, not just the patients who can afford to pay. The private sector has incentives to work with the public sector such as being able to influence government policies on subsidies, regulation, accreditation and quality control. However, collaboration with the for-profit sector raises concerns about cost and quality. While the objective of partnership projects may be easier to define, ensuring appropriate incentives to deliver the right services at the right cost and quality to the right people remain gray areas. And because financial incentives are important, there is a need for the private sector to know which services are profitable and which are not.

The non-profit sector secures considerable benefits by collaborating with the public sector. Apart from more stable financial support, it gains legitimacy in the communities served. It can also expand projects that otherwise would have remained as local pilot initiatives, a good example being the management of Primary Health Centers in India by Karnataka's Karuna Trust. By collaborating with the private non-profit sector the public sector is able to ensure that health care services reach inaccessible terrains, obtain better quality without extensive oversight or regulation and encourage need-based interventions. While government must respect the integrity of the non-profit sector, the latter is well advised to refrain from chronic criticisms that undermine a spirit of partnership. At the same time, non-profit organizations need to realize that regular budgetary support from the government may jeopardize their autonomy.

While government may find it challenging to mainstream a large section of informal and indigenous providers, involving them could ensure better quality and wider reach. Given the strong opposition by professional service providers, this task is not easy but evidence indicates that the poor are more likely to use the informal parts of the private sector such as shopkeepers, drug-sellers and solo practitioners. Of course, the inclusion of informal providers and traditional healers in any form of partnership raises dilemmas in terms of legitimacy, stigma, ethics and quality. But with appropriate legislation, traditional healers could be mainstreamed through access to training, promotion of traditional medicine and institutional referral affiliation.

Finally there are more benefits of working together than working independently. The challenges are to overcome mutual suspicions, identify mutually beneficial areas of engagement and synergy, agree common goals and resolve possible areas of conflict. All these become possible if partnerships are based on prior consultation rather than only through competitive tendering.

## Scope of partnerships

Public-private partnerships seek equity, efficiency, accessibility and quality of services while delivering them to all and particularly to targeted beneficiaries. Partnerships are expected to achieve cost-effective delivery of services, ameliorate economic distress among the poor and facilitate wider as well as easier access by beneficiaries. Partnerships seek to optimize the relative strengths and overcome the deficiencies of each partner.

But partnerships are no substitute for good governance nor are they a lasting solution to deficiencies in the delivery of health services for those who depend on the public sector. Partnerships are desirable in areas where the public sector has not been effective. The public sector has often been found wanting in providing primary care services in geographically remote regions with difficult terrain where government health personnel are hard to retain. Similarly the public sector is not efficient in the use of resources, maintenance of assets or delivery of specialist services. But the public sector has been effective in large-scale public health programs like disease control, immunization campaigns and health communications. These services are frequently finessed by the private sector, but they provide maternal care, sterilization, treatment of communicable diseases such as tuberculosis and control of blindness. Partnerships between the public and private sectors need to be based on rational judgements by both parties about areas of mutual benefit.

Private for-profit clinical providers are more interested in providing specialty diagnostic or clinical services than low-revenue primary care. Evidence world-wide indicates that private institutional providers are generally willing and capable of providing surgical care, inpatient services, telemedicine and diagnostic services involving sophisticated technology. Private for-profit non-clinical contractors provide support services such as laundry, kitchen, equipment maintenance and the supply of drugs and medicine. Small private providers are willing to provide clinical services such as reproductive health care (delivery and sterilization), disease control and child health. Individual private providers are usually interested in services like outpatient day-care that ensure a minimum patient volume and ambulatory care.

Whatever the mode of payment, all private providers are keen to maintain a certain volume of 'business'. The non-profit sector may not have the capacity to undertake super-specialty clinical services but it can provide primary care, health promotion, preventive public health, community mobilization, training, outreach activities, monitoring and evaluation, surveillance and health communications. These tasks are not easy for the for-profit sector or even for government agencies.

Other than non-clinical support, services that are eligible for public-private partnership do not follow any particular pattern or rationale. Partnerships seem to have arisen as ad hoc solutions to various service delivery problems rather than a deliberate long-term strategic vision. Undoubtedly not all services need to be opened for private sector provision and not all private partners are capable of delivering the preferred services. It is also difficult to indicate which services should be kept 'off-limits' to the private sector.

The objectives of any partnership need to be carefully defined in order to identify the outcomes anticipated from the partnership. If the overall objective of a partnership is to improve quality or reduce an economic burden, then specific performance measures and outcome indicators need to be identified and incorporated into the partnership design. There is also a need to indicate whether the partnership is intended to deliver a particular service. The intended beneficiaries under public-private partnership are often groups such as women, children, those with low-incomes and the aged who lack the benefit of services through conventional delivery systems. In developing countries, partnerships seek to alleviate the economic impact of costs associated with acute illness.

## Enabling conditions

Evidence indicates that successful partnerships are triggered by certain enabling, often compelling, conditions. These include:

- the need to maintain a service delivery facility to reach inaccessible populations through efficient use of resources;
- the need to enter a new territory with lower risk for the private for-profit sector of investments in infrastructure or for the private non-profit sector of access to new communities with resources and legitimacy;
- situations in which both partners leverage their relative positions of advantage as well as vulnerabilities in human resource skills, technology, image, outreach, cost-effectiveness and community acceptance;
- visionary leadership by bureaucrats, entrepreneurs and charitable trusts who envision benefits of working together;
- demonstrable merits of collaboration through a successful pilot project that donors or one of the partners seek to upscale; and
- demand for private sector provision of service from the community such as the Chiranjeevi scheme in India and voucher schemes in Africa.

Other conditions that enable successful partnerships are clarity among partners about mutual obligations and benefits, incentives and penalties, community support, stability of the government, a facilitative legal climate and often the driving force of an individual.

Whatever the situation, successful partnerships begin only after a clear understanding of each partner's need, followed by consultations prior to formalizing the partnership. A policy pronouncement by the government alone is not a sufficient condition for partnerships to be initiated. Though informal consultations are a precursor to successful partnerships, there is a need to evolve methods of selecting private partners that will be objective, legal and in the best interests of the community. While construed by some as unethical, eligibility conditions are often tailored to help the private partners to avoid administrative scrutiny.

The process of competitive tendering has proved to be problematic. Evidence indicates that private partners – usually commercial for-profit contactors chosen purely on the basis of competitive tendering – are subsequently either dissatisfied or unable to perform according to the original partnership agreements. During the bidding stage the primary concern of a private partner is to win the contract so it tends to showcase a low-cost bid. Such behaviour is caused by the administrative requirement that government must choose the lowest bid. Because civil servants fear that any procedural lapse will cost them dearly, public sector managers are frequently more concerned about satisfying minute procedural requirements than about the needs of beneficiaries. The contractors may also misjudge the volume of business or they may presume lax supervision by the public partner that would eventually allow them to recover costs by 'cutting corners' or, in some cases, to renegotiate an upward revision of the tariff. In the absence of adjustments, the contractor is unlikely to deliver services at the original level of quality or effectiveness as specified in the contract.

Although open-tendering has certain merits like legal compliance, objective criteria, competitive bids and transparent procedures, it may be more appropriate for large-scale infrastructural development projects where tenders have technical and financial bids that are screened separately. But in the process of finding partners to deliver health services to the poor in a community, conventional tendering has its limitations. To overcome these problems in selecting private partners, prior consultation through a committee structure is advisable – for example, discussions among the private partners, the community, eminent persons and the government – followed by formal negotiations.

Evidence suggests that public-private partnerships based on prior consultation experience fewer difficulties than competitively chosen partners. However, more research is needed on whether private non-profit agencies prefer relationship-based partnerships or whether the private for-profit sector prefers competitive selection processes (or vice versa), and also whether state bureaucrats prefer for-profit or non-profit partners selected through competition or prior consultation. It is also important to identify situations with potential liabilities for partnerships – for example, non-profit organizations run by political leaders and religious sects or private contractors with a tainted past.

## Forms of partnerships

While contracting is the predominant model of partnership in the delivery of health services, other forms of partnership have been thriving too. These include social franchising, social marketing, social insurance (vouchers and service coupons) and joint ventures. The appropriateness of a partnership format depends on the service delivery objectives. For example contracting-in may be an option if a service facility is underused or non-functional. Contracting itself has several formats like contracting-in, contracting-out, contracting for health personnel, procurement contracts, maintenance contracts and management contracts. Governments throughout the world have been experimenting with different models and providing valuable insights about the contextual relevance of one model of partnership over another.

Evidence suggests that, as a formal policy instrument, public-private partnership remains at a nascent stage. Case studies indicate that experimenting with partnership ideas before formalizing a policy is more successful than simply promulgating a policy without prior experience. Lack of success in partnerships was often caused by insufficient consultations with facility managers or other important stakeholders. Partnerships initiated unilaterally by the bureaucracy appear to be less successful than those initiated by private partners. However, the appropriateness of a particular model must be judged on the evidence about its positive and negative aspects, its degree of complexity and its effects on beneficiaries. Also to be considered are the administrative and organizational capacity (both technical and managerial) of the lead partner as well as the model's acceptability at community level.

## Stakeholders

In any partnership for service delivery, there are more stakeholders than if the partners were to deliver services individually. Identifying the stakeholders and understanding their expectations are critical for the success of any partnership. Each stakeholder has its own interests that may be shared or in conflict with other stakeholders. For example, while the government's department of health and the beneficiaries may expect delivery of services free of cost (or highly subsidized), the private partner may want to introduce user-fees that would allow cost recovery and provide for a margin of profit. While beneficiaries of partnerships expect no discrimination in the quality of services they receive free, patients who pay for themselves outside the purview of a partnership expect better quality service or preferential treatment. Cost-control and quality of care have been perennial areas of conflict between managers and clinical personnel.

There are also great risks in handling certain stakeholders. For example, in a community-based partnership, the power dynamics based on political, social and economic strata of the members carry potential risks. Certain stakeholders – government staff, unsuccessful contractors, competitors, activists – could sabotage partnerships, and some stakeholders are more powerful than others. For example, while the poor and the marginalized often are designated beneficiaries at the core of a partnership to deliver health care services, they almost invariably are the least powerful stakeholders. Furthermore, lower-rung civil servants who approve and release periodic payments are sometimes the most influential stakeholders. Community leaders and elected representatives of political parties may also pose serious challenges to partnership.

However, the power and the influence of stakeholders are contextual. Evidence indicates that providing information and consulting relevant stakeholders reduces confrontation and partnership failures. In India the Karuna Trust, which manages several primary health centers under a public-private partnership with the Government of Karnataka, faced protests by the local community and even threats of eviction. Only after intense communication and consultation about the details and the merits of the partnership was it allowed to take control of the primary health centres. In several community-based partnerships, the beneficiaries were neither informed about, nor aware of, a local partnership. Although they perceived a change in the quality of service and expressed satisfaction about it, they remained ignorant of the partnership, especially those managed by non-profit organizations. Partnerships with for-profit organizations were more easily recognized. Among the stakeholders in public-private partnership projects, beneficiaries expressed concerns about sufficiency of services and supplies, staff expressed concerns about working conditions, wages, supervision and interference, and the private sector managers expressed concerns about delayed payments, volume of clients, political interference and attitudes of public sector managers.

## Capacity-building

For partnerships to function effectively, all partners need organizational systems and institutional structures. While the public sector has complex administrative systems, the private sector often lacks them. The non-profit sector usually operates on a small scale in an informal manner; it consciously avoids elaborate structures and systems. The for-profit sector has more complex systems but operates in a flexible manner with an ability to incorporate changes quickly. The private sector tends to be wary of the rigidities and formalities associated with government bureaucracy.

Public systems require extensive documentation and procedural details with which non-profit organizations are not conversant or do not comprehend. Non-profit organizations are often unable to follow the detailed accounting systems required by government agencies. Such differences between public and private sectors cause misunderstandings and conflicts. The public system is unlikely to accept flexible private sector practices so it tries to force the private sector to function like a bureaucracy, thus increasing transaction costs. The private sector requires different sets of skills to manage partnership projects, which are beyond conventional grants-in-aid. In grant-in-aid schemes the non-profit sector shapes the objectives and enjoys considerable functional autonomy. But under a partnership, the public sector sets the objectives and closely supervises the functioning of the delivery agency. Close supervision obviates autonomy.

However, as argued in Chapter 1, autonomy is a foundational component of partnership. A partnership is characterized by relative autonomy for its partners during their day-to-day operations as well as overall management. From the perspectives of private partners, autonomy is non-intrusive liberty to take operational decisions without cumbersome bureaucratic approvals. Evidence indicates that, despite possessing an enormous scope for intervention, the public sector generally does not intrude on a private partner's functional autonomy. Rarely do partnerships fail due to an overbearing public sector. The popular perception that the private sector is vulnerable to losing its autonomy when it works with the public sector is debatable. Indeed evidence suggests that the private sector plays a subtle role by influencing the state's policy on private sector rather than vice versa.

The public sector and the non-profit sector have a long history of working together so transition from grants-in-aid to partnerships is unlikely to be difficult. But the mindset of officials in the bureaucracy toward the non-profit sector tends to be domineering. Apart from concessions and subsidies, the private for-profit sector has had less experience of working with the public sector. In recent years, through pilot projects under health sector reforms, however, governments have begun to learn to understand the intricacies of working with the private sector.

In a common pattern associated with health sector reform departments of health have created separate cells and units whose officials are trained in the modalities of public-private partnership. These officials are able to design guidelines, eligibility conditions, tenders, financial details and performance indicators. But without modifications in the legal, administrative and procedural systems of the bureaucracy, new initiatives with the private sector have not been easy. Although senior civil service officials in the health ministry have been trained, they run the risk of frequent transfer. Officers who initiate partnerships are often posted elsewhere. New officials are rarely able to understand or appreciate the systems developed by their predecessors. Sometimes the strategies and systems are modified or completely abandoned, depending on the likes and dislikes of the new incumbents. Middle-level functionaries, despite their training, do not have decision-making power while lower functionaries in health departments are either unaware or unskilled in handling such initiatives. They are either untrained or inadequately briefed about the objectives of partnership or they do not share the enthusiasm of their superiors.

Health officials at the level of operational facilities lack the necessary skills to understand a partnership proposal, evaluate its benefits, identify performance outcomes or monitor its functioning. Functionaries at all levels must be educated about the merits and intricacies of partnership, including identification of need, scope and objective, contract design, performance and quality indicators. There is also a need to develop capacity in costing services, negotiating with the private sector, competencies for 'oversight', incentives and penalties, and an ability to redesign if partnerships are not viable. Institutional capacity is not only about trained personnel but also creating guidelines, financial management, information systems and evaluation methods. Other issues include the degree of delegation of administrative power and authority, the extent of involvement of critical stakeholders, and incentives for public sector managers. Lack of capacity leads to delayed payment to the private partner. Such laxity influences the private partners' reluctance to bid for further contracts, which leads to higher bids to compensate.

Health systems managers may regard the new initiative as a burdensome task requiring them not only to placate their subordinates but also to seek better performance from the private partner. The latter task is unfamiliar to them or a task in which they have not been successful with their own subordinates. There is no blueprint for improving government capacity about partnerships. Different situations demand different types of partnerships and different types of partnerships require different capacities. Absence of oversight by the public sector can be attributed to lack of technical skills and/or lack of willingness to undertake such responsibility with vigour. Even if the government officials play more active roles in monitoring the partnership projects, a corollary question remains: 'what prevents them taking a similar interest in monitoring their own functionaries?' The capacity of both private partners and public officials to manage partnerships is yet to be fully developed, but key questions are which specific skills are required, where are they available, and how can they be deployed quickly? Capacity development is not restricted only to the public sector. The private sector and its stakeholders also need to cultivate the capacity for partnership.

## Contract design

One justification for partnership with the private sector is to deliver health services more efficiently and at better quality. While designing partnership contracts, however, public sector officials find it difficult to define performance indicators. A sample of partnership contracts in India revealed that very few specified performance indicators, and none defined quality indicators. Access to services is often measured in terms of eligible beneficiary groups but not how to prevent access by non-eligible groups. Partnership agreements generally have clear administrative instructions for the private partner, but there is rarely mention of quality and performance measures.

Setting benchmarks is generally the responsibility of the lead partner but the public sector is yet to be fully geared to setting quality standards and performance criteria. Quality and performance indicators are more evolved in donor-funded projects in Africa, India and Latin America. In India, the urban slum project in Andhra Pradesh – originally funded by the World Bank and now by the state government – has explicit performance parameters based on a weighted score of 200 points. A possible explanation of why performance indicators are conspicuously absent in many partnership contracts could be that, since the public sector itself is unable to provide services efficiently or at desirable levels of quality, it lacks the capacity to design performance contracts. Government contracts tend to focus on input factors like minimum eligibility conditions, competitive bidding and cost rather than on outcome indicators.

Measuring and monitoring performance is essential but can be costly and difficult. While kitchen and laundry services are relatively simple, measurable and easy to monitor, others are not. Performance measures originate from the need to deliver services. For example, if a voucher scheme has been launched to reduce maternal and infant mortality as well as promote institutional delivery, the baseline indicators must allow comparative assessment of its impact in a region. However, such evaluation may occur several months or even years after the launch of a partnership. Operational management indicators like accounting standards, documentation, training, and community outreach targets may be easier to monitor but, if not linked to outcome indicators, these measures are not useful. Likewise it is difficult to measure the quality of services delivered by the private partner. While it is assumed that non-profit providers provide high quality services whereas for-profit partners have few incentives to exceed levels specified in their contracts, evidence suggests that partnerships with private providers rarely monitor costs, quality of care or outcomes.

It may be easier to award contracts for newly created projects than to terminate in-house services. The former strategy reduces the fear of public sector employees about their retrenchment but comparative costs must be accurately assessed. Inappropriately priced contracts lead to poor performance by the private partner, thus eventually incurring even greater costs. Clinical services are particularly prone to such vagaries. Incentives and disincentives, exit clauses and recovery of funds in case of non-delivery of services need to be carefully built into the design of a project agreement.

Feedback from stakeholders suggests the utility of involving them during the design stage of a partnership. Agreements need to incorporate systems of decision-making and conflict management. When the responsibilities and authorities of partners are not clearly defined, major problems occur in coordination. If hospital services are contracted without having involved hospital administrators during negotiations, they are unlikely to understand their responsibilities or authority. They would find it impossible to enforce contract clauses so contractors could defy them. Evidence confirms that 'troubled' partnership initiatives have been caused by insufficient consultations at the facility level with field managers prior to finalizing a partnership contract.

## Compliance

Adherence by each partner to mutual obligations and commitments is critical in any partnership. Failure to fulfill mutual responsibilities leads to disaffection, conflict and lack of trust among the partners and among other stakeholders. In all types of partnership, the public sector is committed to providing funds and in some cases training, premises and even legal facilitation such as registration, licensing and accreditation. In some contracts, the government is obligated to provide equipment, drugs, supplies and fuel or its equivalent in financial terms. The private partners are generally obligated to provide uninterrupted services to the target beneficiaries. Other obligations include employment of qualified staff, upkeep of physical infrastructure, payment of rents and taxes, and submission of periodic accounts. Some partnership projects prescribe additional responsibilities under certain contingencies such as medical emergencies, calamities, public health surveys, national disease control programs, birth control, immunization and other preventive and health promotion services.

While obligations are generally acknowledged, evidence reveals a lack of monitoring mechanisms to ensure that the obligations of each partner are fulfilled both in letter and spirit. While it may be easier for the public sector to find deficiencies in services by the private partner, there is no neutral authority to monitor the obligations of the government. For example, when reimbursement is delayed or payments are not released, how can a private partner – especially a non-profit partner – resolve the issue? There have also been complaints of inadequate equipment, inaccessible amenities and other difficulties faced by private partners in hospital-based delivery. Public-private partnerships should appoint an ombudsman to resolve such eventualities. The ombudsman could be a committee comprised of eminent citizens and legal counsel.

## Benefits and risks

The success of a public-private partnership hinges on an assessment of risks and benefits of partnership by respective partners. All private partners seek to benefit in monetary terms as well as enhancing their reach but the perceived benefits of a for-profit partner differ from those of a non-profit partner. Non-profit partners gauge their benefits in terms of community service, financial sustenance, community support and altruistic satisfaction. For-profit partners expect greater commercial returns, access to government contracts elsewhere and greater business volume although sometimes commercial contractors overestimate their expected benefits from a partnership. The public sector in turn is able to fulfill its commitments by engaging the private sector to deliver services on its behalf.

Though partnerships are generally beneficial for partners, they contain degrees of risk. For the public sector, perceptions of risk differ at different levels of hierarchy and in the scope of services provided by a partnership. At the policy level, the risks are likely to be political in nature. Popular sentiments, expressed through the media, political parties, health action groups and staff unions may inhibit government from making overtures to the private sector, especially to the for-profit sector that is perceived to be interested only in profits. In the context of economic liberalization in which public sector activities are being slowly rolled back, there is a strong suspicion that government may retrench the health sector too. This suspicion is strengthened by the fact that the government, despite its regulatory powers, has not been effective in regulating the asymmetrical growth of the private sector or its misdeeds.

Another area of concern is that the public sector may lose its own capacity to provide similar services if a private partner delivers services under long-term contracts over an extended period of time. This loss may allow the private sector to dictate its own terms in future engagements. Under such circumstances the public sector may be forced to accede to demands under which the intended beneficiaries would suffer. Another possibility is that under the partnership, subsidized or free services to beneficiaries may eliminate competitors from the market and thus give the private partner a monopoly.

The private sector, in turn, has not convincingly demonstrated its interest in public health activities like primary care and preventive health services. It reserves its enthusiasm for collaborating with the government in tertiary care services and for setting up private medical colleges. These patterns of behaviour reinforce the view that collaboration by the private sector with government is intended only to obtain monetary benefits without risk.

Other risks emanate from stereotyping the private sector as exploitative, an image with a social, cultural and historical legacy. Countries that recently embraced a market economy are likely to debate the merits of private sector collaboration in the provision of health care services. Societies with more pervasive political divides between right or left ideologies encounter forceful positions for and against partnership. Resistance is likely to be less when the non-profit sector is involved. Multi-party coalition governments face more diverse views than dominant-party regimes. However, political consent or dissent depends on past experience of collaboration with the private sector as well as popular sentiments about such collaboration. In countries like India the popular debate on the merits and demerits of public-private partnerships is at a nascent stage. Policy debates have often been rhetorical and ideological both for and against partnerships with the private sector.

Not-for-profit organizations, on the other hand, are popularly perceived as 'givers', an image that is advantageous for them. Governments face fewer hurdles when partnering with NGOs although the latter have severe limitations. They are frequently characterized by limited scope of services, limited geographical operations, high dependence for funds and resources, short-term focus, limited sustainability, and lack of technical and managerial capacity. Several recent cases in India of fake organizations masquerading as non-profit NGOs have raised doubts too about the integrity of this sector.

Risk assessment follows other dimensions as well. Financial and reputational risks are high among non-profit agencies. Inadvertent procedural lapses (say in accounting) may lead to administrative strictures, temporary stoppage of funds, audit inspections or, worse, a ban on future bidding by the agency in government tenders. Apart from denting the image of an agency, these actions cripple the delivery of services to the beneficiaries. Of similar concern is accountability for service delivery. Even when partnerships occur, government is ultimately responsible for the delivery of services. If deficiencies occur in services under a partnership, the onus falls on the government health functionaries.

Yet another concern is the nature of relationships among key stakeholders and their personality styles. Sometimes differences in personality lead to conflicts and jeopardize the functioning of a partnership. Sustainable partnerships require the careful handling of relationships. Because partners from different organizational cultures have different work habits, these generate possible areas of disagreement and conflict. One of the best ways to handle conflict is to anticipate its possibility in the design stage by mutually agreeing on methods of conflict resolution, eliminating potential areas of conflict through negotiation, and creating channels of communication among leaders on each side. If needed, a mutually agreeable third party could be used to resolve conflicts and disputes.

A final area of concern is whether, once a partnership agreement expires, another partner would be available under similar terms and conditions. For example, in the management of a tertiary care institution with a huge capital investment by the public sector, what alternatives are available for the government if the chosen partner functions ineffectively or fails? Or, if the partnership is successful, would the government be willing to extend the same concessions to other projects? In the event of a project being unsuccessful, one may ask: 'if ABC could not succeed, who else could?'

More research is required to understand whether partnerships run higher risks if partners are chosen through competitive process than through selective pre-negotiated agreements. A competitive process cannot guarantee the performance of an agency that wins a bid although, given lack of prior intimacy, it may be easier to monitor its activities.

## Equity and fairness

Cost-effectiveness of public-private partnerships cannot be achieved through inequitable treatment of partners and unfair allocation of resources. Uniform guidelines are required for resource allocation to private partners depending on the nature and scope of services, geographical terrain and an area's demographic, and morbidity conditions. Yet evidence suggests that the government is circumspect about granting full budgetary allocation to non-profit agencies whereas for-profit organizations receive extensive concessions.

When inconsistencies exist under a government regime, questions appear about fairness in partnership policy. For example, a state government in India currently finances a non-profit agency to manage primary health centres with a budget grant that is less than the government's own allocation to the health centres. The same government provides a guaranteed profit to a corporate hospital that manages its tertiary care hospital, even after an enormous investment in capital costs. It is unclear whether such a discrepancy is due to better negotiating skills by the private sector or to a pervasive perception that it is not acceptable for non-profit agencies to negotiate cost margins or whether the government is simply more than eager to encourage for-profit agencies in the promotion of its policy on public-private partnerships. Compounding this muddle is a lack of incentives for better performing partnerships or disincentives for poorly performing projects except in terms of renewal or non-renewal of the contract.

A similar area of concern is the timing of grants or reimbursements to non-profit partners whose existence often depends entirely on government funds. Partnership agreements need guidelines about the timely release of payments or, in the event of non-release, the consequences thereof. Evidence suggests that disbursements under public-private partnerships are directed toward primary care services, which repudiates the claim in some quarters that partnerships with the private sector divert government resources toward specialist care. Even in primary care the argument that public-private partnership is a route to privatization is untrue. Without government grants, the private sector cannot sustain operations at these locations so the government's responsibilities have become more indispensable than ever. A future area for research is the impact of partnerships on public sector health budgets.

## Beneficiaries

In almost all the partnerships, the policy of targeting the poor has provided maternal and child health as well as primary and secondary level care. But targeting the poor in tertiary care services poses a challenge. Because economic debilitation of poor patients is higher when tertiary care is needed, there is considerable merit in generating public-private partnerships in tertiary care services. As the amount of government reimbursement for tertiary care services is greater, partnerships at this level need to be better managed.

When powerful members of the local community avail themselves of services under the guise of being poor, however, the poor patients lose. If there is no fixed quota of hospital beds for the poor, and if the government works on a reimbursement mode, hospital administrators have no motivation to prevent ineligible patients from using such services. Partnerships in tertiary care services need to address this issue with appropriate checks and control systems. Currently contracts and documented agreements do not spell out verification mechanisms or designate the authority for verification or establish penalties for violations.

Even if contracts contain such clauses, enforcement at the facility level is difficult or even risky. Identity papers for those below the poverty line are easy to obtain, yet there is no mechanism to verify their authenticity or if patients actually belong to the designated categories of beneficiaries. The private partner may not be able to turn away the ineligible beneficiaries for fear of possible consequences. If the government tries to enforce these restrictions, powerful community groups may lobby against the partnership project itself. There is a need to find ways to prevent misuse of facilities through legal safeguards and to establish stricter penalties for misuse even after the service has been availed. Although public-private partnership has been able to achieve the main objective of reaching the poor and making health services accessible to them, the economic benefit for the poor of the services accessed under partnerships is yet to be empirically verified.

Other countries have reported similar experiences of subsidies not reaching the intended beneficiaries, such as cases of chemically impregnated anti-malarial bed nets in Tanzania and vouchers in Thailand. The very logic of public-private partnership is lost if the poor are marginalized. Evidence indicates that reaching the poor is the toughest challenge under partnerships (Bhatt 1999). It is important to evolve policy to strengthen public facilities along with the development of private sector partnerships and to develop mechanisms such as catastrophic illness insurance or state sickness funds to protect the poor from financially burdensome health care services.

Reportedly the very poor make little use of formal health services in either the public or private sectors but they do use the informal private sector extensively (DFID 2000). The challenge for policy-makers is to ensure that the health care needs of the very poor are met. If regulatory controls on the informal sector do not work, at least the harmful effects of the care they receive from the informal private sector could be reduced. The poor often utilize informal providers who are difficult to monitor. Even if the latter were possible, the resources necessary to achieve such engagement would raise concerns about sustainability. It may be unrealistic to think that partnerships will alleviate the health care needs of this group. It is also clear that providing for the poor and very poor requires that greater attention be focused on strengthening the public system of health care.

## Monitoring and information

The success of public-private partnerships hinges on adequate monitoring systems being in place to assess the means and outcomes of these initiatives. Invariably responsibility for supervision and monitoring lies with the public sector but in practice it has little capacity or willingness to supervise and monitor. In India, concessions and subsidies given to private for-profit hospitals in exchange for delivering benefits to the poor were poorly monitored. Consequently there was litigation as well as intervention by the judiciary.

No monitoring system is in place to enforce the obligations of the private sector. In the absence of effective monitoring, the core objective of the public-private partnership – to protect poor patients from economic debilitation – is unfulfilled. Rare inspections have discovered instances of fake registration of poor patients, of beds earmarked for the poor having been filled by others and admissions to hospitals of patients referred by politicians.

Monitoring could be made easier by a well designed management information system. Information is critical for managing partnerships. Many bottlenecks are due not only to bureaucratic red tape but also to poor information systems. Poor information means poor accountability. Problems such as failure to release payments in a timely manner, sloppy accounting and financial management, inadequate verification of beneficiaries, outdated inventories of stocks and supplies, and lack of indicators about target achievements could all be better managed by a well designed management information system.

However, sometimes the problem is not the availability of information but the lack of incentives for those responsible to collect and use information. For example, in a social insurance scheme among agricultural cooperative society members in southern India, all partner hospitals were required to provide routine data on diagnosis, length of stay, main procedures, etc. But there were long delays in the reporting of these data, which led to problems in monitoring reimbursements by the third party administrator. While it is relatively easy to monitor non-clinical services without sophisticated information systems, the ways in which contractors attempt to save costs or compromise the quality of clinical services are much more subtle and require sophisticated information systems to detect them. Even if such information systems can be set up, the capacity or incentive of managers to process the information produced and the authority to use the information for corrective measures needs to be incorporated in the contract design.

## Sustainability

While it is possible to launch innovative public-private partnerships, it is important to ensure that they are sustainable from financial, institutional and political perspectives. Financial sustainability usually receives the most attention but institutional and political sustainability are equally important. Small-scale programs with intensive management inputs and clear objectives are often not sustainable when scaled up. Donor-funded programs can be sustained as long as donor funds continue but have little prospect of long-term sustainability unless they are fully owned by the government. Financial sustainability does not necessarily mean full cost recovery or self-funding by the private partner. The key question is what kind of partnership is more likely to give better value for money than other investments in the sector.

Concern about sustainability raises questions for which there are no easy answers. If an initiative like the private management of primary health centers is more cost-effective in the use of public money, should the strategy of purchasing service delivery be adopted and scaled up for the entire state? Should government resume managerial responsibility for those partnerships that have proved to be successful? In remote areas that are difficult to reach, should government finance the recurrent costs whatever their value for money?

## Governance and transparency

Good governance is a key issue in all partnerships. All kinds of contractual engagements or financial transactions with private partners are scrutinized by the government at some point in time. Private partners that use public resources must be accountable because partnerships must be able to demonstrate that public resources are effectively used for the public good. Any public-private partnership that goes through a bidding process is likely to undergo public scrutiny. Value-for-money in public-private ventures needs to be demonstrated through documentation and made accessible for public scrutiny. Even failed partnership ventures should be documented and placed in the public domain.

It is important to ensure that all process steps are followed and that there is complete transparency in decisions, communications and procedures. Having adequate monitoring mechanisms in place would ensure such transparency. If the steps in the process of governance are not followed appropriately, partnership initiatives may be suspected of being back-door privatization. Perceptions of this kind may undermine public-private partnerships. Given its inadequate managerial and technical capacity, the public sector could underestimate the time and efforts required or overestimate the chances of success of a partnership. Considerable interdepartmental coordination of activities is also needed.

Both public and private partners search for information about each other. Private partners look for information on opportunities, cost of bids and successful past bids; the public sector looks for characteristics and histories of the private sector bidders. Since the search for information incurs transaction costs, appropriate mechanisms could be instituted to ensure that information is available to all. Such information would obviate opportunistic behavior by the private sector.

## Policy lessons

Public-private partnerships are a formidable alternative to overcome the deficiencies of service delivery by either partner, but they are no panacea for the ills of public sector health systems in developing countries. As an alternative to full privatization, public-private partnerships are a strategy for government to overcome its failure to deliver adequate health care services and to ameliorate the impact of the private sector on the poor. Public-private partnerships hold great potential if public sector can organize itself and develop sufficient capabilities to supervise them. But if a policy of public-private partnerships is to succeed, certain conditions need to be understood as objective policy lessons.

Partnerships should be mutually beneficial arrangements that involve all stakeholders. Whether government, community, NGO or the private for-profit sector, each stakeholder has its own special strengths. By taking advantage of those strengths, synergies can be achieved that lead to better outcomes.

Partnerships are best organized as area specific, demand driven, need based and people centered. Top-down approaches do not work. Local experience needs to be considered when designing programs.

Partnerships allow governments to counter the influence of market forces. Government leadership is a key factor to formulate policy, set standards and hold stakeholders accountable.

Leadership and vision are critical in a complex partnership. The quality of leaders affects partnership at every stage from design onwards. Leaders who get involved at each stage of a partnership are more successful than leaders who see themselves only as facilitators. Partnership requires strong governmental leadership and support systems. Wherever governance is weak, there is an unhealthy tendency to project partnership with the private sector as the solution rather than improving governance per se.

Evidence indicates that public subsidies through partnerships benefit the poor but that a substantial portion of such benefits are garnered by the more well-to-do. The government has an important role in establishing a legal framework to protect the services negotiated under partnership for the intended beneficiaries such as women, the poor and marginalized groups. Government's role goes beyond managing contracts or supervising performance.

The rationale for partnering with the private sector must be clearly articulated and justified. It is important to understand not only the services to be provided under public-private partnerships but also the basis on which such decisions are made.

The public and private sectors do not have uniform objectives, structures, work cultures, values and levels of commitment. The profit motive of the private sector needs to be acknowledged as legitimate, and the altruism of the non-profit sector needs to be balanced with its concern about financial sustenance. Although the non-profit sector may be easier to engage, some of its organizations may bid for government grants like any commercial contractor. Recognition of this difference helps to overcome misconceptions. Partnerships do not mean that the philosophy or the organizational mission of respective partners must change.

While designing contract agreements or signing memoranda of understanding, caution is required in defining performance indicators, incentives or penalties, dispute settlement mechanisms, exit options, quality standards and risks. Guidelines must be developed to avoid or protect against unwanted litigation.

Since public-private partnerships are at the nascent stage in developing countries, all options must be empirically explored through pilot projects instead of debating whether it is more effective to subsidize inputs through a social insurance scheme or provide direct subsidies to the poor by purchasing the services from the private sector through vouchers. After experimentation the more suitable methods should be scaled up. Likewise it is appropriate to examine whether partnership with the private sector has a catalytic effect on public health services in terms of quality of care, accessibility, service utilization level and human resource performance.

Government should review its capacity for public-private partnership and consider developing public-private partnership units at both provincial and national levels. A health policy resource institute could serve as an autonomous policy 'think tank' to provide consultancy to the government. The resource center could review best practices, formulate guidelines for partnership structures, and mobilize public interest and awareness. It could also encourage organizational systems appropriate for national, regional and local partnerships, develop guidelines and codes of conduct for partners, and conduct reviews and evaluations of partnerships. In India the National Health Resource Centre has been established with these purposes. Departments of health at various levels from district through state to nation can draft policy papers on engaging the private sector that are appropriate to the respective health service delivery level. Such policy documents should be based on extensive stakeholder consultation before adoption and approval by respective governments.

Governments could create various partnership scenarios with the help of the private sector to indicate the geographical and clinical areas of collaboration as well as types of services requiring short-term and long-term collaboration. Health informatics would be useful in mapping health resources, morbidity patterns, demographic situations and the nature of services needed and available. Informatics could be used to license, accredit, monitor and regulate the private sector. Such information could be disseminated through clearing houses, networks and other media. Without accurate information, government is comparatively weak during the bargaining stage of establishing a partnership.

In some countries laws pertaining to private sector regulation are either archaic or not enforceable or even non-existent. Occasionally the existing legal framework is not conducive to private sector participation in the delivery of health care services. Some regulations treat the formal private sector harshly, which makes its organizations register as charitable trusts but operate commercially. Since the legal status of these organizations is muddled, they are reluctant to interact with the public sector for fear of being 'caught'. There is need for a thorough review in all countries of legislation about the private sector.

Government must augment its technical and managerial capacity. The public sector in many developing countries lacks systems of employing professionally trained managers in the public health cadre. Physicians are compelled to undertake administrative responsibilities without formal orientation to the skills required. Managing new forms of public systems requires skills that are beyond the realm of conventional bureaucracy. There is a need to create and fill positions of managers, private sector specialists, health economists, legal experts and even professional consultants.

The weakest link in public-private partnership projects is the documentation and dissemination of detailed records. Public-private partnerships are regarded as temporary amalgamations between organizational systems. Barring the long-term contracts for private finance initiatives, most partnerships are short-term pilots with specific targets. In several countries, these projects are driven by the funding agencies on an experimental basis. As a result both partners tend to function in an ad hoc manner with little scope for a partnership system to evolve. At the end of a project, its lessons are documented and disseminated but, due to the lack of detailed information on the merits and demerits of the systems used, similar projects elsewhere tend the 'reinvent the wheel'.

Project managers in partnerships search for details that, if readily available, would help to overcome planning bottlenecks and delays. They could design strategies with complete knowledge about whether a particular strategy would succeed or fail in a given context. Administrative costs could be saved too if documentation were available to policy-makers. Provincial repositories of public-private partnership initiatives could be linked with a national level host and greatly help program managers at the operational level.

It is imperative to create sufficient political consensus and put in place legal systems that delineate the scope for partnership. The legal framework must balance between a system of regulations that ensures accountability of partners and overregulation that stifles innovation. Regulations that interfere with smooth and effective program implementation should be reviewed, modified or, if appropriate, eliminated.

Public-private partnership initiatives cannot be uniform across all regions or suitable under all kinds of political and administrative dispensations. In states where the private sector is prevalent, partnership initiatives are an alternative not necessarily because of their competitive efficiency but to prevent immiseration of the poor and deprived sections of society. Prior experimentation with partnership helps to formulate better policy.

Decentralized partnership initiatives are more likely to be successful, but administrative capabilities are less likely to exist at lower levels of the health care system. Arguments against decentralization of contracting emphasize the lack of capacity to contract at the local level. They also note the dangers of corruption inherent when local-level officials award contracts. However, given the limited evidence about the issue of corruption, it does not necessarily follow that there is greater likelihood of corruption in decentralized contexts. Decentralization may simply move the location of corruption to a more democratic level.

Governments should have a purposeful policy towards public-private partnership. Unless partnerships can be sustained, they should not be initiated. Longer-term strategy should be built into funding arrangements. The primary roles of the government in public-private partnerships are to govern, to define standards, to allocate resources, to ensure safety-nets, to define appropriate health package, to provide legislative support and to control corruption. These roles should be clearly delineated and fully understood by public officials as well as their political masters.

Under public-private partnership, the responsibility of the government increases. These partnerships are under greater scrutiny than when services are provided by either partner individually. Government assumes greater responsibility by inviting the private sector to provide services directly to the public on its behalf, which invitation in turn increases the accountability of the government itself. Government should not treat the private partner merely as a contractor. The role of the private sector partner must be clearly laid out. Whatever the mode of partnership, the initial funding comes from the public sector with a realistic costing of health packages to be delivered by the private partner.

Although partnerships are formed between organizations, they succeed because individuals act as champions for projects and serve as listening-posts for feedback about the partnership. These change-agents are committed to such initiatives. There is need to identify such individuals among the partners, empower them and use their influence to further the cause of effective partnership.

Experience suggests that it is easier to develop new structures and to introduce relatively radical reforms where there is little prior provision. It is more difficult to introduce new approaches that replace existing services where vested interests have been built up and stakeholders may be wary of change.

Public-private partnerships should not deprive public agencies of government funding. While promoting private sector collaboration, governments should strengthen their public facilities with equal vigor and adopt the best practices from the private sector in the provision of services. When engaging in public-private partnerships, governments are actually more at risk. Taking up this new task is a major test of skills and capacity for the government.

Modes of payment are critical in shaping the efficiency, partner motivation and eventual success of a partnership when delivering services. Prospective, global and case-based payments are all relevant under different partnership models and under different service delivery strategies. Whatever the payment model, the ability of the public sector to release timely payments is of paramount concern.

Factors that facilitate successful public-private partnerships at the operational level include regular exchange of communication, joint planning of activities as well as problem-solving, supervision and monitoring, training, and stability of key personnel. Other helpful factors are informal communication channels, uniform management information systems, regular field visits, geographical proximity of the project management unit, and the ability to tolerate mistakes as well as to learn from them.

Factors that hinder partnerships at the operational level are lack of communication between partners to discuss problems and solutions, lack of regular meetings, incomplete exchange of information or reluctance to share information, and lack of consultation about quality and service standards. Other problematic factors include frequent turnover of key personnel, lack of authority by field managers to take decisions, authoritarian or overbearing supervision, lack of awareness about partnerships by lower-level officials and prejudices or misconceptions about the motives of partners or their so-called hidden agenda.

Any policy initiative to strengthen public sector health services would be welcome and public-private partnerships promise better outcomes. However, a government that fails to deliver quality services due to a lack of administrative capacity would not be able to contract either clinical or non-clinical services. The first step must be to improve basic administrative systems.

# References

Abramson, W.B. 1999. Partnerships between the Public Sector and Non-Governmental Organizations: Contracting for Primary Health Care Services. A State of the Practice Paper. *Partnerships for Health Reform (PHR), Latin American and Caribbean Health Sector Reform Initiative* (LAC/HSR), No. 25. Bethesda: Abt Associates Inc.

Abramson, W.B. 2001. Monitoring and Evaluation of Contracts for Health Service Delivery in Costa Rica. *Health Policy and Planning* 16: 404–411.

Abrantes, A. 2003. Contracting Public Health Care Services in Latin America. In *Innovations in Health Service Delivery: The Corporatization of Public Hospitals* edited by A.S. Preker and A. Harding. Washington, DC: The World Bank, pp. 239–262.

ADBI. 2000. *Public Private Partnerships in Health*. Executive Summary Series No. S34/01, Executive Summary of Proceedings (30 October–3 November), Ayutthaya, Thailand. Tokyo: Asian Development Bank Institute.

ADBI. 2001. *Partnership Issues in the Social Sector*. Executive Summary Series No. S51/01. Tokyo: Asian Development Bank Institute.

Agha, S., A.M. Karim, A. Balal and S. Sossler. 1997. *Evaluation Report: Green Star Clinic Network Pilot Project*. Washington, DC: Population Services International.

Agha, S., A.M. Karim, A. Balal and S. Sossler. 2003. *A Quasi Experimental Study to Assess the Performance of a Reproductive Health Franchise in Nepal*. Country Research Series Paper 14. Washington, DC: Commercial Market Strategies.

Ahmed, M. 2000. Promoting Public-Private Partnership in Health and Education: The Case of Bangladesh. In *Public Private Partnership in the Social Sector: Issues and Country Experiences in Asia and the Pacific* edited by Y. Wang. ADBI Policy Paper No. 1. Tokyo: Asian Development Bank Institute, pp. 219–291.

Aljunid, S. 1995. The Role of Private Medical Practitioners and their Interactions with Public Health Services in Asian Countries. *Health Policy and Planning* 10: 333–349.

Allen, P. 1995. Contracts in the National Health Service Internal Market. *Modern Law Review* 58: 321–342.

Allen, P. 2002. A Socio-Legal and Economic Analysis of Contracting in the NHS Internal Market using a Case Study of Contracting for District Nursing. *Social Science and Medicine* 54: 255–266.

Ambegaokar, M. and L. Lush. 2004. Family Planning and Sexual Health Organizations: Management Lessons for Health System Reform. *Health Policy and Planning* 19: 22–30.

Annigeri, V.B., L. Prosser, J. Reynolds and R. Roy. 2004. *An Assessment of Public-Private Partnership Opportunities in India*. POPTECH Publication Number 2004–207–032, USAID/India Contract HRN-C-00–00–00007–00. Online, available at: www.poptechproject.com.

Armand, F. 2003. *The Sustainability Challenge: Identifying Appropriate Financing Models for Social Marketing Programs.* Washington, DC: Commercial Market Strategies.

Asenova, D., W. Stein, C. McCann and A. Marshall. 2007. Private Sector Participation in Health and Social Care Services in Scotland: Assessing the Risk. *International Review of Administrative Sciences* 73: 275–292.

Ashman, D. 2001. Strengthening North-South Partnerships for Sustainable Development. *Nonprofit and Voluntary Sector Quarterly* 30: 74–98.

Ashton, T. 1998. Contracting for Health Services in New Zealand: A Transaction Cost Analysis. *Social Science and Medicine* 46: 357–367.

Ashton, T., J. Cummin and J. McLean. 2004. Contracting for Health Services in a Public Health System: The New Zealand Experience. *Health Policy* 69: 21–31.

Auerbach, L. 2002. *Issues Raised by Public Private Partnerships in Ontario's Hospital Sector.* Centre for Voluntary Sector Research and Development. Ontario, Canada: Carleton University. Online, available at: www.ochu.on.ca/ochu/section-07/reports/auerbacj_report.doc.

Avery, G. 2000. Outsourcing Public Health Laboratory Services: A Blueprint for Determining Whether to Privatize and How? *Public Administration Review* 60: 330–337.

Axelsson, H., F. Bustreo and A. Harding. 2003. *Private Sector Participation in Child Health: A Review of World Bank Projects, 1993–2002.* Washington, DC: World Bank.

Banks, D. and M. Shahrouri. 2003. *The Provision of Reproductive Health Services in Private Hospitals in Amman, Jordan.* Bethesda: The Partners for Health Reform*plus* Project, Abt Associates Inc.

Barnett, C. and P. Putney. 2000. *Contracting NGOs to Deliver HIV/AIDS Services in Guatemala: Case Study Report.* Bethesda: Partnerships for Health Reform, Abt Associates Inc.

Barnett, C., C. Connor, and P. Putney. 2001. *Contracting Nongovernmental Organizations to Combat HIV/AIDS. Special Initiative Report No. 33.* Bethesda: Partnerships for Health Reform, Abt Associates Inc.

Bartlett, W. 1991. Quasi Markets and Contracts: A Markets and Hierarchies Perspective on NHS Reforms. *Public Money and Management* 11: 53–61.

Baru, R. 1998. *Private Health Care in India: Social Characteristics and Trends.* New Delhi: Sage Publications.

Batley, R. 2004. The Politics of Service Delivery Reform. *Development and Change* 35: 31–56.

Bazzoli, G., R. Stein, J.A. Alexander, D.A. Conrad, S. Sofaer and S.M. Shortell. 1997. Public-Private Collaboration in Health and Human Service Delivery: Evidence from Community Partnerships. *The Milbank Quarterly* 75: 533–561.

Belmartino, S. 1994. The Role of the State in Health Systems. *Social Science and Medicine* 39: 1315–1321.

Bennett, J. 2001. *Public-Private Partnerships for Ontario Hospital Capital Projects.* Background report prepared for the Ontario Hospital Association's Committee on Hospital Capital Development. Ontario, Canada.

Bennett, S. 1991. *The Mystique of Markets: Public and Private Health Care in Developing Countries.* Departmental Publication No. 4. London: London School of Hygiene and Tropical Medicine.

Bennett, S. and A. Mills. 1998. Government Capacity to Contract: Health Sector Experiences and Lessons. *Public Administration and Development* 18: 307–326.

Bennett, S. and E.E. Ngalande-Banda. 1994. *Public and Private Roles in Health: A*

*Review and Analysis of Experience in Sub-Saharan Africa.* Geneva: World Health Organization.

Bennett, S., G. Dakpallah, P. Garner, L. Gilson, S. Nittayaramphong, B. Zurita and A. Swi. 1994. Carrot and Stick: State Mechanisms to Influence Private Provider Behaviour. *Health Policy and Planning* 9: 1–13.

Bennett, S., B. McPake and A. Mills. 1997. The Public/Private Mix Debate in Health Care. In *Private Health Providers in Developing Countries* edited by S. Bennett, B. McPake and A. Mills. London: Zed Books, pp. 1–18.

Berman, P. 1995. Health Sector Reform: Making Health Development Sustainable. In *Health Sector Reform in Developing Countries: Making Health Development Sustainable* edited by P. Berman. Boston: Harvard University Press, pp. 13–33.

Berman, P. and P. Dave. 1994. Experiences in Paying for Health Care in India's Voluntary Sector. In *Reaching India's Poor: Non-governmental Approaches to Community Health* edited by S. Pachauri. New Delhi: Sage Publications, pp. 355–373.

Bhatt, R. 1999. Characteristics of Private Medical Practice in India: A Provider Perspective. *Health Policy and Planning* 14: 26–37.

Birchall, J. 2002. Mutual, Non-profit or Public Interest Company? *Annals of Public and Co-operative Economics* 73: 181–213.

Bitrán, R. and W. Yip. 1998. *A Review of Health Care Provider Payment Reform in Selected Countries in Asia and Latin America.* Bethesda: Partnerships for Health Reform, Abt Associates Inc.

Björkman, J.W. 2005. Health, Development and Governance. In *International Development Governance* edited by A.S. Huque and H. Zafarullah. New York: Dekker/CRC Press, pp. 777–294.

Blagescu, M. and J. Young. 2005. *Partnerships and Accountability: Current Thinking and Approaches among Agencies Supporting Civil Society Organizations.* Working Paper 255. London: Overseas Development Institute.

Blair, J.D. and J.A. Bussler. 1998. Competitive Forces in the Medical Group Industry: A Stakeholder Perspective. *Health Care Management Review* 23(2): 7–27.

Blair, J.D. and M.D. Fottler. 1998. Effective Stakeholder Management: Challenges, Opportunities and Strategies. In *Handbook of Health Care Management* edited by W.J. Duncan, P.M. Ginter and L.E. Swayne. Malden: Blackwell, pp. 39–54.

Blair, J.D. and C.J. Whitehead. 1988. Too Many on the Seesaw: Stakeholder Diagnosis and Management for Hospitals. *Hospital and Health Services Management* 33: 153–166.

Bloom, D.E., P. Craig and M. Mitchell. 2000. Public and Private Roles in Providing and Financing Social Services: Health and Education. In *Public Private Partnership in the Social Sector: Issues and Country Experiences in Asia and the Pacific* edited by Y. Wang. Tokyo: Asian Development Bank Institute Policy Paper No. 1, pp. 17–29.

Bossert, T., W. Hsiao, M. Barrera, L. Alarcon, M. Leo and C. Casares. 1998. Transformation of Ministries of Health in the Era of Health Reform: The Case of Colombia. *Health Policy and Planning* 13: 59–77.

Bouchet, B. and W. Abramson. 1998. *Health Sector Reforms in Developing Countries: How Quality Assurance Methods Can Make a Difference* (manuscript). Bethesda: Abt Associates, Inc.

Bovaird, T. 2006. Developing New Forms of Partnership with the 'Market' in the Procurement of Public Services. *Public Administration* 84: 81–102.

Bowman, L. 2000. P3–Problem, Problem, Problem. *Project Finance* (June): 25–27.

Bowman, L. 2001. Pfist Fight. *Project Finance* (September): 26–28.

Boycko, M., A. Shleifer and R.W. Vishny. 1996. A Theory of Privatization. *The Economic Journal* 106: 309–319.

Brinkerhoff, D.W. 1999. Exploring State-Civil Society Collaboration: Policy Partnerships in Developing Countries. *The Implementing Policy Change Project – II.* Bethesda: Abt Associates, Inc.

Brinkerhoff, J.M. 2002. Government-Nonprofit Partnership: A Defining Framework. *Public Administration and Development* 22: 19–30.

Broomberg, J., P. Masobe and A. Mills. 1997. To Purchase is to Provide? The Relative Efficiency of Contracting versus Public Provision of Hospital Services in South Africa. In *Private Health Providers in Developing Countries: Serving the Public Interest?* edited by S. Bennett, B. McPake and A. Mills. London: Zed Books, pp. 214–236.

Brugha, R. and S. Pritze-Aliassime. 2003. Promoting Safe Motherhood through the Private Sector in Low and Middle-income Countries. *Bulletin of the World Health Organization* 81: 616–623.

Brugha, R. and Z. Varvasovszky. 2000. Stakeholder Analysis: A Review. *Health Policy and Planning* 15: 239–246.

Brunsson, N. and K. Sahlin Andersson. 2000. Constructing Organizations: The Example of Public Sector Reform. *Organization Studies* 21: 721–746.

Busse, R., T. van der Grinten and P.G. Svensson. 2002. Regulating Entrepreneurial Behavior in Hospitals: Theory and Practice. In *Regulating Entrepreneurial Behaviour in European Health Care Systems* edited by R.B. Saltman, R. Busse and E. Mossialo. Buckingham: Open University Press (European Observatory on Health Care Systems).

Campbell, D. 1996. The Relational Constitution of the Discrete Contract. In *Contract and Economic Organization* edited by D. Campbell and P. Vincent-Jones. Dartmouth: Aldershot.

Campbell, D. and D. Harris.1993. Flexibility in Long Term Contractual Relationships: The Role of Co-operation. *Journal of Law and Society* 20: 166–191.

Carr, G. 1998. *Public-Private Partnerships: The Canadian Experience.* Oxford: Oxford School of Project Finance. July 9–11. Online, available at: www.pppcouncil.ca/pdf/oxford.pdf.

Carvel, J. 2003. Headhunt for NHS Boardrooms, *The Guardian*, March 3. Online, available at: www.guardian.co.uk/society/2003/mar/03/nhs2000.politics.

Carvel, J. 2004a. Jarvis Involved in Health Centres, *The Guardian*, January 17. Online, available at: www.guardian.co.uk/society/2004/jan/17/nhs2000.politics.

Carvel, J. 2004b. NHS Trusts Bullied into Private Contracts, *The Guardian*, June 1. Online, available at: www.guardian.co.uk/society/2004/jun/01/nhs2000.politics.

Central Bureau of Health Intelligence (CBHI). 2007. *Health Information India 2004 and 2005.* Online, available at: http://cbhidghs.nic.in/hia.

Chong, E., F. Huet, S. Saussier and F. Steiner. 2006. Public-Private Partnerships and Prices: Evidence from Water Distribution in France. *Review of Industrial Organization* 29: 149–169.

Chowdhury, S. 2002. Educating Mothers for Health: Output-based Incentives for Teaching Oral Dehydration in Bangladesh. In *Contracting for Public Health Services: Output-based Aid and Its Application*, edited by P.J. Brook and S.M. Smith. Washington, DC: The World Bank.

CII-McKinsey Report. 2004. *Healthcare in India: The Road Ahead.* New Delhi: Indian Health Care Federation and Confederation of Indian Industries.

Clarkson, M.B.E. 1995. A Stakeholder Framework for Analyzing and Evaluating Corporate Social Performance. *Academy of Management Review* 20: 92–117.

Cohen, M. 2006. The Privatization of Health Care Cleaning Services in Southwestern British Columbia, Canada: Union Responses to Unprecedented Government Actions. *Antipode* 19: 626–644.

Commission on Macroeconomics in Health. 2003. *India Health Report*. New Delhi: Government of India.

Connor, C. 2000. Contracting Nongovernmental Organizations for HIV/AIDS: Brazil Case Study. *PHR Project's Special Initiative Report No. 30*. Bethesda: Partnerships for Health Reform, Abt Associates Inc.

Coston, J.M. 1998. A Model and Typology of Government-NGO Relationships. *Nonprofit and Voluntary Sector Quarterly* 27: 358–382.

Croxson, B. 1999. *Organizational Costs in the New NHS: An Introduction to the Transaction Costs and Internal Costs of Delivering Health Care*. London: Office of Health Economics.

Dansky, K.H. and L.S. Gamm. 2004. Accountability Framework for Managing Stakeholders of Health Programs. *Journal of Health Organization and Management* 18: 290–304.

De Angelis, A. 2002. *Project Finance and PPP in Italy*. Rome: The International Project Finance Association (IPFA) July26.

Dean, M. 2003. New Prescription for Hospitals, *Guardian*, January 8. Online, available at: www.guardian.co.uk/society/2003/jan/08/hospitals.nhs2000.

Deber, R.B. 2002. *Delivering Health Care Services: Public, Not-For-Profit, or Private?* Toronto: Commission on the Future of Health Care in Canada. Discussion Paper 17.

Dees, J.G. 1998. Enterprising Nonprofits: What Do You Do When Traditional Sources of Funding Fall Short? *Harvard Business Review* 76: 58–67.

Delay, S., L. Gilson, D. Hemson, K.M. Lewin, M. Motimele, R. Scott and H. Wadee. 2004. *South Africa: A Study of Non-state Providers of Basic Services*. School of Public Policy, University of Birmingham. Research Report.

DFID. 1995. (Part 1) *Technical Note on Enhancing Stakeholder Participation in Aid Activities* (Part 2) *Guidance Note on Stakeholder Analysis of Aid Projects and Programs* (Part 3) *Guidance Note on Indicators for Measuring and Assessing Primary Stakeholder Participation*. London: Department for International Development.

DFID. 2000. *Making the Most of the Private Sector*. Workshop organized on behalf of the Department for International Development. London: Health Systems Resource Centre (12 May).

Domberger, S. and P. Fernandez. 1999. Public Private Partnership for Service Delivery. *Business Strategy Review* 10(4): 29–39.

Dunnigan, M. and A. Pollock. 2003. Downsizing of Acute Inpatient Beds Associated with Private Finance Initiative: Scotland's Case Study. *British Medical Journal* 326: 905–908.

Edwards, P. and J. Shaoul. 2003. Partnerships: For Better, For Worse? *Accounting, Auditing and Accountability Journal* 16: 397–421.

Eichler, R., P. Auxila and J. Pollock. 2002. Promoting Preventive Health Care: Paying for Performance in Haiti. In *Contracting for Public Health Services: Output-based Aid and Its Application* edited by P.J. Brook and S.M. Smith. Washington, DC: The World Bank.

El-Gohary, N., H. Osman and T.E. El-Diraby. 2006. Stakeholder Management for Public-Private Partnerships. *International Journal of Project Management* 24: 595–604.

England, R. 2000. *Contracting and Performance Management in the Health Sector: A Guide for Low and Middle Income Countries*. London: DFID Health Systems Resource Centre.

England, R. 2004. *Experiences of Contracting with the Private Sector: A Selective Review*. London: DFID Health Systems Resource Centre.

Entwistle, T. and S. Martin. 2005. From Competition to Collaboration in Public Service Delivery: A New Agenda for Research. *Public Administration* 83: 233–242.

Erulkar, A. 2003. Increasing the Quality of Adolescent Girls; Education: A Vital Development and Reproductive Health Measure. In *Adolescent and Youth Sexual and Reproductive Health: Charting Directions for a Second Generation of Programming*. New York: Population Council, pp. 77–89.

Escobar, A. 1995. *Encountering Development: The Making and Unmaking of the Third World*. Princeton: Princeton University Press.

Essig, M. and A. Batran. 2005. Public-Private Partnership: Development of Long-term Relationships in Public Procurement in Germany. *Journal of Purchasing and Supply Management* 11: 221–231.

Farnsworth, K. and C. Holden. 2006. The Business Policy Nexus: Corporate Power and Corporate Inputs into Social Policy. *International Journal of Social Policy* 35: 473–494.

Ferguson, J. 1990. *The Anti-Politics Machine*. Cambridge: Cambridge University Press.

Flinders, M. 2002. Governance in Whitehall. *Public Administration* 80: 51–75.

Flinders, M. 2005. The Politics of Public-Private Partnerships *The British Journal of Politics & International Relations* 7: 215–239.

Fooks, C. and L. Maslove. 2003. *Assessing the Impact of Changing the Public/Private Mix in Canada's Health Care System*. Background paper prepared for The Canadian Cancer Society. Toronto: Canadian Policy Research Networks Inc.

Foreit, K. 1998. *The Role of the Provider in Family Planning and Reproductive Health Services Marketing*. Washington, DC: The Futures Group International.

Fottler, M. 1987. Health Care Organizational Performance: Present and Future Research. *Journal of Management* 13: 179–203.

Fottler, M., J.D. Blair, C.J. Whitehead, M. Laus and G.T. Savage. 1989. Assessing Key Stakeholders: Who Matters to Hospitals and Why? *Hospital and Health Services Administration* 34: 525–546.

Fowler, A. 2000. *Partnerships: Negotiating Relationships, A Resource for Non-Governmental Development Organizations*. Occasional Paper No. 32. Oxford: International NGO Training and Research Centre.

Freeman, R.E. 1984. *Strategy Management: A Stakeholder Approach*. Marshfield: Pittman Publishers.

Friedland, R.B. 2005. How Medicare Works. *Generations* 29: 30–34.

Gaffney, D. and A. Pollock. 1999. Pump-priming the PFI: Why are Privately Financed Hospital Schemes being Subsidized? *Public Money and Management* 19: 55–62.

Gauri, V., J. Cercone and R. Briceno. 2004. Separating Financing from Provision: Evidence from 10 Years of Partnership with Health Cooperatives in Costa Rica. *Health Policy and Planning* 19: 292–301.

Gazley, B. and J.L. Brudney. 2007. The Purpose (and Perils) of Government-Nonprofit Partnership. *Nonprofit and Voluntary Sector Quarterly* 36: 389–415.

Gill, M. 2003. *Policy Partnerships: Essential Elements of Effective Government/NGO Relationships*. Synergy Associates. Online, available at: www.synergyassociates.ca/publications/PolicyPartnerships.htm.

Gilson, L., J. Adusei, D. Arhin, C. Hongoro, P. Mujinja and K. Sagoe. 1997. Should African Governments Contract out Clinical Services to Church Providers? In *Private Health Providers in Developing Countries: Serving the Public Interest?* edited by S. Bennett, B. McPake and A. Mills. London: Zed Books, pp. 276–302.

Ginter, P.M., L.E. Swayne and W.J. Duncan. 2002. *Strategic Management of Health Care Organizations*, 4th edition. London: Blackwell Business.

Glennerster, H. 2003. *Understanding the Finance of Welfare: What Welfare Costs and How to Pay For It*. London: Policy Press.

Gotsadze, G. and A. Levan. 2003. *Private-Public Partnership in Georgia: Case Study of Contracting an NGO to Provide Non-core Specialist Services*. London: DFID Health Systems Resource Center.

Government of India. 1988. *Directory of Hospitals*. New Delhi: Ministry of Health and Family Welfare.

Government of India. 2000. *Annual Report (1999–2000)*. New Delhi: Ministry of Health and Family Welfare.

Government of India. 2001. *Tenth Five Year Plan, 2002–2007*. New Delhi: Planning Commission.

Government of India. 2002a. *Fifty-seventh Round on Unorganised Sector, 2000–2001*. New Delhi: National Sample Survey Organization.

Government of India. 2002b. *National Health Policy 2001*. New Delhi: Ministry of Health and Family Welfare.

Government of India. 2004. *Health Sector Reforms in India: Initiatives from Nine States*. New Delhi: Bureau of Planning, Directorate General of Health Services in collaboration with the World Heath Organization Country Office for India.

Government of India. 2005. *Concept Note on Public Private Partnerships*. New Delhi: Department of Family Welfare, Ministry of Health and Family Welfare.

Greve, C. 2003. Public-Private Partnerships in Scandinavia. *International Public Management Review* 4: 59–69.

Grimmeisen, S. and H. Rothgang. 2004. *The Changing Role of the State in Europe's Health Care Systems*. Second Annual ESPAnet Conference, University of Oxford. September 9–11. Online, available at: www.apsoc.ox.ac.uk/Espanet/espanetconference/papers/ppr.9.SG.pdf.

Hammami, M., J.F. Ruhashyankiko and E.B. Yehoue. 2006. *Determinants of Public-Private Partnerships in Infrastructure*. Washington, DC: IMF Working Paper WP/06/99.

Heilman, J. and G. Johnston. 1992. *The Politics of Economics of Privatisation*. Tuscaloosa: University of Alabama Press.

Hildebrand, M.E. and M.S. Grindle. 1994. *Building Sustainable Capacity: Challenges for the Public Sector*. Unpublished paper, prepared for UNDP.

Hodge, G.A. 2004. The Risky Business of Public-Private Partnerships. *Australian Journal of Public Administration* 63(4): 37–49.

Hodge, G.A. and C. Greve. 2007. Public-Private Partnerships: An International Performance Review. *Public Administration Review* 67: 545–558.

Hodgkin, C. 2005. *PPP in Brief*. Online, available at: www.kit.nl/specials/html/ppp_in_brief.asp.

Hongoro, C. and L. Kumaranayake. 2000. Do They Work? Regulating For-Profit Providers in Zimbabwe. *Health Policy and Planning* 15: 368–377.

Horev, T. and Y.M. Babad. 2005. Healthcare Reform Implementation: Stakeholders and their Roles – The Israeli Experience. *Health Policy* 71: 1–21.

Hudson, B. and B. Hardy. 2001. Localization and Partnership in the 'New National Health Service': England and Scotland Compared. *Public Administration* 79: 315–335.

IIED (International Institute for Environment and Development). 2005. *Stakeholder Power Analysis*. (Tool developed by James Mayers.)

Institute for Public Policy Research (IPPR). 2001. *Building Better Partnerships*. London: Institute of Public Policy Research.

Jakab, M., A. Preker and A. Harding. 2002. Linking Organizational Structure to the External Environment: Experiences from Hospital Reform in Transition Economies. In *Hospitals in a Changing Europe* edited by M. McKee and J. Healy. Buckingham: Open University Press (European Observatory on Health Care Systems series), pp. 177–201.

Jeong, H. 2005. Health Care Reform and Change in Public-Private Mix of Financing: A Korean Case. *Health Policy* 74: 133–145.

Jeugmans, J. 2000. *Mongolia: Health Sector Reforms and the Private Sector*. In *Public-Private Partnership in the Social Sector: Issues and Country experiences in Asia and the Pacific* edited by Y. Wang. Policy Paper No. 1. Tokyo: Asian Development Bank Institute, pp. 113–143.

Jorgensen, M. 2006. *Evaluating Cross Sector Partnerships*. Copenhagen: Copenhagen Business School.

Jutting, J. 1999. *Public-Private-Partnership and Social Protection in Developing Countries: The Case of the Health Sector*. Geneva: ILO workshop on the Extension of Social Protection.

Keramidas, O. and L. Bout-Colonna. 2007. Public-Private Partnership: A New Way of Thinking for Health Management. *International Journal of Public Sector Performance Management* 1: 83–99.

Kigondu, J. and J. Naisho. 2003. Afriafya Program Evaluation Report. April–May. Online, available at: www.afriafya.org/doc/AfriAfya_EvaluationReport_May_2003_pdf.

Kirkpatrick, I., M. Kitchener and R. Whipp. 2001. 'Out of Sight – Out of Mind': Assessing the Impact of Markets for Children's Residential Care. *Public Administration* 79: 49–71.

Knowles, J.C. and C. Leighton. 1997. *Measuring Results of Health Sector Reform for System Performance: A Handbook of Indicators*. Bethesda: Abt Associates.

Kulkarni, S. 2003. *India Sector Paper: Health Overview and Prospects*. New Delhi: Centre for Media Studies (submitted to Asian Development Bank).

Lasker, R.D. and E.S. Weiss. 2003. Creating Partnership Synergy: The Critical Role of Community Stakeholders. *Journal of Health and Human Services Administration* 26: 119–138.

Laurie, N. and L. Bondi. 2005. *Working the Spaces of Neoliberalism: Activism, Professionalisation and Incorporation*. Oxford: Blackwell.

Lavadenz, F., N.S. Schwab and Y.H. Straatman. 2001. Redes Públicas, Descentralizadas y Comunitarias de Salud en Bolivia. *Pan-American Journal of Public Health* 9: 182–189. Cited in Liu *et al.* 2004.

LaVake, S.D. 2003. *Applying Social Franchising Techniques to Youth Reproductive Health/HIV Services*. Youth Issues Paper 2. Family Health International–Youth Net Program. Online, available at: www.fhi.org/en/Youth/YouthNet/Publications/YouthIssuesPapers.htm.

LeGrand, J and W Bartlett. 1993. Quasi-markets and Social Policy: The Way Forward? In *Quasi-markets and Social Policy* edited by J LeGrand and W Bartlett. Basingstoke: Macmillan.

Levine, P. 2002. Building the Electronic Commons. *The Good Society* 11(3): 1–9.

Lewis, D. 1998. Inter-Agency Partnership in Aid-Recipient Countries: Lessons from an Aquaculture Project in Bangladesh. *Non-profit and Voluntary Sector Quarterly* 27: 323–338.

Lienhard, A. 2006. Public Private Partnerships (PPPs) in Switzerland: Experiences – Risks – Potentials. *International Review of Administrative Sciences* 72: 547–563.

Linder, S. 1999. Coming to Terms with the Public-Private Partnership: A Grammar of Multiple Meanings. *The American Behavioral Scientist* 43: 35–51.

Lister, S. 2000. Power in Partnership? An Analysis of an NGO's Relationship with its Partners. *Journal of International Development* 12: 227–239.

Liu, X., D.R. Hotchkiss, S. Bose, R. Bitran and U. Giedion. 2004. *Contracting for Primary Health Services: Evidence on Its Effects and a Framework for Evaluation.* Bethesda: ABT Associates.

Loevinsohn, B. 2001. *Contracting for Delivery of Primary Health Care in Cambodia: Design and Initial Experience of a Large Pilot Test.* Washington, DC: The World Bank.

Loevinsohn, B. 2002. *Practical Issues in Contracting for Primary Health Care Delivery: Lessons from Two Projects in Bangladesh.* Washington, DC: The World Bank.

Loevinsohn, B. and A. Harding. 2004. *Contracting for the Delivery of Community Health Services: A Review of Global Experience.* Washington, DC: The World Bank.

Loevinsohn, B. and A. Harding. 2005. Buying Results? Contracting for Health Service Delivery in Developing Countries. *The Lancet* 366: 676–681.

Lönnroth, K., M. Uplekar and L. Blanc. 2006. Hard Gains through Soft Contracts: Productive Engagement of Private Providers in Tuberculosis Control. *Bulletin of the World Health Organization* 84: 876–883.

Luís-Manso, P. 2005. Economic Risks in the Drinking Water Sector. *IWA International Conference on Water Economics, Statistics and Finance.* Rethymno, Greece, July 8–10.

Maceira, D. 1998. *Provider Payment Mechanisms in Health Care: Incentives, Outcomes and Organizational Impact in Developing Countries.* Bethesda: Partnerships for Health Reform, Abt Associates Inc.

McKee, M. and J. Healy. 2002. Editors. *Hospitals in a Changing Europe.* Buckingham: Open University Press.

Macneil, I. 1978. Contracts: Adjustment of Long-term Economic Relations under Classical, Neoclassical and Relational Contract Law. *Northwestern University Law Review* 72: 854–905.

McPake, Barbara and Charles Hongoro. 1995. Contracting Out of Clinical Services in Zimbabwe. *Social Science and Medicine* 41: 13–24.

Mahal, A., J. Singh, F. Afridi, V. Lamba, A. Gumber and V. Selvaraju. 2002. *Who Benefits from Public Sector Health Spending in India.* New Delhi: National Council for Applied Economic Research.

Mahal, A., V. Srivastava and D. Sanan. 2000. Decentralisation and its Impact on Public Service Provision in the Health and Education Sectors: The Case of India. In *Governance, Decentralisation and Reform in China, India and Russia* edited by J. Dethier. London: Kluwer Academic Publishers, pp. 235–270.

Mahmud, H., A. Ullah Khan and S. Ahmed. 2002. Mid-Term Health Facility Survey – Urban Primary Health Care Project, Bangladesh: Report. Dhaka: Mitra and Associates.

Makin, T. 2003. The Changing Public-Private Infrastructure Mix: Economy-wide Implications. *Australian Journal of Public Administration* 62(3): 32–39.

Maltby, P. 2003. Public Interest Companies: Fad or Permanent Fixture? *New Economy* 10: 21–27.

Marek, T., D. Issakha, N. Biram and R. Jean. 1999. Successful Contracting of Prevention Services: Fighting Malnutrition in Senegal and Madagascar. *Health Policy and Planning* 14: 382–389.

Marek, T., C. O'Farrell, C. Yamamoto and I. Zable. 2005. *Trends and Opportunities in Public-Private Partnerships to Improve Health Service Delivery in Africa.* Washington, DC: The World Bank.

Mills, A. 1997. Contractual Relationships between Government and the Commercial Private Sector in Developing Countries. In *Private Health Providers in Developing Countries: Serving the Public Interest?* edited by S. Bennett, B. McPake and A. Mills. London: Zed Books, pp. 189–213.

Mills, A. 1998. To Contract or Not To Contract? Issues for Low and Middle Income Countries. *Health Policy and Planning* 13: 32–40.

Mills, A. and J. Broomberg. 1998. *Experiences of Contracting Health Services: An Overview of the Literature.* London: Working paper 01/98, London School of Hygiene and Tropical Medicine.

Mills, A., C. Hongoro, and J. Broomberg. 1997. Improving the Efficiency of District Hospitals: Is Contracting an Option? *Tropical Medicine and International Health* 2: 116–126.

Misra, R., S. Rao, and R. Chatterjee. 2003. *India Health Report.* New Delhi: Oxford University Press.

Mitchell, M. 1986. *Monitoring of the Pakistan Primary Health Care Project.* Boston: Harvard Institute for International Development.

Mitchell, M. 2000. Models of Service Delivery. In *Public-Private Partnerships in the Social Sector: Issues and Country Experiences in Asia and the Pacific* edited by Y Wang. Tokyo: Asian Development Bank Institute.

Mitchell, R.K., B.R. Agle and D.J. Wood. 1997. Toward a Theory of What Really Counts. *Academy of Management Review* 22: 853–886.

Mitchell-Weaver, C. and B. Manning. 1992. Public-Private Partnerships in Third World Development: A Conceptual Overview. *Studies in Comparative International Development* 26(4): 45–67.

Montagu, D. 2002. Franchising of Health Services in Low-Income Countries. *Health Policy and Planning* 17: 121–130.

Montagu, D. 2003. *Output-based Services for Health and Their Potential Application in Kenya.* Online, available at: www.cfwshops.org.

Moore, M. 1992. Competition and Pluralism in Public Bureaucracies. *IDS Bulletin* 23(4): 65–77.

Morse, S. and N. McNamara. 2006. Analyzing Institutional Partnerships in Development: A Contract between Equals or a Loaded Process? *Progress in Development Studies* 6: 321–336.

Moser, P. 2000. Partnerships in the Provision of Health Care in Asia. In *Public Private Partnership in the Social Sector: Issues and Country Experiences in Asia and the Pacific* edited by Y. Wang. Policy Paper No. 1. Tokyo: Asian Development Bank Institute, pp. 119–130.

Mosse, D. 2004. Is Good Policy Unimplementable? Reflections on the Ethnography of Aid Policy and Practice. *Development and Change* 35: 639–671.

Mossialos, E., A. Dixon, J. Figueras and J. Kutzin. 2002. (eds). *Funding Health Care: Options for Europe.* Buckingham: Open University Press (European Observatory on Health Care Systems).

Moulton, L. and H.K. Anheier. 2001. *Public-Private Partnerships in the United States: Historical Patterns and Current Trends.* Centre for Civil Society Working Paper 16. London: London School of Economics and Political Science.

Mukhopadhyay, A. 2000. Public-Private Partnership in the Health Sector in India. In

*Public Private Partnership in the Social Sector: Issues and Country Experiences in Asia and the Pacific* edited by Y. Wang. Policy Paper No. 1. Tokyo: Asian Development Bank Institute, pp. 343–356.

Murthy, K.J., T.R. Frieden, A. Yazdani, and P. Hreshikes. 2001. Public-private Partnership in Tuberculosis Control: Experience in Hyderabad, India. *International Journal of Tuberculosis and Lung Diseases.* 5: 354–359.

Mushi, A.K., R.M. Joanna, A. Schellenberg, H. Mponda and C. Lengeler. 2003. Targeted Subsidy for Malaria Control with Treated Nets using a Discount Voucher Scheme in Tanzania. *Health Policy and Planning* 18: 163–171.

Naimoli, J. 2003. *Partnerships within the Public Sector to Achieve Health Objectives: Performance-based Management in an Evolving Decentralized Public Health System in West Africa: The Case of Burkina Faso.* Washington, DC: The World Bank.

Najam, A. 2000. The Four C's of Third Sector-Government Relations: Cooperation, Confrontation, Complementarity and Co-optation. *Nonprofit Management and Leadership* 10: 374–396.

National Commission on Macroeconomics in Health (NCMH). 2005. New Delhi: Ministry of Health and Family Welfare, Government of India.

National Family Health Survey-3. 2007. *Fact Sheets.* Mumbai. International Institute for Population Sciences. Online, available at: http://nfhsindia.org/factsheet.html.

National Health Accounts Report, India 2000–2001. 2005. Ministry of Health and Family Welfare, Government of India. Online, available at: http://mohfw.nic.in/NHA/2001–02.pdf.

National Rural Health Mission (NRHM). 2007. Ministry of Health and Family Welfare, Government of India. Online, available at: http://mohfw.nic.in/NRHM/Task_grp/ Draft_Report_Task_Group_on_PPP7_9_06.pdf.

Nellis, J. 1994. *Is Privatization Necessary? Public Policy for the Private Sector.* Washington, DC: The World Bank.

Newman, C.L. 2000. Comparative Study of NGO/Government Partnerships. *International Centre for Not-for-Profit Law* 2(3). Online, available at: www.icnl.org/ journal/VOL21ISS3/p_ngogov.htm.

O'Connor, D.R. 2002. *Report of the Walkerton Inquiry: The Events of May 2000 and Related Issues. Part One: A Summary.* Toronto: Ontario Ministry of Attorney General. Online, available at: www.attorneygeneral.jus.gov.on.ca/english/about/pubs/walkerton/part1/WI_Summary.pdf.

O'Faircheallaigh, C., J. Wanna and P. Weller. 1999. *Public Sector Management in Australia: New Challenges, New Directions*, 2nd edition. Brisbane: Centre for Australian Public Sector Management.

Osewe, P. 2006. *Strengthening the Role of the Private Sector in Expanding Health Coverage in Africa.* Princeton: Woodrow Wilson International Center for Scholars.

Oyaya, C.O. and S.B. Rifkin. 2003. Health Sector Reforms in Kenya: An Examination of District Level Planning. *Health Policy* 64: 113–127.

Pallavi. 2005. *Forms and Discourse of NGO/Government Partnerships: The Case Study of Pratham and Childline Indian Foundation.* Unpublished MA Research Paper in Public Policy and Management. The Hague: Institute of Social Studies.

Palmer, N. 2003. Does Duty Call: Contracts and GPs in South Africa. *Insights Health.* Online, available at: www.id21.org/zinter/id21zinter.exe?a=14&i=InsightsHealth3art 7&u=47be9c78.

Palmer, N. and A. Mills. 2003. Classical versus Relational Approaches to Understanding Controls on a Contract with Independent GPs in South Africa. *Health Economics* 12: 1005–1020.

Paoletto, G. 2000. Public Private Sector Partnerships: An Overview of Cause and Effect. In *Public Private Partnership in the Social Sector: Issues and Country Experiences in Asia and the Pacific* edited by Y. Wang. Policy Paper No. 1. Tokyo: Asian Development Bank Institute, pp. 35–54.

Peters, D.H., G.G. Mirchandani and P.M. Hansen. 2004. Strategies for Engaging the Private Sector in Sexual and Reproductive Health: How Effective Are They? *Health Policy and Planning* 19: i5-i21 (Supplement 1).

Pollock, A., J. Shaoul, D. Rowland and S. Player. 2001. *Public Services and the Private Sector*. London: Catalyst.

Pollock, A., J. Shaoul and N. Vickers. 2002. Private Finance and Value for Money in NHS Hospitals: A Policy in Search of a Rationale? *British Medical Journal* 324: 1205–1209.

Pongsiri, N. 2002. Regulation and Public Private Partnerships. *The International Journal of Public Sector Management* 15: 487–495.

Putney, P. 2000. *Partnerships between the Public Sector and Non-governmental Organizations: The NGO Role in Health Sector Reform*. Health Sector Reform Initiative. No. 26. Online, available at: www.americas.health-sector-reform.org.

Ramsey, C. 1995. *Labour in the Hospital Sector*. Vancouver: The Fraser Institute.

Rangan, S., R. Samii and L.N. Wassenhove. 2006. Constructive Partnerships: When Alliances between Private Firms and Public Actors Can Enable Creative Strategies. *Academy of Management Review* 31: 738–751.

Rao, K.S., G.N.V. Ramana and H.V.V. Murthy. 1997. *Financing of Primary Health Care in Andhra Pradesh*. New Delhi: World Health Organization.

Roberts, J.A. 1993. Managing Markets. *Journal of Public Health Medicine* 15: 305–310.

Roberts, M., W. Hsia, D. Berman and M.R. Reich. 2004. *Getting Health Reform Right: A Guide to Improving Performance and Equity*. New York: Oxford University Press.

Robison, D., T. Hewitt and J. Harriss (eds) 2000. *Managing Development: Understanding Inter-Organizational Relationships*. London: Sage Publications.

Roe, E.M. 1991. Development Narratives, or Making the Best of Blueprint Development. *World Development* 19: 297–300.

Roemer, M.I. 1984. Private Medical Practice: Obstacle to Health for All. *World Health Forum* 5: 195–210.

Roemer, M.I. and J.E. Roemer. 1982. The Social Consequences of Free Trade in Health Care: A Public Health Response to Orthodox Economics. *International Journal of Health Services* 12: 111–129.

Romanow, R.J. 2002. *Building on Values: The Future of Health Care in Canada*. Ottawa: The Commission on the Future of Health Care in Canada. Final Report.

Rosen, J.E. 2000. *Contracting for Reproductive Health Care: A Guide*. Washington, DC: The World Bank. Online, available at: www.worldbank.org/documents/contractingforRH.

Rosenthal, G. 2000. State of the Practice: Public-NGO Partnerships for Quality Assurance. *HSR Health Sector Reform Initiative, Family Planning Management Development Project*. Boston: Management Sciences for Health. Online, available at: www.lachsr.org/documents/stateofthepracticepublishingpartershiponsetodecentralisation.

Sako, M. 1992. *Prices, Quality and Trust: Inter-firm Relations in Britain and Japan*. Cambridge: Cambridge University Press.

Salim, M.A.H., M. Uplekar, P. Daru, M. Aung, E. Declercq and K. Lönnroth. 2006. Turning Liabilities into Resources: Informal Village Doctors and Tuberculosis Control in Bangladesh. *Bulletin of the World Health Organization* 84: 479–484.

Saltman, R.B., R. Busse, E. Mossialos (eds) 2002. *Regulating Entrepreneurial Behavior in European Health Care Systems.* Buckingham: Open University Press. (European Observatory on Health Care Systems.)

Scharle, P. 2002. Public Private Partnerships as a Social Game. *Innovation* 15: 227–252.

Selvaraju, V. and V.B. Annigeri. 2001. *Trends in Public Spending on Health in India.* New Delhi: National Institute of Public Finance and Policy. Background paper for the Commission on Macro-Economics and Health (India).

Shaoul, J. 2004. Railpolitik: The Financial Realities of Operating Britain's National Railways. *Public Money and Management* 24: 27–36.

Shaoul, J. 2005. The Private Finance Initiative or the Public Funding of Private Profit. In *The Challenge of Public-Private Partnerships: Learning from International Experience* edited by G. Hodge and C. Greve. Cheltenham: Edward Elgar, pp. 190–206.

Shleifer, A. 1998. State versus Private Ownership. *Journal of Economic Perspectives* 12: 133–150.

Siddiqi, S., T.I. Masud and B. Sabri. 2006. Contracting but Not without Caution: Experience with Outsourcing of Health Services in Countries of the Eastern Mediterranean Region. *Bulletin of the World Health Organization* 84: 867–875.

Skibiak, J.P., M. Chambeshi-Moyo and Y. Ahmed. 2001. *Testing Alternative Channels for Providing Emergency Contraception to Young Women.* New York: Population Council.

Slack, K. and W.D. Savedoff. 2001. *Public Purchaser-Private Provider Contracting for Health Services: Examples from Latin America and the Caribbean.* Washington, DC: Inter-American Development Bank.

Smith, E., R. Brugha and A. Zwi. 2001. *Working with Private Sector Providers for Better Health Care: An Introductory Guide.* London: London School of Health and Tropical Medicine.

Smith, S.R. and M. Lipsky. 1993. *Nonprofits for Hire: The Welfare State in the Age of Contracting.* Cambridge: Harvard University Press.

Stinson, J., N. Pollak and M. Cohen. 2005. *The Pains of Privatization: How Contracting Out Hurts Support Workers, Their Families and Health Care.* Vancouver: Canadian Centre for Policy Alternatives.

Sunseri, R. 1999. Outsourcing on the Outs. *Hospitals and Health Networks* 73(10): 46.

Tandon, R. 1991. *NGO Government Relations: A Source of Life or a Kiss of Death?* New Delhi: Society for Participatory Research in Asia.

Taylor, R. and S. Blair. 2002. *Public Hospitals: Options for Reform through Public-Private Partnerships.* World Bank Note 241. Online, available at: www.worldbank.org/html/fpd/notes.

Teicher, J., Q. Alam and B.V. Gramberg. 2006. Managing Trust and Relationships in PPPs: Some Australian Experiences. *International Review of Administrative Sciences* 72: 85.

Teisman, G.R. and E.H. Klijn. 2002. Partnership Arrangements: Governmental Rhetoric or Governance Scheme? *Public Administration Review* 62: 189–198.

Thomason, J.A. 2002. *Health Sector Reform in Developing Countries: A Reality Check.* Online, available at: www.sph.uq.edu.au/acithn/conf97/papers97/thomason.htm.

Thompson, C.R. and M. McKee. 2004. Financing and Planning of Public and Private Not-for-profit Hospitals in the European Union. *Health Policy* 67: 281–291.

Towne, J. and S. Hoppszallern. 2003. 13th Annual Contract Management Survey. *Hospitals and Health Networks* 77(10): 52.

Trescoli, C. 2002. 'Alzira' Model: A PFI Based on a Capitation System. *British Medical Journal*. Online, available at: www.bmj.com/cgi/eletters/324/7347/1205#22452.

Tuohy, C.A., C. Flood and M. Stabile. 2004. How Does Private Finance Affect Public Health Care Systems? Marshalling Evidence from OECD Nations. *Journal of Public Health Politics, Policy and Law* 29: 359–396.

Van Ham, H. and J. Koppenjan. 2001. Building Public-Private Partnerships: Assessing and Managing Risks in Port Development. *Public Management Review* 3: 593–616.

Varvasovszky, A. and R. Brugha. 2000. A Stakeholder Analysis. *Health Policy and Planning* 15: 338–345.

Varvasovsky, Z. 1998. *Alcohol Policy in Hungary*. London: London School of Hygiene and Tropical Medicine.

Venkat Raman, A. 2002. *Institutional Reforms in Health Sector: A Study of Personnel and Organizational Issues in Health Sector Reforms*. Robert McNamara Research Fellowship Report (World Bank), Faculty of Management Studies, University of Delhi.

Venkat Raman, A. 2004. Those Who Matter: Group-based Stakeholder Analysis. In *The 2004 Pfeiffer Annual (Consulting)* edited by E. Biech. San Francisco: John Wiley & Sons Inc., pp. 97–108.

Venkat Raman, A. and J.W. Björkman. 2006. *Public-Private Partnership in the Provision of Health Care Services to the Poor*. Indo-Dutch Programme for Alternatives in Development. Research Report, Faculty of Management Studies, University of Delhi.

Vladescu, C. and S. Radulescu. 2002. Improving Primary Health Care: Output-based Contracting in Romania. In *Contracting for Public Health Services: Output-Based Aid and Its Application* edited by P.J. Brook and S.M. Smith. Washington, DC: World Bank.

Walsh, K. 1995. *Public Services and Market Mechanisms: Competition, Contracting and the New Public Management*. London: Macmillan.

Wang, Y. 2000. (ed.). *Public-Private Partnerships in the Social Sector: Issues and Country Experiences in Asia and the Pacific*. Policy Paper No. 1. Tokyo: Asian Development Bank Institute.

Waters, H., L. Hatt and H. Axelsson. 2002. *Working with the Private Sector for Child Health*. Washington, DC: The World Bank.

Widdus, R. 2001. Public-Private Partnerships for Health: Their Main Targets, Diversity and their Future Directions. *Bulletin of the World Health Organization* 79: 713–720.

Wildridge, V., S. Childs, L. Cawthra and B. Madge. 2004. How to Create Successful Partnerships: A Review of the Literature. *Health Information and Libraries Journal* 21 (June): 3–19.

Williamson, O.E. 1985. *The Economic Institutions of Capitalism: Firms, Markets and Relational Contracting*. New York: The Free Press.

World Bank. 1993. *Investing in Health: World Development Report, 1993*. Oxford: Oxford University Press.

World Bank. 1997. *The State in a Changing World: World Development Report 1997*. Oxford: Oxford University Press.

World Bank. 2001. *India: Raising the Sights: Better Health Systems for India's Poor*. Washington, DC: HNP Unit-India, Report # 22304.

World Bank. 2004. *India: Private Health Services for the Poor*. Draft Policy Note. Online, available at: www.sasnet.lu.se/EASASpapers/11IsmailRadwan.pdf.

World Bank. 2005. *A Guide to Competitive Vouchers in Health*. Washington, DC: The World Bank.

World Economic Forum. 2005. *Building on the Monterrey Consensus: The Growing Role* of *Public-Private Partnerships in Mobilising Resources for Development.* Geneva: United Nations high-level plenary meeting on financing for development (September).

World Health Organization. 1997. *Public-Private Sector Partnerships for Health: Role of Governments.* SEA/HSD/212, WHO Project: ICP ICO001/ICP RPS002. New Delhi: WHO Regional Office.

World Health Organization. 1999. *WHO Guidelines on Collaborations and Partnership with Commercial Enterprise.* Geneva: WHO.

World Health Organization. 2000. *Health Systems: Improving Performance: The World Health Report.* Geneva: WHO.

World Health Organization. 2001. Making a Public-Private Partnership Work: An Insider's View. (Interview of Amadou Diarra by John Maurice.) *Bulletin of the World Health Organization* 79: 795–796.

World Health Organization. 2002a. *Key Points: WHO Traditional Medicine Strategy 2002–2005.* Geneva: WHO.

World Health Organization. 2002b. *The Role of the Private Sector and Privatization in European Health Systems.* Copenhagen: Regional Committee for Europe, 52nd Session.

Wortzel, H.V. and L.H. Wortzel. 1989. Privatization: Not the Only Answer. *World Development* 17: 633–641.

Wouters, A. 1998. *Alternative Provider Payment Methods: Incentives for Improving Health Care Delivery.* Primer for Policymakers. Bethesda: Partnerships for Health Reform, Abt Associates Inc.

Zahariadis, N. 1999. The Rise and Fall of British State Ownership: Political Pressure or Economic Reality? *Comparative Politics* 31: 445–463.

# Index